Instant Pot®
Miracle

Instant Pot® Miracle

Miracle

From Gourmet to Everyday, 175 Must-Have Recipes

HOUGHTON MIFFLIN HARCOURT
BOSTON · NEW YORK

INSTANT POT® and the Instant Pot® logo are registered trademarks of Double Insight Inc. Used under license.

Copyright © 2017 by Houghton Mifflin Harcourt

For information about permission to reproduce selections from this book, write to trade.permissions@hmhco.com or to Permissions, Houghton Mifflin Harcourt Publishing Company, 3 Park Avenue, 19th Floor, New York, New York 10016.

www.hmhco.com

Library of Congress Cataloging-in-Publication Data is available.

ISBN 978-1-328-85105-5 (pbk)

ISBN 978-1-328-85106-2 (ebk)

Book design by Waterbury Publications, Inc.

Printed in the United States of America

DOC 20 19 18 17 16 15

4500733047

"Pumpkin-Spice Steel-Cut Oats," "Chickpea Broccoli Salad," "Maple & Vinegar-Braised Parsnips," and "Spicy Brown Rice and Bean Soup" from *VEGAN UNDER PRESSURE: Perfect Vegan Meals Made Quick and Easy in Your Pressure Cooker* by Jill Nussinow, MS, RDN. Copyright © 2016 by Jill Nussinow, MS, RDN. Used by permission of Houghton Mifflin Harcourt. All rights reserved.

Contents

The Story of the Instant Pot®

The idea for the Instant Pot®—a multipurpose cooker that relies on the latest technologies—started with a simple, basic, and universal desire.

In 2008, Robert Wang and two colleagues (who along with Wang would eventually be founders of the company that produces the Instant Pot®) began brainstorming ideas for kitchen appliances that could address the very personal concerns they had about being able to fix quick, healthy, delicious meals after long days at work. All three had worked in the Canadian high-tech industry. Wang's wife worked in the high-tech field as well—and the couple had two young children. There was another motivating factor: Wang and his colleagues observed changes in the lifestyles of North Americans. Although people were busier than ever and had less time to cook, they wanted to eat more healthfully.

The trio settled on rebooting the pressure cooker—traditionally a stovetop pot with a locked-on lid fitted with a rubber or plastic gasket and heated up until enough pressure built up in the pot to cook foods far more quickly than regular braising and steaming methods. Although once popular, pressure cooking had fallen out of favor because of tales told of exploding pots that catapulted hot beef stew or cooked beans all over the kitchen. Safety was their first hurdle. They decided to make it their top priority followed by innovation. Their appliance would not just be a pressure cooker but also a slow cooker, rice cooker, steamer, sauté pan, and yogurt maker—all in one.

They partnered with three other investors and set up a business called Double Insight in Ottawa to manufacture their brainchild. The first Instant Pot® came on the market in 2010. The rest, as they say, is history.

Word spread—primarily through social media—about the convenience the pot provides to the home cook and the creativity it allows for meal making even on the busiest days. Nearly everyone who acquires an Instant Pot® becomes an instant fan—and they enthusiastically spread the word to friends, family members, and coworkers. Words used to describe the Instant Pot® veer toward the passionate. "Love!" and "life-changing" are two of the most common praises.

And then of course there are the results: Butter-knife-tender roasts in minutes, creamy risottos with no stirring, hearty bean soups and chili with no overnight soaking and a fraction of the traditional cooking time—and the creamiest, fluffiest cheesecake you will ever taste.

The creators of the Instant Pot® do not rest on their laurels and the tremendous success of their invention. They are constantly seeking to improve it based on feedback from their customers. Each iteration released to the market—every 12 to 18 months—has enhancements to make using it easier and more satisfying.

It may sound too good to be true, but it's not. With a little bit of prep work and the push of a button, you can get wonderful, healthful meals on the table with speed and ease and (we dare say) have a lot of fun doing it!

Happy cooking!

How to Use the Instant Pot®

The User Manual that came with your Instant Pot® has detailed information on how to use the appliance. Read through it and refer to it as often as necessary. Here are the basics, plus some points that should be highlighted.

The Basics

• When you plug in your Instant Pot®, the display will read **OFF**. After you have selected the cooking function and adjusted the time, if necessary, the pot will automatically go on and start cooking 10 seconds after you push the last button.

• Press **CANCEL** if you need to start over.

• Press **CANCEL** when you are switching functions in the middle of a recipe—for instance, from **SAUTÉ** to **MANUAL** or from **SLOW COOK** to **SAUTÉ** to reduce a sauce.

• For both the **SAUTÉ** and **SLOW COOK** functions, there are three temperature settings: **LESS**, **NORMAL**, and **MORE**. **Note:** If you have an Ultra 10-in-1 Multi-Use Programmable Pressure Cooker, Low/Medium/High correspond to Less/Normal/More on the Duo 7-in-1 Multi-Use Programmable Pressure Cooker.

• For all cooking functions except **SLOW COOK**, **YOGURT**, and **SAUTÉ** (when you don't use the lid), the pressure-release valve should be in the closed or sealed position.

Pressure Cooking in the Instant Pot®

Pressure cooking can be done in one of two ways:

The selection of **MANUAL** (choosing high or low pressure) and the setting of the cook time using the **+** and **-** buttons is one way. The other is through the use of the pre-set buttons. Each of the pre-set buttons defaults to high pressure, with the exception of **RICE**, which defaults to low pressure. Each pre-set button also has a default (**NORMAL**) cook time, but can be adjusted to **LESS** or **MORE**. Each pre-set can also be customized to any time you like using the **+** and **-** buttons. To see the **NORMAL**, **LESS**, and **MORE** cook times for each pre-set function, press the **ADJUST** button to toggle among them. (Note that these times only refer to the cook time—not the Closed Pot Time; see "Understanding the Timings," page 13.) To clear the machine from a previously customized cook time, press the **ADJUST** button for 3 seconds, until you hear a beep.

Slow Cooking in the Instant Pot®

The **SLOW COOK** function on the Instant Pot® defaults to a 4-hour cook time. Use the **+** or **-** buttons to set the time and the **ADJUST** button to toggle among the three temperature settings—**NORMAL, LESS**, and **MORE**. In this book, **SLOW COOK** is most often used on **MORE**. This temperature level is the equivalent of medium-high if there was such a setting on a stand-alone slow cooker, so the timings are somewhere between what would be low and high on a regular slow cooker.

Sautéing in the Instant Pot®

The **SAUTÉ** function on the Instant Pot® has three temperature settings—**NORMAL, LESS**, and **MORE**. Although you don't need to set a cook time for the **SAUTÉ** function, it automatically shuts off after 30 minutes. In this book, **SAUTÉ** is most often used on **NORMAL** (although there are few exceptions). **MORE** can be used to very quickly sear and brown a piece of meat, and **LESS** can be used to simmer or reduce a sauce.

Other Functions

The **YOGURT** program involves a two-stage process to make homemade yogurt—first to boil and cool down the milk, then to incubate the yogurt for a minimum of 8 hours after the live cultures are added. See page 293 for the Homemade Yogurt recipe.

Use the **DELAY START** button (or **TIMER** on older models) to delay the start of cooking. Select a cooking function, make any adjustments, then press the **DELAY START** button and adjust with the **+** and **-** buttons. Press the button once for hours and again for minutes.

Use **KEEP WARM/CANCEL** to cancel a function or turn off the Instant Pot®. The **SLOW COOK** and all pressure-cooking functions switch over to **KEEP WARM** after the cook time is complete and the pressure has been released from the pot, whether by a natural or quick release.

1. To open the lid, grasp the handle and rotate lid about 30 degrees counterclockwise in the direction of "Open" until the ▼ mark on the lid is aligned with the ▲ mark on the cooker base. When the lid can be lifted off of the pot, you will hear a chime.

2. The inner pot of the Instant Pot® is removable for easy cleaning and so that you can better read the volume-level markings on the inside. You can either add the food and liquid to the inner pot when it is outside of the Instant Pot® or when it has been placed inside the Instant Pot®. Be sure the outside is clean and free of drips before you return the inner pot to the Instant Pot® for cooking.

3. For pressure cooking, the total amount of food and liquid should never exceed the maximum level marking of the inner pot. It's recommended that you do not fill the inner pot more than ⅔ full. For foods such as rice, beans, and dried vegetables, do not fill pot more than ½ full.

4. Secure the lid on the pot by the opposite method of opening it. You will hear a chime when it is locked on.

Turn the pressure-release valve to the proper setting—open or closed—for your recipe.

5. Select cooking function and program the cooker. Adjust pressure, temperature, and cook times according to the directions in your recipe if necessary.

6. For pressure cooking, release the pressure in one of two ways according to what is specified in the recipe.

Quick Release: Turn the pressure-release valve to the open or venting position to quickly release steam until the float valve drops down. In general, do not use quick release for foods with a large volume of liquid or high starch content, such as grains and starchy soups. Food may splatter out of the valve.

Natural Release: Leave the pressure-release valve in the closed position. This method allows the cooker to cool down naturally until the float valve drops down. This can take 10 to 15 minutes or even longer. The cooker will not go into the **KEEP WARM** cycle until all of the pressure has been released.

How to Use Our Recipes

In addition to knowing how to use the Instant Pot® from a technical standpoint, understanding how the recipes in this book are written will make cooking with it that much easier.

Recipe Selection

With the exception of the blogger favorites, every recipe in this book was created new for the Instant Pot®. We wanted this book to be comprehensive—to be largely built on classic dishes everyone loves to make and eat adapted for the Instant Pot®. You know you can turn to this book for superlative versions of your favorite foods. But we also included a selection of innovative dishes or standards with a twist to keep things fresh and interesting. The recipes are written so that if even if you've never used the Instant Pot® before, you can easily follow them.

How We Tested

Every recipe in this book was tested in a 6-quart Duo 7-in-1 Multi-Use Programmable Pressure Cooker. (Note that the size of Instant Pot® you use can affect the timings slightly. A larger pot will take slightly more time to come up to pressure, while a smaller one will take slightly less.)

The purpose of recipe testing is to make sure a recipe works every time you make it, that the timings are accurate, that it tastes great, and that the finished product is of the highest quality possible. We tested these recipes until we got the results we wanted: Perfectly cooked meats and poultry that were juicy, tender, and never dried out. Vegetables that maintained their bright colors and fresh flavors, with an optimum texture that was appropriate to the dish—whether that was creamy and tender baby potatoes or barely cooked zucchini that still had a bit of a bite. And fish and shellfish that came out of the cooker with their delicate textures and flavors intact.

Understanding the Timings

One of strongest advantages of the Instant Pot®—inherent in its name—is its ability to help you make fresh food fast. So the timings in the banners at the top of each recipe contain very important information. Here's how we define each term:

Prep Time: This refers to everything in the method that is done before the lid is secured on the pot and the button is selected for the first (and often only) closed-pot cooking function. That includes preparing and chopping fresh vegetables and browning and searing meats and poultry. Some recipes require a little bit of additional prep work while the pot is cooking—and if so, that time is included in the Total Time—but most don't, so you can walk away and do other things.

Function: This simply refers to which function(s) on the Instant Pot® is used to make that recipe and at which level it is used.

Closed Pot Time: This is important to note. It is not the cook time, which is specified in the recipe, but rather the entire time the lid is on the pot, which—in the case of pressure cooking—includes the time it takes for the pot to come up to pressure, cook, and depressurize, whether by a natural or quick release. For slow cooking, it refers to the minimum cooking time given in the recipe.

Total Time: This refers to the Prep Time and Closed Pot Time totals, plus any additional steps that are not part of that (such as marinating, chilling, standing, or simmering). Those are noted separately after a + sign in the Total Time box.

Reading the Recipes

The recipe method is broken down into three sections: Prep, Cook, and Serve.

Prep: See the "Understanding the Timings" section at left for a definition of Prep. This step always ends with securing the lid on the pot and either closing the pressure-release valve (for pressure-cooking and steaming) or opening the pressure-release valve (for slow-cooking and all other functions except sautéing, which is done with no lid).

Cook: This includes the selection of the cook function and, if pressure cooking, the type of release that should be used when cooking is complete. If there are a few additional cooking steps that follow, they are also included in this step.

Serve: This refers to the last steps in the method—often it is simply seasoning a dish, sprinkling it with fresh herbs, or transferring it to a bowl or platter—that are done to get ready to serve the dish.

*Note: The recipes in this book refer to the steam rack that came with your Instant Pot® as "the trivet." This is to distinguish it from a collapsible basket-style vegetable steamer—both of which are used in these recipes. Sometimes just one is used; sometimes both. Particularly if your vegetable steamer doesn't have legs, it is helpful to stack it on top of the trivet in the pot to keep foods out of the water or other liquid at the bottom of the pot.

Breakfast

Chai-Spiced Breakfast Quinoa with Berries

Instead of getting your chai fix in a cup, try it in a bowl—in this healthy and nicely spiced grain-based breakfast dish. Fresh berries are stirred into the creamy grains and placed on top—with a drizzle of honey.

PREP TIME	FUNCTION	CLOSED POT TIME	TOTAL TIME
10 minutes	Slow Cook (More)	2 hours	2 hours 10 minutes

SERVES: 6

- 2 cups quinoa
- 5 cups water
- ¼ cup honey
- 1 tablespoon coconut oil
- 2 teaspoons minced fresh ginger
- 1 teaspoon ground cardamom
- 1 teaspoon ground cinnamon
- ¼ teaspoon ground cloves
- ¼ teaspoon ground nutmeg
- ¼ teaspoon salt
- 1 cup refrigerated coconut milk (full fat) or half-and-half
- 2 cups raspberries, chopped strawberries, blueberries, and/or blackberries
- Honey

PREP
Place quinoa in a sieve and rinse well under cool running water; let drain. Combine quinoa, the water, honey, coconut oil, ginger, cardamom, cinnamon, cloves, nutmeg, and salt in the Instant Pot®. Secure the lid on the pot. Open the pressure-release valve.

COOK
Select **SLOW COOK** and adjust to **MORE**. Cook for 2 to 3 hours or until grains are tender. Press **CANCEL**.

SERVE
Stir in the coconut milk and 1 cup of the fresh berries. Top each serving with the remaining berries and drizzle with honey.

Coconut-Lime Breakfast Porridge

Coconut and lime give this creamy breakfast cereal a tropical touch. Topped with fresh, juicy blackberries, it's a healthful, eye-opening way to start your day.

PREP TIME	FUNCTION	CLOSED POT TIME	TOTAL TIME	RELEASE
5 minutes	Porridge (Less)	30 minutes	35 minutes	Natural

SERVES: 3 to 4

Nonstick cooking spray

1 **cup steel-cut oats**

1 **cup refrigerated coconut milk**

½ **teaspoon finely shredded lime zest**

2 **tablespoons freshly squeezed lime juice**

1 **tablespoon honey or agave nectar**

2 **cups cold water**

⅛ **teaspoon salt**

2 **cups fresh blackberries, washed**

PREP
Spray the inner pot of the Instant Pot® lightly with cooking spray (this helps reduce foaming and aids in cleanup). Combine the oats, coconut milk, lime zest, lime juice, honey, the water, and salt in the pot. Stir well. Secure the lid on the pot. Close the pressure-release valve.

COOK
Select **PORRIDGE** and adjust to **LESS.** When cooking is complete, use a natural release to depressurize. Remove lid; set aside. Stir porridge well, allowing any excess liquid to be absorbed.

SERVE
Serve porridge in warm bowls topped with fresh blackberries.

Jill Nussinow blogs at TheVeggieQueen.com and is the author of *Vegan Under Pressure*.

Pumpkin-Spice Steel-Cut Oats

The wildly popular pumpkin-spice combo infuses this hearty oatmeal flavored with warm spices and maple syrup and studded with dried cranberries. Crunchy toasted nuts on top add texture and nutrition. Perfect for a fall morning!

PREP TIME	FUNCTION	CLOSED POT TIME	TOTAL TIME	RELEASE
10 minutes	Pressure/Manual (High)	20 minutes	30 minutes	Natural

SERVES: 4

Nonstick cooking spray (optional)

2¼ cups water

1 cup unsweetened plain or vanilla almond, soy, or cashew milk

Pinch of salt

½ teaspoon grated nutmeg

¼ teaspoon ground cardamom

1 to 2 cinnamon sticks

¼ cup dried cranberries

1 cup steel-cut oats

½ cup pumpkin puree or ½ cup diced pumpkin or other squash

1 to 2 teaspoons pumpkin pie spice

Maple syrup

¼ cup chopped toasted pecans or walnuts

PREP

Spray the inner pot of the Instant Pot® lightly with cooking spray if desired (this helps reduce foaming and aids in cleanup). Combine the water and milk in the pot. Stir in the salt, nutmeg, cardamom, cinnamon sticks, and cranberries. Add the oats and pumpkin, but do not stir. Secure the lid on the pot. Close the pressure-release valve.

COOK

Select **MANUAL** and cook at high pressure for 10 minutes. When cooking is complete, use a natural release to depressurize.

Carefully remove the lid, tilting it away from you.

SERVE

Stir the mixture. If it seems watery, place the lid back on and let sit 5 minutes. Open carefully. Use long tongs to remove and discard the cinnamon sticks. Add the pumpkin pie spice and maple syrup to taste.

Top each bowl with toasted nuts.

PUMPKIN-SPICE BUCKWHEAT: Make this dish with buckwheat groats (kasha) instead of steel-cut oats. Follow the same directions.

Breakfast Sausage Meatballs
with Maple-Apricot Glaze

Meatballs for breakfast? You bet! Especially when they're seasoned with classic breakfast-sausage herbs and spices, such as sage, mustard, and caraway—and a hint of heat from cayenne. The sweetness of the apricots and maple syrup beautifully balances the savory flavors.

PREP TIME	FUNCTION	CLOSED POT TIME	TOTAL TIME	RELEASE
55 minutes	Sauté (Less); Pressure/Manual (High)	20 minutes	1 hour 15 minutes	Quick

SERVES: 6

- 1 egg
- 1 medium cooking apple, peeled, cored, and finely chopped
- ½ cup quick-cooking oats
- ¼ cup thinly sliced green onions
- 1 teaspoon dried sage, crushed
- ½ teaspoon salt
- ½ teaspoon ground mustard
- ¼ teaspoon caraway seeds or fennel seeds, finely crushed* (optional)
- ¼ teaspoon black pepper
- ⅛ to ¼ teaspoon cayenne pepper (optional)
- 1 to 1¼ pounds ground turkey
- 1 to 2 tablespoons cooking oil
- ⅓ cup water
- ⅓ cup chopped dried apricots
- ½ cup pure maple syrup
- ½ cup apricot preserves

PREP
In a large bowl beat egg lightly. Stir in apple, oats, green onions, sage, salt, mustard, caraway seeds (if using), black pepper, and cayenne pepper (if using). Add turkey; mix well.

Shape mixture into eighteen 2-inch meatballs. Select **SAUTÉ** on the Instant Pot® and adjust to **LESS**. Once hot, add 1 tablespoon of the oil. Cook meatballs, half at a time, in hot oil until meatballs are browned, carefully turning occasionally to lightly brown all sides evenly, for about 10 minutes. If necessary, add remaining oil to pot to prevent sticking. Transfer meatballs to a large plate when browned. Press **CANCEL**.

Add the water, apricots, syrup, and preserves to pot. Stir until combined. Place the trivet in the bottom of the pot. Arrange browned meatballs on trivet, stacking as needed so all fit in the pot. Secure the lid on the pot. Close the pressure-release valve.

COOK
Select **MANUAL** and cook at high pressure for 6 minutes. When cooking is complete, use a quick release to depressurize.

SERVE
Transfer meatballs to a large shallow serving bowl. Remove trivet from pot. Stir sauce in bottom of pot. Pour over meatballs. Toss gently to coat meatballs with sauce. Serve warm.

*TIP: Use a spice grinder or clean coffee grinder to easily crush seeds.

Spinach, Tomato & Feta Frittatas

These individual frittatas are made in 6-ounce ramekins or custard cups. To give the Greek flavor profile a boost, substitute dried oregano for the dried basil.

PREP TIME	FUNCTION	CLOSED POT TIME	TOTAL TIME	RELEASE
15 minutes	Pressure/Manual (High)	15 minutes	30 minutes	Quick

SERVES: 4

- 1½ cups water
- Nonstick cooking spray
- ¼ cup chopped, seeded tomato
- ¼ cup coarsely chopped baby spinach
- 1 green onion, sliced
- ¼ cup crumbled feta cheese, divided
- 4 eggs, beaten
- 1 tablespoon milk
- ¼ teaspoon dried basil, crushed
- ⅛ teaspoon salt
- Dash black pepper

PREP

Place the trivet—with handles under the rack—in the Instant Pot®. Add the water to pot.

Coat four 6-ounce ramekins or custard cups with cooking spray. Divide tomato, spinach, green onion, and half of the feta cheese among the ramekins. In a small bowl combine eggs, milk, basil, salt, and pepper. Pour egg mixture into ramekins. Cover each ramekin with foil. Arrange 3 of the ramekins evenly on the trivet. Set remaining ramekin on top of the other three.

Secure the lid on the pot. Close the pressure-release valve.

COOK

Select **MANUAL** and cook at high pressure for 5 minutes. When cooking is complete, use a quick release to depressurize.

SERVE

Carefully remove ramekins from pot. Remove foil and top with remaining feta cheese.

Barbara Schieving is the creator of the blog PressureCookingToday.com.

Crustless Tomato-Spinach Quiche

This veggie quiche is especially delicious when made with ripe, juicy summer tomatoes.

PREP TIME	FUNCTION	CLOSED POT TIME	TOTAL TIME	RELEASE
20 minutes	Pressure/Manual (High)	1 hour 15 minutes	1 hour 35 minutes	Natural

SERVES: 6

- 1½ cups water
- 12 large eggs
- ½ cup milk
- ½ teaspoon salt
- ¼ teaspoon black pepper
- 3 cups fresh baby spinach, roughly chopped (one 5-ounce package)
- 1 cup diced, seeded tomato
- 3 large green onions, sliced (green part only)
- 4 tomato slices
- ¼ cup shredded Parmesan cheese

PREP

Place the trivet in the pot. Pour the water into the Instant Pot®.

In a large bowl whisk together the eggs, milk, salt, and pepper. Add spinach, diced tomato, and green onions to egg mixture and stir to combine. Lightly grease a 1½-quart baking dish. Transfer to prepared dish. Gently place sliced tomatoes on top and sprinkle with Parmesan cheese.

Cover top of dish with foil. Tear an 18-inch-long sheet of foil. Fold the sheet lengthwise into thirds to make a long, narrow sling. Use the sling to place the dish on the trivet in the pot. Secure the lid on the pot. Close the pressure-release valve.

COOK

Select **MANUAL** and cook at high pressure for 20 minutes. When cooking is complete, use a natural release to depressurize.

Carefully open the lid and lift out the dish.

SERVE

If desired, broil until top is lightly browned.

Eggs Shakshuka

Pronounced [shahk-SHOO-kah], this dish of eggs poached in rich, spicy tomato sauce (the degree of heat varies from recipe to recipe) is a popular breakfast in North Africa and the Middle East. The heat level of this version is fairly mild.

PREP TIME	FUNCTION	CLOSED POT TIME	TOTAL TIME	RELEASE
30 minutes	Sauté (Normal); Pressure/Manual (High, Low)	20 minutes	50 minutes	Quick

SERVES: 6

- 1 tablespoon olive oil
- 1 medium onion, chopped
- 1 clove garlic, minced
- 1 large red sweet pepper, chopped
- 4 cups diced ripe red tomatoes (4 to 6 medium tomatoes)
- 2 tablespoons tomato paste
- 1 teaspoon chili powder
- 1½ teaspoons ground cumin
- 1 teaspoon sweet paprika
- ¼ teaspoon cayenne
- ½ teaspoon caraway seeds, crushed
- 6 eggs
- 6 ounces feta cheese, crumbled
- 1 cup thinly sliced spinach leaves

PREP
Select **SAUTÉ** on the Instant Pot® and adjust to **NORMAL**. When hot, add the olive oil, onion, and garlic. Cook and stir for 3 minutes or until onion is soft. Press **CANCEL**.

Add sweet pepper, tomatoes, tomato paste, chili powder, cumin, paprika, cayenne, and caraway. Stir to combine. Secure the lid on the pot. Close the pressure-release valve.

COOK
Select **MANUAL** and cook at high pressure for 5 minutes. When cooking is complete, use a quick release to depressurize.

Once steam is released, open lid. Working one egg at a time, break eggs on top of the hot sauce, spacing evenly.* Secure the lid on the pot. Close the pressure-release valve. Select **MANUAL** and cook at low pressure for 1 minute. When cooking is complete, use a quick release to depressurize.

SERVE
Using a large spoon, transfer eggs and sauce onto serving plates. Sprinkle each serving with feta cheese and sliced spinach; serve immediately.

*TIP: It's easiest to first crack each egg into a 1-cup glass measure and gently pour it into the hot tomato sauce.

Bagel-Lox Strata

This elegant strata is perfect for entertaining company for brunch. Serve it with a crisp green salad, ripe tomato wedges, or fresh fruit—and a little bit of something bubbly, if you'd like.

PREP TIME	FUNCTION	CLOSED POT TIME	TOTAL TIME	RELEASE
20 minutes	Pressure/Manual (High)	35 minutes	55 minutes	Quick

SERVES: 6

- 1   cup water
- 2   everything bagels, cut into bite-size pieces
- 1   ounce cream cheese, cut into ½-inch pieces
- 2   ounces thinly sliced smoked salmon (lox-style), cut into small pieces
- 2   tablespoons finely chopped onion
- 1   tablespoon snipped fresh chives
- 4   eggs
- 1   cup milk
- ½   cup cream-style cottage cheese
- 2   teaspoons snipped fresh dill

PREP

Place the trivet in the bottom of the Instant Pot®. Add the water to the pot.

Lightly grease a 1½-quart round ceramic or glass baking dish. Arrange half of the bagel pieces in the prepared dish. Top with cream cheese, salmon, onion, and chives. Arrange the remaining bagel pieces over salmon mixture.

In a medium bowl combine eggs, milk, cottage cheese, and dill. Pour evenly over ingredients in dish. Press lightly with the back of a large spoon to moisten all of the bagels. Cover with foil. Place the dish on the trivet. Secure the lid on the pot. Close the pressure-release valve.

COOK

Select **MANUAL** and cook at high pressure for 25 minutes. When cooking is complete, use a quick release to depressurize.

SERVE

Carefully remove the dish from the cooker. Uncover the dish. If desired, broil the strata 4 inches from the heat for 3 to 4 minutes or until the top is lightly browned.

Bacon & Egg Breakfast Bowl

The Instant Pot® makes quick work of steel-cut oats, but instead of the standard sweetened cereal, this recipe turns the oats into a savory breakfast bowl topped with bacon and eggs.

PREP TIME	FUNCTION	CLOSED POT TIME	TOTAL TIME	RELEASE
15 minutes	Sauté (Normal); Porridge (Normal)	30 minutes	45 minutes	Natural

SERVES: 4

- 4 slices bacon, coarsely diced
- ½ cup diced onion
- 2 garlic cloves, minced
- ½ cup steel-cut oats
- 2 cups chicken broth
- ¼ teaspoon black pepper
- ⅛ teaspoon crushed red pepper
- 4 eggs
  Salt and black pepper
- 1 avocado, sliced
  Snipped fresh chives

PREP
Select **SAUTÉ** on Instant Pot® and adjust to **NORMAL**. When hot, add the bacon and cook, stirring occasionally, until bacon is crisp. Remove bacon to a paper towel-lined plate. Press **CANCEL**. Remove all but 1 tablespoon of the grease from the pot, reserving extra grease in a small dish.

Select **SAUTÉ** and adjust to **NORMAL**. Add onion and garlic to pot. Cook, stirring, for 2 to 3 minutes or just until fragrant. Press **CANCEL**. Add oats, broth, black pepper, and crushed red pepper. Secure the lid on the pot. Close the pressure-release valve.

COOK
Select **PORRIDGE** and adjust to **NORMAL**. Once cooking is complete, use a natural release to depressurize.

When pressure release is nearly complete, heat remaining bacon grease in a skillet. Add eggs and cook 3 to 4 minutes or until whites are nearly set. Season with salt and black pepper to taste. Carefully flip, if desired, and cook for 1 to 3 minutes until desired doneness.

SERVE
Release any remaining steam from the pot by opening pressure-release valve. Divide oats among four bowls. Top with bacon, egg, and avocado. Sprinkle with chives.

Cinnamon-Spiced Breakfast Bake with Bacon

Looking for something a little naughty and indulgent? This bread-pudding-style casserole is made with a combination of torn French bread and doughnuts and finished off with maple syrup and powdered sugar. Smoky, salty bacon provides a nice contrast to all of that sweetness.

PREP TIME	FUNCTION	CLOSED POT TIME	TOTAL TIME	RELEASE
20 minutes	Sauté (Less); Pressure/Manual (High)	45 minutes	1 hour 5 minutes + 15 minutes stand	Quick

SERVES: 6

- 2 cups French bread cubes (½-inch cubes)
- 4 cups torn doughnuts (cinnamon sugar cake and/or glazed raised doughnuts)
- 6 eggs
- 2 cups 2% milk
- ¼ teaspoon pumpkin pie spice or ground cinnamon
- ¼ teaspoon salt
- 1 tablespoon pure vanilla extract
- 4 slices bacon, diced
  Nonstick cooking spray
- 2 cups water
  Pure maple syrup
  Powdered sugar

PREP

Combine bread cubes and torn doughnuts in a large bowl. Whisk together eggs, milk, pumpkin pie spice, salt, and vanilla in a mixing bowl. Pour over bread and doughnuts. Stir to combine; set aside.

Select **SAUTÉ** on the Instant Pot® and adjust to **LESS**. Sauté diced bacon for 5 minutes. Press **CANCEL**. Remove bacon pieces to a paper towel-lined plate. Drain grease and wipe pot clean with a paper towel.

Stir bacon into doughnut and egg mixture. Pour into a 1½- or 2-quart soufflé dish coated with cooking spray. Cover with foil. Add water to pot. Place soufflé dish in the pot. Secure the lid on the pot. Close the pressure-release valve.

COOK

Select **MANUAL** and cook at high pressure for 35 minutes. When cooking is complete, use a quick release to depressurize. Remove foil and let stand for 15 minutes before serving.

SERVE

Spoon into serving bowls. Drizzle with maple syrup and powdered sugar.

Hearty Eggs Benedict Breakfast Casserole

This breakfast casserole has all of the flavors of traditional Eggs Benedict without the egg poaching—and with a healthy dose of veggies.

PREP TIME	FUNCTION	CLOSED POT TIME	TOTAL TIME	RELEASE
30 minutes	Sauté (Normal); Pressure/Manual (High)	30 minutes	1 hour + 20 minutes bake/stand	Quick

SERVES: 6

- 1 tablespoon olive oil
- 1 cup sliced fresh button mushrooms
- ½ cup chopped red sweet pepper
- 3 green onions
- 5 eggs
- 1¼ cups whole milk
- ¼ teaspoon black pepper
- 4 English muffins, split and toasted
- 6 ounces thinly sliced Canadian bacon or cooked ham, chopped
- 1½ cups water

MOCK HOLLANDAISE SAUCE

- ⅓ cup sour cream
- ⅓ cup mayonnaise
- 2 teaspoons lemon juice
- 2 teaspoons yellow mustard
- Milk (optional)
- Sliced green onion (optional)

PREP

Select **SAUTÉ** on the Instant Pot® and adjust to **NORMAL**. When hot, add oil, mushrooms, and sweet pepper. Cook for 5 minutes, stirring occasionally. Thinly slice green onions, keeping white bottoms separate from green tops. Add white parts of green onions to pot with vegetables. Cook for 2 minutes more, stirring occasionally. Press **CANCEL**.

Meanwhile, in a large bowl whisk together eggs, milk, and black pepper. Cut or tear toasted English muffins into 1-inch pieces. Add to milk mixture. Stir in bacon. Add vegetables from the pot along with sliced green onion tops and Canadian bacon. Stir to combine.

Transfer bread mixture to a greased 1½-quart round ceramic or glass casserole (make sure the dish will fit in the Instant Pot® first). Spread to an even layer. Cover top with foil. Tear an 18-inch-long sheet of foil. Fold the sheet lengthwise into thirds to make a long, narrow sling.

Place the trivet in the bottom of the pot. Add the water to the pot. Place filled casserole in the center of the foil sling. Use the sling to lower the casserole into the pot until it sits on the steam rack. Tuck foil into pot so the lid will fit. Secure the lid on the pot. Close the pressure-release valve.

COOK

Select **MANUAL** and cook at high pressure for 20 minutes. When cooking is complete, use a quick release to depressurize.

SERVE

Lift the casserole out of the pot using the foil sling. Uncover casserole. Bake casserole in a 400°F oven for 10 to 15 minutes or until top is browned. Let casserole stand 10 minutes before serving.

Meanwhile, for Mock Hollandaise Sauce, combine sour cream, mayonnaise, lemon juice, and yellow mustard in a small saucepan. Cook and stir over medium-low heat until warm. If desired, stir in a little milk to thin. If desired, stir in sliced green onion. Drizzle sauce over each serving.

Three-Cheese Bacon-Scallion Crustless Quiche

Cheddar, Parmesan, and blue cheese add tanginess and rich flavor to this yummy quiche. Substitute smoked paprika for the regular paprika if you like.

PREP TIME	FUNCTION	CLOSED POT TIME	TOTAL TIME	RELEASE
15 minutes	Pressure/Manual (High)	40 minutes	55 minutes + 10 minutes stand	Natural

SERVES: 4 to 6

- 1½ **cups water**
- 6 **eggs**
- ¾ **cup milk**
- ½ **cup thinly sliced scallions**
- ½ **cup shredded sharp cheddar cheese**
- ¼ **cup crumbled blue cheese**
- 6 **slices bacon, crisp-cooked and crumbled**
- 3 **tablespoons grated Parmesan cheese**
- ½ **teaspoon freshly ground black pepper**
- ¼ **to ½ teaspoon paprika**
- **Sliced scallions**

PREP
Place the trivet in the pot. Add the water to Instant Pot®. Grease a 1-quart soufflé dish.

In a medium bowl whisk together eggs, milk, scallions, cheddar cheese, blue cheese, bacon, 2 tablespoons of the Parmesan cheese, and the pepper. Pour into prepared dish. Sprinkle with the remaining 1 tablespoon Parmesan cheese and the paprika. Cover dish with foil. Place covered dish on trivet. Secure the lid on the pot. Close the pressure-release valve.

COOK
Select **MANUAL** and cook at high pressure for 20 minutes. When cooking is complete, use a natural release to depressurize.

SERVE
Let cool for at least 10 minutes before serving. Sprinkle with additional sliced scallions just before serving.

Appetizers & Snacks

Savory Blue Cheese Appetizer Cheesecake

With a crust of crushed buttery crackers and chopped pecans, this savory cheesecake takes the standard cheeseball to a new level. Paired with crisp, sweet slices of apple and pear, it's perfect for a fall party.

PREP TIME	FUNCTION	CLOSED POT TIME	TOTAL TIME	RELEASE
45 minutes	Manual/Pressure (High)	1 hour 5 minutes	1 hour 50 minutes + 1 hour cool + 4 hours chill	Natural

SERVES: 12

Nonstick cooking spray

- 1 **cup finely crushed buttery crackers**
- ½ **cup finely chopped pecans**
- 3 **tablespoons melted butter**
- 16 **ounces cream cheese, softened**
- 4 **ounces blue cheese, crumbled**
- ¼ **cup heavy cream**
- 1 **teaspoon dried basil**
- ½ **teaspoon garlic powder**
- ¼ **teaspoon ground white pepper**
- 3 **eggs, room temperature**
- ¼ **cup diced green onions**
- 2 **cups water**

Crackers or crostini and pear and/or apple slices, for serving

PREP

Lightly spray a 6- or 7-inch springform pan with cooking spray. Cut a piece of parchment paper to fit the bottom of the pan. Place in the pan and spray again; set aside.

Combine crackers, pecans, and butter; mix well. Press into bottom and about 1½ inches up the sides of the springform pan.

Beat cream cheese, blue cheese, and cream in a large bowl until smooth and creamy. Beat in basil, garlic powder, and white pepper. Add eggs, one at a time, beating just until egg is combined. Fold in green onions. Pour into prepared crust. (Pan will be full.) Tent with foil.

Place trivet in the bottom of the pot. Pour the water into the Instant Pot®. Cut a piece of foil the same size as a paper towel. Place the foil under the paper towel and place the pan on top of the paper towel. Wrap the bottom of the pan in the foil with the paper towel as a barrier.

Fold an 18-inch-long piece of foil into thirds lengthwise. Place under the pan and use the two sides as a sling to place cheesecake on the trivet in the pot. Secure the lid on the pot. Close the pressure-release valve.

COOK

Select **MANUAL** and cook at high pressure for 40 minutes. When cooking is complete, use a natural release to depressurize.

SERVE

Remove the cheesecake from the pot using the sling. Cool on the rack for 1 hour and refrigerate for at least 4 hours. Carefully remove pan sides.

Serve cheesecake with crackers or crostini and pear and/or apple slices.

Greek Stuffed Grape Leaves

These delicate parcels of lamb or beef and rice flavored with lemon, parsley, mint, and dill—called *dolmades*—are a classic Greek *meze,* or appetizer. Boiling the leaves before filling and cooking tenderizes them.

PREP TIME	FUNCTION	CLOSED POT TIME	TOTAL TIME	RELEASE
45 minutes	Pressure/Manual (High)	40 minutes	1 hour 25 minutes	Natural

SERVES: about 34

1 **pound ground lamb or beef**

2 **cups uncooked instant rice**

3 **tablespoons fresh lemon juice**

2 **tablespoons finely chopped fresh flat-leaf parsley**

2 **tablespoons finely chopped fresh mint**

2 **tablespoons finely chopped fresh dill**

2 **tablespoons finely chopped green onions**

1 **teaspoon salt**

1 **15- to 16-ounce jar grape leaves (about 30 to 36 leaves)**

½ **cup water**

½ **cup lemon juice**

Plain Greek yogurt (optional)

PREP

To make the filling, in a large bowl combine lamb, rice, the 3 tablespoons lemon juice, parsley, mint, dill, green onions, and salt; set aside.

Bring a large pot of water to a boil. Add grape leaves. Boil for 5 minutes. Drain well.

To assemble the grape leaves, place four to six whole grape leaves at a time on a work surface with the stem sides up and stem ends pointing toward you. Pinch or trim off any long or tough stems. Depending on the size of the leaf, shape 1 to 2 tablespoons of the filling into a 1½- to 2-inch log and place it on the leaf perpendicular to the stem end. Roll the end of the leaf over the filling, tuck in the sides, and roll tightly into a cigar shape. Repeat with remaining grape leaves and filling.

Place the rolled grape leaves in the Instant Pot®, packing them together tightly and keeping them in the same direction. Once you finish a layer, turn the second layer of grape leaves in the opposite direction. After all the grape leaves are packed into the pot, add the water and the ½ cup lemon juice to the pot. Secure the lid on the pot. Close the pressure-release valve.

COOK

Select **MANUAL** and cook at high pressure for 15 minutes. When cooking is complete, use a natural release to depressurize.

SERVE

Serve stuffed grape leaves warm. If desired, serve yogurt for dipping. (They can also be chilled and served cold.)

Asian Chicken Sliders with Pickled Cucumbers & Onions

This slider features the famous Asian flavor quartet—sweet, sour, salt, and heat—but the flavors are subtle enough to appeal to both kids and adults.

PREP TIME	FUNCTION	CLOSED POT TIME	TOTAL TIME	RELEASE
45 minutes	Sauté (Normal); Pressure/Manual (High)	15 minutes	1 hour	Quick

SERVES: 12

SRIRACHA MAYONNAISE

½ cup mayonnaise

2 to 3 teaspoons sriracha sauce

PICKLED CUCUMBERS

1 cup thinly sliced cucumber

¼ cup thinly sliced red onion

¼ cup rice vinegar (unseasoned)

2 teaspoons sugar

¼ teaspoon crushed red pepper

SLIDERS

1 pound ground chicken breast

⅓ cup panko bread crumbs

¼ cup sliced green onions

1 egg, slightly beaten

1 tablespoon tamari sauce

1 tablespoon sriracha

2 teaspoons black bean garlic sauce

¼ teaspoon salt

1 tablespoon vegetable or olive oil

1 cup reduced-sodium chicken broth or water

12 sweet cocktail or slider buns

PREP

For the mayonnaise, stir together mayonnaise and desired amount of sriracha. Refrigerate until ready to use.

For the pickled cucumbers, combine cucumber, red onion, vinegar, sugar, and crushed red pepper in a bowl. Refrigerate until ready to use.

For the sliders, place chicken, bread crumbs, and green onions in a large bowl. Add beaten egg, tamari, sriracha, black bean sauce, and salt to chicken. Mix thoroughly to combine. Using wet hands (to keep the mixture from sticking), divide and shape into 12 equal-size meatballs, about 1½ inches in diameter.

Select **SAUTÉ** on the Instant Pot® and adjust to **NORMAL**. Add 1 tablespoon oil. When hot, cook half of the meatballs until browned on all sides, carefully turning, for about 6 minutes. Remove browned meatballs and repeat with remaining half. Return all meatballs to pot. Press **CANCEL**. Add broth. Secure the lid on the pot. Close the pressure-release valve.

COOK

Select **MANUAL** and cook at for 5 minutes on high pressure. When cooking is complete, use a quick release to depressurize.

SERVE

Remove meatballs from pot using a slotted spoon. For each slider, spread about 2 teaspoons sriracha mayonnaise on each bottom bun. Top each with a meatball and pickled cucumbers. Add bun tops and serve.

Italian Cocktail Meatballs

There aren't too many nonvegetarians who don't love a good meatball—whether it's served with sauce and spaghetti for dinner or as an appetizer on the end of a cocktail pick.

PREP TIME	FUNCTION	CLOSED POT TIME	TOTAL TIME	RELEASE
45 minutes	Sauté (Normal); Pressure/Manual (High)	20 minutes	1 hour 5 minutes	Quick

SERVES: 10 to 12

MEATBALLS

- 1 egg
- ¼ cup fine dry bread crumbs
- ¼ cup finely shredded Parmesan cheese
- 2 tablespoons milk
- 1 tablespoon chopped fresh basil
- 1 tablespoon chopped fresh flat-leaf parsley
- 2 cloves garlic, minced
- ½ teaspoon salt
- ¼ teaspoon black pepper
- 1 pound ground beef
  Finely shredded Parmesan (optional)

SAUCE

- 1 tablespoon olive oil
- ¾ cup chopped onion
- ¼ teaspoon salt
- ¼ teaspoon crushed red pepper
- 2 cloves garlic, minced
- 1 28-ounce can crushed tomatoes
- 1 8-ounce can tomato sauce
- 2 tablespoons chopped fresh basil

PREP

For the meatballs, in a medium bowl beat egg with a fork. Stir in bread crumbs, Parmesan, milk, basil, parsley, garlic, salt, and black pepper. Add ground beef; mix well. Shape mixture into 1-inch meatballs.

For the sauce, select **SAUTÉ** on the Instant Pot® and adjust to **NORMAL**. Heat oil in pot; add onion, salt, and crushed red pepper and cook for 2 to 3 minutes or until softened, stirring frequently. Add garlic; cook and stir 1 minute more. Press **CANCEL**. Add crushed tomatoes and tomato sauce; stir well. Add meatballs to sauce. Secure the lid on the pot. Close the pressure-release valve.

COOK

Select **MANUAL** and cook at high pressure for 6 minutes. When cooking is complete, use a quick release to depressurize.

SERVE

Stir basil into sauce and meatball mixture. If desired, top with additional Parmesan cheese.

Roasted Garlic Cheesy Crab Dip

Pressure cooking the garlic before mixing it with the other ingredients turns it mellow, creamy, and sweet so that it enhances the flavor of the dip but doesn't overwhelm the delicate flavor of the crab.

PREP TIME	FUNCTION	CLOSED POT TIME	TOTAL TIME	RELEASE
25 minutes	Pressure/Manual (High, Low)	45 minutes	1 hour 10 minutes	Natural/Quick

SERVES: 12 to 16

- ½ cup water
- 2 heads garlic
- 2 teaspoons olive oil
- 1 8-ounce package cream cheese, cut into cubes
- ½ cup finely shredded Parmesan cheese
- ½ cup mayonnaise
- 1 tablespoon Dijon mustard
- ¼ teaspoon celery seeds (optional)
- ¼ teaspoon black pepper
- ⅛ to ¼ teaspoon cayenne pepper
- 2 6-ounce cans lump crabmeat, drained, flaked, and cartilage removed
- ⅓ cup chopped fresh flat-leaf parsley
- 2 tablespoons lemon juice
- 1 green onion (green top only), thinly sliced
- Crostini* or crackers

PREP

Place the trivet in the bottom of the Instant Pot®. Add the water to pot. Cut a ½-inch-thick slice off the top of each head of garlic to expose the cloves; remove any loose papery skin from the garlic heads. Place garlic, cut sides up, on trivet in the pot. Drizzle tops of heads with half the olive oil. Secure the lid on the pot. Close the pressure-release valve.

Select **MANUAL** and cook at high pressure for 12 minutes. When cooking is complete, use a natural release to depressurize. Transfer garlic to a plate; set aside until cool enough to handle.

In a 3- to 4-cup glass bowl combine cream cheese, Parmesan cheese, mayonnaise, mustard, celery seeds (if using), black pepper, and cayenne pepper. Squeeze the base of each garlic head to push out cloves into a small bowl. Add remaining 1 teaspoon olive oil to garlic. Mash with a fork to a paste. Stir into cream cheese mixture. Gently stir in crabmeat. Place bowl on trivet in pot. Secure the lid on the pot. Close the pressure-release valve.

COOK

Select **MANUAL** and cook at low pressure for 8 minutes. When cooking is complete, use a quick release to depressurize. Stir in parsley and lemon juice. Sprinkle with green onion top slices. Serve with crostini or crackers.

***TO MAKE CROSTINI:** Cut a baguette crosswise into ¼-inch-thick slices. Arrange slices in a single layer on a large baking sheet. Brush tops and bottoms lightly with olive oil. Broil 3 to 4 inches from the heat for 1 to 2 minutes or until tops are lightly toasted. Flip bread slices. Broil for 1 to 2 minutes more or until tops are lightly toasted. Transfer to a wire rack; cool.

Lemon-Dill Snack Mix

This lively mix of crisped cereal, pretzel sticks, and toasted nuts will disappear in minutes, no matter the size of the crowd.

PREP TIME	FUNCTION	CLOSED POT TIME	TOTAL TIME
5 minutes	Slow Cook (More)	1 hour 30 minutes	1 hour 35 minutes + cool

SERVES: 14 (makes 7 cups)

Nonstick cooking spray

5 cups bite-size rice, corn, and/or wheat square cereal

2 cups pretzel sticks

1 cup coarsely chopped pecans

1 1-ounce dry ranch salad dressing mix

2 tablespoons dried dill

¼ cup olive oil

1 tablespoon lemon zest

PREP

Lightly coat the Instant Pot® with cooking spray. Add the cereal, pretzel sticks, pecans, dressing mix, and dill to the pot. Drizzle with the oil and toss to coat. Secure the lid on the pot. Open the pressure-release valve.

COOK

Select **SLOW COOK** and adjust to **MORE**. Cook, covered, for 1½ hours, stirring from the bottom every 30 minutes.

Sprinkle the lemon zest over the snack mix and toss gently to combine.

Spread the snack mix on a large baking pan and cool completely.

Laura Pazzaglia is the creator of the blog HipPressureCooking.com.

Artichoke Dip

There is some version of this delicious dip at nearly any gathering. This one incorporates white beans into the mix and swaps low-fat yogurt for the usual sour cream and mayonnaise. It's every bit as flavorful as the standard stuff—and lots better for you.

PREP TIME	FUNCTION		CLOSED POT TIME	TOTAL TIME	RELEASE
10 minutes	Pressure/Manual (High)		45 minutes	55 minutes	Natural

SERVES: 16 (¼-cup servings)

- ½ cup dried Great Northern beans, soaked overnight or quick-soaked
- 1 cup water
- 2 14-ounce cans artichoke hearts, drained
- 2 cloves garlic, smashed
- ¾ cup plain low-fat yogurt
- 1 teaspoon salt, or to taste
- ¼ teaspoon black pepper
- ¾ cup Parmigiano Reggiano cheese

  Crostini and/or bagel chips

PREP
Place beans, the water, and artichoke hearts in the Instant Pot®. Secure the lid on the pot. Close the pressure-release valve.

COOK
Select **MANUAL** and cook at high pressure for 25 minutes. When cooking is complete, use a natural release to depressurize.

SERVE
Add the garlic, yogurt, salt, pepper, and cheese to the pot. Blend with an immersion blender.

Serve warm with crostini and/or bagel chips or refrigerate tightly covered and remove from refrigerator 30 minutes before serving. The dip can be frozen up to 3 months.

Green Chile Chicken Dip

This decadent blend of cream cheese and Monterey Jack is spiked with Mexican seasonings and salsa verde. Choose a salsa that fits your personal tolerance for heat. Either fire-roasted or regular salsa works just fine.

PREP TIME	FUNCTION	CLOSED POT TIME	TOTAL TIME
20 minutes	Sauté (Normal); Slow Cook (More)	2 hours	2 hours 20 minutes

SERVES: 24 to 32

- 1 tablespoon olive oil
- ½ cup chopped onion
- 1 medium poblano pepper, seeded and chopped
- 2 cloves garlic, minced
- 3 cups chopped cooked chicken
- 1 16-ounce jar salsa verde tomatillo salsa
- 1 8-ounce package cream cheese, cubed
- 2 cups shredded Monterey Jack cheese
- 1 teaspoon chili powder
- ½ teaspoon ground cumin
- 1 cup sour cream
- 2 tablespoons chopped fresh cilantro
- Diced tomato (optional)
- Sliced jalapeño pepper (optional)
- Tortilla chips, for serving

PREP
Select **SAUTÉ** on the Instant Pot® and adjust to **NORMAL**. Heat oil in pot. Add the onion and poblano. Cook for 3 to 5 minutes or until softened, stirring frequently. Add the garlic. Cook and stir for 1 minute more. Press **CANCEL**.

Add chicken, salsa, cream cheese, shredded cheese, chili powder, and cumin. Secure the lid on the pot. Open the pressure-release valve.

COOK
Select **SLOW COOK** and adjust to **MORE**. Cook for 2 to 2½ hours, until heated through and cheese is melted; stir well to combine.

SERVE
Stir in sour cream and cilantro. Press **CANCEL**.

If desired, garnish with diced tomato and sliced jalapeño, if desired. Serve with tortilla chips.

Buffalo Chicken Wings with Blue Cheese Dressing

Whip up a batch of these before watching a game with friends, or—because they're so fast and easy—simply because you're craving that irresistible combination of vinegary, spicy chicken cooled down with creamy blue cheese dressing and crunchy veggies.

PREP TIME	FUNCTION	CLOSED POT TIME	TOTAL TIME	RELEASE
20 minutes	Pressure/Manual (High)	25 minutes	45 minutes + 10 minutes broil	Quick

SERVES: 12 to 16

- 1 cup water
- 3 pounds chicken wing pieces*
- ½ cup unsalted butter (1 stick)
- ½ cup hot pepper sauce (such as Frank's)
- 1 tablespoon apple cider vinegar
- ¼ teaspoon Worcestershire sauce
- ¼ teaspoon cayenne pepper
- ¼ teaspoon garlic powder
- Blue cheese dressing
- Celery and carrot sticks

PREP
Place the trivet in the Instant Pot®. Add the water to pot. Add the chicken to the pot. Secure the lid on the pot. Close the pressure-release valve.

COOK
Select **MANUAL** and cook at high pressure for 10 minutes. When cooking is complete, use a quick release to depressurize.

Meanwhile, for the sauce, in a microwave-safe bowl melt the butter. Stir in the hot sauce, vinegar, Worcestershire sauce, cayenne, and garlic powder.

Place the oven rack about 5 inches from the heat source. Preheat the oven on broil. Line a large baking pan with foil. Using tongs, arrange the wings in a single layer on the baking pan. Pat the wings dry with paper towels. Brush the wings with half the sauce. Broil the wings for 5 minutes. Brush with remaining sauce and broil 5 minutes more or until wings are lightly browned.

SERVE
Serve the wings with blue cheese dressing and carrot and celery sticks.

*TIP: Or purchase 3½ pounds chicken wings and cut at the joint to make about 36 pieces.

Sesame-Chile Edamame

Steaming edamame in the Instant Pot® is an ideal way to cook them. The pods get tender enough so you can easily strip them directly into your mouth with your teeth (yes, the proper way to eat edamame), but the beans retain an appealing crisp-tender bite. (Discard the pods.)

PREP TIME	FUNCTION	CLOSED POT TIME	TOTAL TIME	RELEASE
5 minutes	Steam	20 minutes	25 minutes	Quick

SERVES: 4 to 6

- 1 **cup water**
- 1 **to 1¼ pounds frozen edamame (in shells)**
- 1 **tablespoon thinly sliced fresh chives**
- 2 **teaspoons toasted sesame oil**
- 2 **teaspoons sesame seeds**
- 1 **teaspoon flaked sea salt**
- ½ **teaspoon crushed red pepper**
- ½ **teaspoon garlic powder**
- ¼ **teaspoon black pepper**

PREP

Place a vegetable steamer basket in the Instant Pot®; add the water to pot. Place the edamame in the steamer basket. Secure the lid on the pot. Close the pressure-release valve.

COOK

Select **STEAM** and cook for 2 minutes. When cooking is complete, use a quick release to depressurize.

SERVE

Meanwhile, in a small bowl combine the chives, oil, sesame seeds, sea salt, crushed red pepper, garlic powder, and black pepper. Lift out the steamer basket, allowing excess water to drip away. Transfer edamame to a bowl. Toss with sesame oil. Sprinkle with spice mixture; toss gently to coat evenly.

Beef, Pork & Lamb

Kitchen-Sink Pot Roast

This dish features the simple, satisfying flavors of old-school pot roast with a modern touch—a few handfuls of baby kale tossed in at the end for a splash of bright color and a nutritional boost.

PREP TIME	FUNCTION	CLOSED POT TIME	TOTAL TIME	RELEASE
35 minutes	Sauté (Normal); Pressure/Manual (High)	1 hour 30 minutes	2 hours 5 minutes	Quick

SERVES: 6 to 8

- 1 3½- to 4-pound boneless beef rump roast
- 1 teaspoon salt
- 1 teaspoon dried thyme
- ½ teaspoon black pepper
- 2 tablespoons vegetable oil
- 1½ cups beef broth
- 1 cup dry red wine
- 4 medium Yukon gold potatoes, halved (unpeeled)
- 2 medium yellow onions, quartered
- 4 large carrots, cut into 2-inch lengths
- 4 stalks celery, cut into 2-inch lengths
- 4 cups baby kale

PREP

Season roast with salt, thyme, and pepper. Select **SAUTÉ** on the Instant Pot® and adjust to **NORMAL**. When hot, add oil to the pot. Add the roast to the pot and brown on all sides for about 10 minutes. Press **CANCEL**. Add the broth and wine to the pot. Secure the lid on the pot. Close the pressure-release valve.

COOK

Select **MANUAL** and cook at high pressure for 50 minutes. When cooking time is complete, use a quick release to depressurize. Add the potatoes, onions, carrots, and celery. Secure the lid on the pot. Close the pressure-release valve. Select **MANUAL** and cook at high pressure for 10 minutes. When cooking time is complete, use a quick release to depressurize.

SERVE

Remove vegetables and meat to a serving platter. Stir kale into hot juices in cooker and allow to just wilt for 1 to 2 minutes. Remove with a slotted spoon and transfer to platter. Spoon some of the juices over meat and vegetables.

Beef Shank Osso Buco with Citrus Gremolata

Traditional osso buco is made with veal shanks. This version takes a tougher cut of meat—bone-in beef shanks—and turns them meltingly tender. A sprinkle of gremolata—a blend of lemon, orange, garlic, and parsley—right before serving gives the finished dish bright, fresh flavor.

PREP TIME	FUNCTION	CLOSED POT TIME	TOTAL TIME
45 minutes	Sauté (Normal); Slow Cook (More)	6 hours	6 hours 45 minutes

SERVES: 4

- ½ cup all-purpose flour
- 1 teaspoon salt
- ½ teaspoon freshly ground black pepper
- 4 crosscut bone-in beef shanks (2½ to 3 pounds)
- 2 tablespoons olive oil
- 1 cup chopped onion
- 1 cup chopped carrots
- ½ cup chopped celery
- 4 cloves garlic, minced
- ¼ cup tomato paste
- ⅓ cup dry white wine
- ½ teaspoon dried marjoram
- ½ teaspoon dried thyme
- 1¼ cups beef broth
- 1 tablespoon balsamic vinegar
- 2 bay leaves
- Citrus Gremolata
- Cooked polenta (optional)

PREP

In a shallow dish combine flour, salt, and pepper. Mix well. Dredge beef shanks in flour mixture, coating well.

Select **SAUTÉ** on the Instant Pot® and adjust to **NORMAL**. Add olive oil. Brown beef shanks in hot oil, one shank at a time, adding additional oil as needed. Set aside. Add onion, carrots, and celery. Cook and stir vegetables for 5 to 6 minutes or until onions are tender. Stir in garlic, tomato paste, and wine. Stir, scraping up any browned bits in bottom of pot. Press **CANCEL**. Arrange beef shanks on top of vegetables; sprinkle with marjoram and thyme. Add broth, vinegar, and bay leaves. Secure the lid on the pot. Open the pressure-release valve.

COOK

Select **SLOW COOK** and adjust to **MORE**. Cook for 6 to 7 hours or until beef is fork tender. Press **CANCEL**.

When cooking is complete, transfer beef shanks to an oven-safe platter; cover with foil and keep warm in a 200°F oven. Remove and discard bay leaves. Skim excess fat from sauce.

SERVE

If desired, serve beef shanks over polenta. Spoon sauce over beef shanks. Sprinkle with Citrus Gremolata. Serve immediately.

CITRUS GREMOLATA: Combine the finely shredded zest of 2 lemons, the finely shredded zest of 1 orange, 1 tablespoon minced garlic, and 1 cup finely chopped fresh flat-leaf parsley. Mix well. May be prepared up to 2 days ahead when tightly covered and refrigerated.

Barbacoa-Style Shredded Beef

Although *barbacoa* has traditionally referred to meat that is slow-cooked over an open fire or in a hole in the ground above hot coals, this version is inspired by some contemporary Mexican interpretations that call for steaming. The results are the same—tender, juicy, highly seasoned meat. Serve with tortillas or rice.

PREP TIME	FUNCTION	CLOSED POT TIME	TOTAL TIME
45 minutes	Sauté (Normal); Slow Cook (More)	5 hours	5 hours 45 minutes

SERVES: 8

1   2½- to 2¾-pound beef chuck roast

2   teaspoons paprika

1½   teaspoons dried oregano, crushed

1½   teaspoons ground cumin

1   teaspoon salt

½   teaspoon black pepper

¼   teaspoon ground cloves

1   tablespoon cooking oil

½   cup reduced-sodium beef broth

1   medium onion, cut into wedges

1   canned chipotle pepper in adobo sauce + 1 tablespoon adobo sauce from can

4   cloves garlic, minced

1   bay leaf

1   8-ounce can tomato sauce

¼   cup cider vinegar

1   tablespoon honey

16   corn tortillas, warmed

Salsa

Chopped avocado

Pickled Red Onion Slivers

Chopped fresh cilantro

Lime wedges

PREP

Trim fat from beef; cut beef into four portions. In a small bowl combine paprika, oregano, cumin, salt, black pepper, and cloves. Sprinkle over all sides of beef portions, rubbing in with your fingers. Select **SAUTÉ** on the Instant Pot® and adjust heat to **NORMAL**. When hot, add oil and beef pieces, half at a time if needed. Brown beef portions, turning to brown all sides evenly, for about 10 minutes. Press **CANCEL**. Add beef broth, onion, chipotle pepper and adobo sauce, garlic, and bay leaf to pot with beef. Secure the lid on the pot. Open the pressure-release valve.

COOK

Select **SLOW COOK** and adjust to **MORE**. Cook for 5 to 6 hours or until meat is tender. Press **CANCEL**.

SERVE

Transfer meat to a cutting board using a slotted spoon; cover to keep warm. Remove bay leaf from cooking juices and discard. Skim fat from top of cooking juices. Add tomato sauce, vinegar, and honey to cooking juices in pot. Use an immersion blender* to blend cooking juices until very smooth.

Using two forks, shred the cooked beef. Add beef back to pot with cooking juices. Toss to coat meat with juices. Using a slotted spoon, serve meat in tortillas topped with salsa, avocado, Pickled Red Onion Slivers, and cilantro. Serve with lime wedges for squeezing.

PICKLED RED ONION SLIVERS: In a medium bowl combine ½ cup slivered red onion and ⅓ cup lime juice. Toss to coat; press down on onion to cover as much with the juice as possible. Cover; let stand at room temperature for 30 minutes or chill for up to 3 days, stirring occasionally. Drain onion to serve.

*If you don't have an immersion blender, transfer the cooking juices to a regular blender; cover and blend until smooth. Return blended juice to the pot.

Korean Beef Tacos with Sriracha Slaw

It was a beautiful day when someone decided to fuse the Korean seasonings for beef—soy, sugar, garlic, sesame, and hot chiles—with the Mexican habit of enjoying cooked meat wrapped in a tortilla.

PREP TIME	FUNCTION	CLOSED POT TIME	TOTAL TIME
20 minutes	Sauté (Normal); Slow Cook (More)	6 hours	6 hours 20 minutes

SERVES: 8

BEEF

- 1 tablespoon vegetable oil
- 2 to 2½ pounds boneless beef chuck roast, cut into 3 to 4 chunks
- 1 Asian or Bosc pear, cored
- ¼ cup reduced-sodium soy sauce
- 3 tablespoons brown sugar
- 4½ teaspoons minced garlic
- 1 tablespoon sesame oil
- Dash cayenne pepper
- 1 tablespoon sesame seeds, toasted
- 16 6-inch flour tortillas
- Fresh cilantro

SRIRACHA SLAW

- ¼ cup mayonnaise
- 2 teaspoons sriracha sauce
- 1 bag (14 to 16 ounces) coleslaw mix

PREP

Select **SAUTÉ** on the Instant Pot® and adjust to **NORMAL**. Add oil to pot. When hot, add the chunks of chuck roast and cook for 5 to 8 minutes or until well browned. Drain fat.

Shred pear into a medium bowl. Add soy sauce, brown sugar, garlic, sesame oil, and cayenne pepper. Mix well. Pour over the beef. Press **CANCEL**. Secure the lid on the pot. Open the pressure-release valve.

COOK

Select **SLOW COOK** and adjust to **MORE**. Cook for 6 to 7 hours until beef is very tender. Press **CANCEL**.

SERVE

Combine mayonnaise and sriracha in a large bowl. Add coleslaw mix and toss to coat. Refrigerate until beef is ready. Shred beef with two forks. Sprinkle with sesame seeds.

Portion beef into tortillas and top with slaw and cilantro.

Beef Stroganoff Sandwiches

The nostalgic, old-school dish your mother might have made with French onion soup mix gets a modern remix. This version is made with a blend of natural seasonings and is served on toasted French bread with sliced baby sweet peppers and melty cheese on top.

PREP TIME	FUNCTION	CLOSED POT TIME	TOTAL TIME	RELEASE
10 minutes	Sauté (Normal); Pressure/Manual (High)	35 minutes	1 hour 10 minutes + 5 minutes broil	Natural

SERVES: 4

- 1 pound lean ground beef
- ½ cup chopped onion
- 2 cloves garlic, minced
- 1 8-ounce package button mushrooms, sliced
- 2 tablespoons flour
- 1½ cups beef broth
- ¼ teaspoon salt
- ½ teaspoon coarsely ground black pepper
- 1 8-ounce carton sour cream
- 1 teaspoon Worcestershire sauce
- 1 loaf French bread, ends trimmed and cut into four 4-inch pieces
- Butter, softened
- 4 to 6 mini sweet peppers, sliced
- 1 cup shredded cheddar cheese

PREP
Select **SAUTÉ** on the Instant Pot® and adjust to **NORMAL**. Add the ground beef, onion, garlic, and mushrooms. Cook for 5 minutes or until the meat is browned. Press **CANCEL**. Drain off any fat. Stir in the flour to coat. Add the broth, salt, and pepper. Secure the lid on the pot. Close the pressure-release valve.

COOK
Select **MANUAL** and cook at high pressure for 10 minutes. When cooking is complete, use a natural release to depressurize.

SERVE
Stir in the sour cream and Worcestershire sauce.

Adjust an oven rack 4 inches from the heat source and preheat the broiler. Place bread, cut sides up, on a baking sheet and lightly spread with butter. Broil for 2 to 3 minutes or until bread is lightly toasted.

Spoon the stroganoff onto the toasted bread. Top with pepper slices and cheese. Broil for 3 to 4 minutes or until cheese is melted.

Grown-Up Sloppy Joes

The "adult" element in the filling for these saucy sandwiches is a splash of stout beer, which gives the meat mixture a rich, malty taste. No harm done if you leave it out.

PREP TIME	FUNCTION	CLOSED POT TIME	TOTAL TIME
20 minutes	Sauté (Normal); Slow Cook (More)	5 hours	5 hours 20 minutes

SERVES: 8

- 1½ pounds lean ground beef
- 1 large onion, coarsely chopped
- 1 large red sweet pepper, coarsely chopped
- 3 cloves garlic, minced
- ½ teaspoon salt
- 1 teaspoon coarse-ground black pepper
- ½ teaspoon dried thyme
- 2 tablespoons all-purpose flour
- 1 8-ounce can tomato sauce
- ½ cup chili sauce
- 1 tablespoon Dijon mustard
- 1 tablespoon Worcestershire sauce
- ½ cup stout beer
- 8 hamburger buns, split and toasted

PREP
Select **SAUTÉ** on the Instant Pot® and adjust to **NORMAL**. Add the ground beef, onion, sweet pepper, and garlic; cook for 8 to 10 minutes or until the meat is browned. Press **CANCEL**. Drain off any fat. Add the salt, black pepper, thyme, and flour to the pot; stir to combine. Add the tomato sauce, chili sauce, mustard, Worcestershire sauce, and beer. Secure the lid on the pot. Open the pressure-release valve.

COOK
Select **SLOW COOK** and adjust to **MORE**. Cook for 5 to 6 hours. If mixture is too saucy, press **CANCEL**. Select **SAUTÉ** and adjust to **NORMAL**. Cook, stirring, until desired consistency. Press **CANCEL**.

SERVE
Spoon mixture onto bun bottoms and top with bun tops.

Philly-Cheese French Dip Sandwiches

This sandwich takes the classic Philly favorite of juicy, slow-cooked beef served on a crusty roll with sweet peppers and melted cheese and makes it even better with the flavorful "jus" served with French dips.

PREP TIME	FUNCTION	CLOSED POT TIME	TOTAL TIME
40 minutes	Sauté (Normal/More); Slow Cook (More)	5 hours 30 minutes	6 hours 10 minutes + 10 minutes rest

SERVES: 8

- 2 teaspoons onion powder
- 2 teaspoons garlic powder
- 3 teaspoons Italian seasoning
- 1 teaspoon salt
- 1 teaspoon black pepper
- 1 3- to 4-pound beef rump roast
- 2 to 3 tablespoons olive oil
- 2 onions, thinly sliced
- 2 green sweet peppers, thinly sliced
- ½ cup red wine
- 1 14.5-ounce can beef broth
- 2 tablespoons Worcestershire sauce
- Hoagie buns
- Butter
- Sliced provolone cheese

PREP

In a small bowl combine onion powder, garlic powder, Italian seasoning, salt, and black pepper. Rub spice mixture all over the beef roast.

Select **SAUTÉ** on the Instant Pot® and adjust to **NORMAL**. Add 2 tablespoons of the olive oil to the pot. When the oil is hot, place beef in the pot. Brown until deep brown on all sides for about 15 minutes. Remove roast and add the onions and the remaining 1 tablespoon olive oil. Cook the onions until softened and lightly browned, stirring occasionally, for about 5 minutes. Stir in sweet peppers; cook for 1 minute. Add red wine; scrape up any browned bits in the pan. Press **CANCEL**. Select **SAUTÉ** and adjust to **MORE**. Add beef broth and Worcestershire sauce. Bring to boiling. Simmer for 10 minutes or until reduced by almost half. Press **CANCEL**.

Return the roast to the pot. Secure the lid on the pot. Open the pressure-release valve.

COOK

Select **SLOW COOK** and adjust to **MORE**. Cook for 5½ to 6 hours or until meat is tender. Press **CANCEL**.

SERVE

Transfer roast to a cutting board. Let rest for 10 minutes. Slice the meat. Use a slotted spoon to transfer the peppers and onions to a bowl.

Meanwhile, preheat oven to 425°F. Spread hoagie buns with butter. Arrange bun halves on a baking sheet, buttered sides up. Bake for 10 minutes or until lightly toasted.

Layer beef, the peppers and onions, and provolone cheese onto the bottoms of the rolls. Bake for about 5 minutes more or until cheese is melted. Serve sandwiches with the juices left in the pot for dipping.

Asian Short Rib-Noodle Bowl

Short ribs are ideal for the Instant Pot®—whether they're slow-cooked, as they are here—or are cooked under pressure. Either way, this tough cut turns so tender it literally falls off the bone. In this case, that's into a flavorful broth bursting with chewy udon noodles and sweet, crisp snap peas.

PREP TIME	FUNCTION	CLOSED POT TIME	TOTAL TIME
30 minutes	Slow Cook (More); Sauté (Normal)	5 hours + 1 hour marinate	6 hours 30 minutes

SERVES: 8

- ¾ cup reduced-sodium soy sauce
- 3 cups low-sodium beef broth
- 3 tablespoons sugar
- 1 teaspoon salt
- 3 tablespoons minced garlic
- 2 tablespoons minced fresh ginger
- 2 tablespoons toasted sesame oil
- 3 tablespoons minced green onion
- ½ teaspoon crushed red pepper
- 5 pounds beef short ribs (8 ribs)
- 2 cups fresh sugar snap peas
- 1 14.2-ounce package (or two 7.1-ounce pouches) ready-to-serve udon stir-fry noodles
  Sesame seeds (optional)
  Sliced green onions (optional)

PREP

In a large nonmetal container or large resealable plastic bag combine soy sauce, beef broth, sugar, salt, garlic, ginger, sesame oil, minced green onion, and crushed red pepper. Mix until sugar dissolves. Add short ribs, pressing to fully immerse ribs in marinade. Let ribs marinate for 1 hour at room temperature or in the refrigerator overnight.

Transfer ribs and marinade to Instant Pot®. Secure the lid on the pot. Open the pressure-release valve.

COOK

Select **SLOW COOK** and adjust to **MORE**. Cook for 5 to 6 hours or until meat is tender. Press **CANCEL**.

SERVE

Once cooking is complete, transfer ribs to a large bowl. Cover to keep warm. Skim the fat from the liquid in the pot. Select **SAUTÉ** and adjust to **NORMAL**. When liquid is simmering, add noodles and snap peas. Return to a simmer and cook for 4 minutes. Press **CANCEL**.

Divide noodle mixture among large, flat soup bowls. Top each serving with a short rib. If desired, sprinkle with sesame seeds and green onions.

Beef & Pork Meatloaf with Rustic Mashed Potatoes

Do your meatloaf and mashed potatoes at the same time—in the same pot—for a satisfying, home-style dinner.

PREP TIME	FUNCTION	CLOSED POT TIME	TOTAL TIME	RELEASE
35 minutes	Pressure/Manual (High)	60 minutes	1 hour 35 minutes + 5 minutes broil	Natural

SERVES: 8

MEATLOAF

- 2 **eggs**
- ¼ **cup ketchup**
- 2 **tablespoons Worcestershire sauce**
- 2 **teaspoons spicy brown mustard**
- 4 **cloves garlic, minced**
- 1 **teaspoon salt**
- 1 **teaspoon dried thyme, crushed**
- ½ **teaspoon black pepper**
- 1 **medium onion, finely chopped (about ¾ cup)**
- 1 **stalk celery, finely chopped**
- ½ **cup dried bread crumbs**
- 1 **pound ground beef**
- 1 **pound ground pork**

RUSTIC MASHED POTATOES

- 8 **medium Yukon gold potatoes (1½ to 2 pounds total), scrubbed and quartered**
- ¾ **cup water**
- ½ **teaspoon salt**
- ½ **cup milk**
- 2 **tablespoons butter**
- **Salt and black pepper to taste**

PREP

For meatloaf, in a large bowl whisk together eggs, ketchup, Worcestershire sauce, mustard, garlic, salt, thyme, and pepper. Stir in onion, celery, and bread crumbs. Add beef and pork; mix well. On an 18×12-inch piece of heavy foil shape meat mixture into an 8-inch-long loaf in the center of the foil. Wrap foil up around mixture to completely enclose the loaf. Poke several holes in the foil on top of the foil to allow steam to escape. Set aside.

For mashed potatoes, add potatoes, the water, and ½ teaspoon salt to the Instant Pot®. Set wrapped meatloaf on top of potatoes in pot. Secure the lid on the pot. Close the pressure-release valve.

COOK

Select **MANUAL** and cook at high pressure for 30 minutes. When cooking is complete, use a natural release to depressurize.

SERVE

Remove the lid; carefully remove meatloaf from the pot. Unwrap meatloaf and place in a 2-quart shallow broilerproof gratin dish or baking dish. Make the Sweet & Tangy Topper* and spread it evenly over the whole surface.

Broil the meatloaf 8 inches from the heat for 5 to 6 minutes or until topper is heated through and just starting to bubble.

Meanwhile, drain off most of the liquid from potatoes in the pot. Add milk and butter to potatoes in pot. Use a potato masher to mash potatoes to desired texture. Season to taste with salt and pepper.

Slice meatloaf crosswise and serve with potatoes.

*SWEET & TANGY TOPPER: In a small bowl whisk together ½ cup ketchup, 1 to 2 tablespoons packed brown sugar, and 2 to 3 teaspoons spicy brown mustard.

Carla Bushey blogs at AdventuresofaNurse.com.

One-Pot Instant Lasagna

Love lasagna but not all of the layering—and then waiting for it to bake while hungry kids ask when dinner will be ready? The active prep time on this family-pleasing dish is just 20 minutes—quick and easy enough for any day of the week.

PREP TIME	FUNCTION	CLOSED POT TIME	TOTAL TIME	RELEASE
20 minutes	Sauté (Normal); Pressure/Manual (High)	25 minutes	45 minutes	Quick

SERVES: 8

½ pound ground beef

½ pound ground sausage

1 16-ounce box mafalda pasta or one 16-ounce package lasagna noodles, broken into 1½- to 2-inch pieces

1 32-ounce jar pasta sauce

4 cups water

8 ounces ricotta cheese

8 ounces shredded mozzarella cheese

PREP

Select **SAUTÉ** on the Instant Pot® and adjust to **NORMAL**. Add ground beef and sausage to the pot and cook just until browned. When cooking is complete, press **CANCEL**. Stir in the pasta, pasta sauce, and the water. Secure the lid on the pot. Close the pressure-release valve.

COOK

Select **MANUAL** and cook at high pressure for 5 minutes. When cooking is complete, use a quick release to depressurize.

SERVE

Stir in the ricotta cheese and half the mozzarella (mixture will look curdled from the ricotta cheese). Pour mixture into a baking pan and top with the rest of the mozzarella. If desired, place the baking pan under the broiler for 2 to 3 minutes or until cheese is melted.

Pulled Pork with Sweet & Tangy Coleslaw

There are as many versions of this Southern-style favorite as there are cooks. This is a solid, classic take on traditional recipes that is ideal for feeding a crowd inexpensively.

PREP TIME	FUNCTION	CLOSED POT TIME	TOTAL TIME
30 minutes	Slow Cook (More)	5 hours 30 minutes	6 hours + 5 minutes stand

SERVES: 6 to 8

- 3 **pounds boneless pork shoulder, visible fat trimmed**
- ¼ **cup Barbecue Seasoning**
- ¼ **cup water**

BARBECUE SEASONING

- ¼ **cup brown sugar**
- 2 **tablespoons chili powder**
- 1 **tablespoon dehydrated minced onion**
- 1 **tablespoon garlic powder**
- 1 **teaspoon ground mustard**
- 1 **teaspoon salt**
- ½ **teaspoon black pepper**

PREP
Cut pork into three to four portions. Make Barbecue Seasoning by combining all the ingredients in a small bowl. Sprinkle ¼ cup seasoning on the pork. Add the water and pork to the Instant Pot®. Secure the lid on the pot. Open the pressure-release valve.

COOK
Select **SLOW COOK** and adjust to **MORE**. Cook for 5 hours and 30 minutes.

SERVE
Remove pork to cutting board; tent with foil for 5 minutes. Shred pork using two forks and return to pot, if desired. Serve with Sweet & Tangy Coleslaw.

SWEET & TANGY COLESLAW: Combine one 16-ounce bag coleslaw mix, 1 cup thinly sliced mini sweet peppers, ¼ cup minced red onion, and ⅓ cup chopped Italian parsley in a large bowl. In a small bowl stir together ⅓ cup mayonnaise, 2 tablespoons unseasoned rice wine vinegar, ½ teaspoon celery seed, ¼ teaspoon ground mustard, ½ teaspoon salt, and ¼ teaspoon black pepper. Add to slaw; mix well and refrigerate until ready to serve.

Mojo-Marinated Cuban-Style Pork

The bright, fresh flavors of Cuban *mojo* [MOH-hoh]—a sauce of cilantro, orange, garlic, oregano, and cumin— offer a way to enjoy pork shoulder apart from the more common BBQ-sauced version.

PREP TIME	FUNCTION		CLOSED POT TIME	TOTAL TIME		RELEASE
30 minutes	Meat/Stew		1 hour 5 minutes	1 hour 35 minutes + 24 hours marinate		Natural

SERVES: 8 to 10

- 1 cup tightly packed fresh cilantro leaves, coarsely chopped
- 1 tablespoon finely shredded orange zest
- ¾ cup freshly squeezed orange juice
- ½ cup freshly squeezed lime juice
- ¼ cup mint leaves, coarsely chopped
- 8 cloves garlic, peeled and minced
- 2 teaspoons dried oregano
- 2 teaspoons ground cumin
- 1 teaspoon salt
- 1 teaspoon black pepper
- ½ cup extra-virgin olive oil
- 1 4-pound skinless, boneless pork shoulder, trimmed of excess fat

PREP
In a large nonmetal bowl combine cilantro, orange zest, orange juice, lime juice, mint, garlic, oregano, cumin, salt, and pepper. Mix well; reserve ½ cup of the mixture for the finishing sauce; cover tightly and store in the refrigerator.

Add olive oil to remaining mixture in bowl. Pierce meat in several places with a small thin knife or skewer. Immerse pork shoulder in marinade, turning once to coat. Cover tightly; refrigerate for 24 hours.

Remove pork from marinade; discard marinade. Place pork in the Instant Pot®. Secure the lid on the pot. Close the pressure-release valve.

COOK
Select **MEAT/STEW** and adjust cook time to 45 minutes. When cooking time is complete, use a natural release to depressurize.

SERVE
Transfer pork to a cutting board. Slice thinly and arrange on a serving platter. Drizzle with reserved marinade.

Pork Ragu

A *ragu* is a thick, full-bodied Italian meat sauce—usually cooked for hours on the stovetop to create the rich depth of flavor. This pressure-cooked version takes less time to achieve that than the traditional cooking method—and you can walk away from it.

PREP TIME	FUNCTION	CLOSED POT TIME	TOTAL TIME	RELEASE
30 minutes	Sauté (Normal); Pressure/Manual (High)	1 hour 30 minutes	2 hours	Natural

SERVES: 8

- 3 pounds boneless pork shoulder
- 1½ teaspoons kosher salt
- ½ teaspoon black pepper
- 1 tablespoon cooking oil
- 1 medium onion, chopped
- 2 medium carrots, chopped
- 4 cloves garlic, minced
- ½ cup dry red wine
- 1 28-ounce can crushed tomatoes
- 1 cup chicken broth
- 2 sprigs fresh thyme
- 1 bay leaf
- ½ teaspoon crushed red pepper
- Cooked polenta or pasta

PREP

Cut pork shoulder into three equal pieces; season with salt and black pepper.

Select **SAUTÉ** on the Instant Pot® and adjust to **NORMAL**. Add oil to pot. When hot, add pork and cook for 10 minutes or until browned, turning occasionally. Remove pork to a plate. Add onion and carrots to pot; cook for 6 to 8 minutes or until browned, stirring frequently. Add garlic; cook and stir for 1 minute more. Add wine; cook and stir for 2 to 3 minutes or until most of the liquid is absorbed. Press **CANCEL**.

Stir in tomatoes, broth, thyme, bay leaf, and crushed red pepper. Return pork to pot. Secure the lid on the pot. Close the pressure-release valve.

COOK

Select **MANUAL** and cook at high pressure for 45 minutes. When cooking is complete, use a natural release to depressurize.

SERVE

Remove and discard thyme sprigs and bay leaf. Use two forks to shred pork in pot. Season with additional salt and black pepper.

Serve over polenta or pasta.

Carnitas

Serve this classic braised Mexican-style pork shoulder in warm tortillas or alongside hot cooked rice. After the fork-tender meat is shredded, it's crisped under the broiler.

PREP TIME	FUNCTION	CLOSED POT TIME	TOTAL TIME	RELEASE
15 minutes	Sauté (Normal); Meat/Stew (More)	1 hour 15 minutes	1 hour 30 minutes + 5 minutes broil	Natural

SERVES: 6

- 1 tablespoon olive oil
- 4 cloves garlic, minced
- 2 teaspoons kosher salt
- ½ teaspoon black pepper
- 2 teaspoons dried oregano
- 1 teaspoon ground cumin
- 1 teaspoon ground cinnamon
- 2 pounds boneless pork shoulder, cut into 2-inch cubes
- 1 cup coarsely chopped onion
- 1 bay leaf
- ½ cup fresh orange juice
- 1½ cups beef or chicken broth
- 12 corn or flour tortillas, warmed
  Fresh salsa
  Queso fresco, crumbled
  Chopped fresh cilantro
  Lime wedges

PREP

In a small bowl combine the oil, garlic, salt, pepper, oregano, cumin, and cinnamon. Rub the seasoning over all of the pork. Place the onion, bay leaf, orange juice, and broth in the Instant Pot®. Add the seasoned pork. Secure the lid on the pot. Close the pressure-release valve.

COOK

Select **MEAT/STEW** and adjust to **MORE**. When cooking is complete, use a natural release to depressurize.

Set a large fine-mesh strainer over a bowl. Using a slotted spoon, transfer the pork the strainer and let drain for 5 minutes. Then transfer the pork to a baking pan. Use two forks to shred the pork and spread into an even layer on the pan. Strain the cooking liquid in the pot; skim and discard the fat.

Adjust an oven rack to about 4 inches from the heat source. Turn on the broiler and cook the pork for 5 minutes or until browned and crisp. If desired, add some of the cooking liquid to the carnitas to moisten.

SERVE

Meanwhile, heat tortillas according to package directions. Serve the carnitas in the tortillas with salsa, queso fresco, cilantro, and lime wedges.

Sausage-Stuffed Carnival Squash

Striped and speckled carnival squash is a cross between sweet dumpling and acorn squash and is about the same size as acorn squash. If you can't find it, acorn squash works just fine in this recipe. The sweetness of the squash is a wonderful contrast to the savory, sage-infused sausage—tastes just like fall!

PREP TIME	FUNCTION	CLOSED POT TIME	TOTAL TIME
20 minutes	Sauté (Normal); Slow Cook (More)	2 hours	2 hours

SERVES: 4

- 1 small carnival or acorn squash (about 1 to 1½ pounds)
- ⅛ teaspoon salt
- 6 ounces pork sausage
- ⅓ cup chopped onion
- ⅓ cup chopped celery
- ¾ cup apple cider
- 1 cup herb-flavor stuffing cubes
- ½ cup water
- Fresh flat-leaf parsley, minced

PREP
Slice stem end off each squash. Cut each squash in half. Using a spoon, scrape seeds from each squash half. Turn squash halves cut sides up. (If necessary, cut a thin slice from the bottom of each half so that it sits flat.) Season each half lightly with salt.

Select **SAUTÉ** on the Instant Pot® and adjust to **NORMAL**. Cook and stir sausage, onion, and celery until sausage is no longer pink for about 5 minutes. Stir in cider; bring to boiling, scraping up the browned bits from the bottom of the pot. Press **CANCEL**. Pour sausage-cider mixture over stuffing cubes in a large bowl; mix lightly until stuffing cubes are moistened.

Fill squash evenly with dressing mixture, packing lightly. Pour water in pot. Place trivet in the pot. Transfer stuffed squash to pot. (Squash will be very close together.) Secure the lid on the pot. Open the pressure-release valve.

COOK
Select **SLOW COOK** and adjust to **MORE**. Cook for 2 hours or until squash is tender.

SERVE
Top with parsley.

Any-Night Porchetta with Veggies

The classic version of this Italian dish usually calls for seasoning and stuffing the meat and then letting it marinate overnight before slow-roasting it in the oven. While this version isn't a 30-minute meal, it is certainly doable any day of the week. Better yet, it's fancy enough for a special occasion or for company on a weekend!

PREP TIME	FUNCTION	CLOSED POT TIME	TOTAL TIME	RELEASE
50 minutes	Sauté (Normal); Pressure/Manual (High)	45 minutes	1 hour 35 minutes	Quick

SERVES: 8 to 10

- 1 2½- to 3-pound pork loin roast
- 1½ teaspoons salt
- ½ teaspoon freshly ground black pepper
- 4 tablespoons olive oil
- 4 cloves garlic, minced
- 1 tablespoon chopped rosemary
- 1 tablespoon finely shredded lemon zest
- 1 tablespoon fennel seeds, bruised
- 2 teaspoons fresh sage, chopped
- 2 teaspoons fresh oregano, chopped
- ½ cup dry white wine
- ½ cup chicken broth
- 1 large onion, coarsely chopped
- 3 cloves garlic, thinly sliced
- 20 baby potatoes, quartered
- 2 large carrots, coarsely chopped
- 20 Brussels sprouts, halved
- 1 teaspoon dried thyme leaves

PREP

Butterfly the pork roast by making a lengthwise cut down the center of the roast, cutting to within ½ inch of the other side. Spread the roast open. Place the knife in the V cut, facing it horizontally toward one side of the V, and cut to within ½ inch of the side. Repeat on the other side of the V. Spread the roast open and cover with plastic wrap. Working from the center to the edges, pound the roast until it is about ¾ inch thick. Remove and discard plastic wrap. Season with ½ teaspoon of the salt and the pepper.

In a small bowl combine 2 tablespoons of the olive oil, minced garlic, rosemary, lemon zest, fennel seeds, sage, and oregano. Spread mixture evenly over meat. Roll pork loin back up; tie to secure in four places with 100%-cotton kitchen string. Cut loin crosswise in half.

Select **SAUTÉ** on the Instant Pot® and adjust to **NORMAL**. Add remaining 2 tablespoons oil to the pot. When oil is hot, brown roast, one piece at a time, on all sides, carefully turning with tongs. Press **CANCEL**. Pour wine and chicken broth into pot. Secure the lid on the pot. Close the pressure-release valve.

COOK

Select **MANUAL** and cook at high pressure for 20 minutes. While pork cooks, combine onion, sliced garlic, potatoes, carrots, Brussels sprouts, remaining 1 teaspoon salt, and thyme. Using hands, mix well.

When cooking is complete, use a quick release to depressurize. Remove meat from pot. Tent lightly with foil and let rest.

Add vegetables to pot. Secure the lid on the pot. Close the pressure-release valve. Select **MANUAL** and cook at high pressure for 3 minutes. When cooking is complete, use a quick release to depressurize.

SERVE

Remove strings from meat and cut into thin slices. Serve meat with vegetables.

Spicy Sausage-Corn Bread Stuffed Peppers

To add a slightly smoky edge to these colorful stuffed peppers, swap fire-roasted diced tomatoes for the regular ones.

PREP TIME	FUNCTION	CLOSED POT TIME	TOTAL TIME	RELEASE
30 minutes	Sauté (Normal); Pressure/Manual (High)	20 minutes	50 minutes	Quick

SERVES: 4

- 1 tablespoon cooking oil
- 1 stalk celery, thinly sliced
- ½ cup chopped onion
- 3 cloves garlic, minced
- 8 ounces andouille sausage, chopped
- 1 cup torn, trimmed fresh kale
- 1 cup corn bread stuffing mix
- ¾ cup undrained canned diced tomatoes
- ⅛ to ¼ teaspoon crushed red pepper
- 4 medium green, red, and/or yellow sweet peppers*
- ⅔ cup water

PREP

Select **SAUTÉ** on the Instant Pot® and adjust to **NORMAL**. Once hot, add oil, celery, and onion. Cook for 5 minutes, stirring occasionally. Stir in garlic. Transfer vegetables to a large bowl. Press **CANCEL**. Add sausage, kale, stuffing mix, tomatoes, and crushed red pepper to vegetables in bowl. Stir gently to combine.

Slice off the top of each pepper, reserving the tops. Use a small sharp knife to remove the seeds and membranes from the peppers, keeping the peppers intact. Spoon sausage mixture evenly into peppers, gently patting it down into the peppers.

Place trivet in the pot. Pour the water into the pot. Arrange stuffed peppers, top sides up, on the trivet. Set the pepper tops on top of the stuffed peppers. Secure the lid on the pot. Close the pressure-release valve.

COOK

Select **MANUAL** and cook at high pressure for 5 minutes. Once cooking is complete, use a quick release to depressurize.

SERVE

Carefully lift each pepper out of the pot and place on a serving platter.

*TIP: Choose peppers that have a flat, wide base.

Sausage & Mushroom Pasta Bolognese

This classic meat sauce from the northern part of Italy never goes out of style. This recipe gives you options—choose ground beef or turkey and red wine or white wine to deglaze the bottom of the pot and add flavor to the sauce.

PREP TIME	FUNCTION	CLOSED POT TIME	TOTAL TIME	RELEASE
35 minutes	Sauté (Normal); Pressure/Manual (High)	1 hour	1 hour 35 minutes	Natural

SERVES: 8

- 1 tablespoon olive oil
- 1 onion, chopped
- 2 carrots, chopped
- 2 stalks celery, chopped
- 4 cloves garlic, minced
- 1 pound fresh Italian sausage, casings removed if present
- 1 pound lean ground beef or turkey
- 8 ounces fresh cremini or button mushrooms, sliced
- 1 cup red wine or white wine
- 1 28-ounce can Italian whole tomatoes, undrained and cut up
- 2 teaspoons dried oregano, crushed
- 2 teaspoons dried basil, crushed
- 1 teaspoon fennel seeds
- ½ cup chopped fresh basil
  Cooked pasta
  Grated Parmesan cheese (optional)

PREP

Select **SAUTÉ** on the Instant Pot® and adjust to **NORMAL**. Add the olive oil to the pot. When hot, add the onion, carrots, celery, and garlic. Cook for 5 minutes or until the vegetables are softened and lightly browned. Add sausage and ground beef. Cook, stirring occasionally, until meat is browned for about 10 minutes. Drain fat. Add mushrooms; cook for 3 more minutes.

Add wine to the pot. Simmer for 2 minutes. Press **CANCEL**. Stir in the tomatoes, oregano, basil, and fennel seeds. Secure the lid on the pot. Close the pressure-release valve.

COOK

Select **MANUAL** and cook at high pressure for 15 minutes. When cooking is complete, use a natural release to depressurize.

SERVE

Stir in fresh basil. Serve sauce over cooked pasta. If desired, sprinkle each serving with Parmesan cheese.

Jenny Hartin is the cookbook promotions manager at Eat Your Books and owner of The Cookbook Junkies.

German Pork Roast

This gorgeous one-dish meal has a decidedly German accent. Flavored with onion, garlic, allspice, and caraway and served with sauerkraut, sweet-and-sour red cabbage, and applesauce, it has the hallmarks of that country's traditional cuisine.

PREP TIME	FUNCTION	CLOSED POT TIME	TOTAL TIME	RELEASE
40 minutes	Sauté (Normal); Pressure/Manual (High, Low)	35 minutes	1 hour 15 minutes	Quick

SERVES: 6

- 2 pounds pork loin
- ½ teaspoon garlic powder
- ½ teaspoon onion powder
- ¼ teaspoon allspice
- ½ teaspoon salt
- ¼ teaspoon black pepper
- 2 tablespoons olive oil
- 6 potatoes, scrubbed and cut in half lengthwise (about 1½ pounds)
- 6 carrots, scrubbed and trimmed (about 1 pound)
- 1 red onion, sliced
- 2 cloves garlic, sliced
- 1½ cups sauerkraut
- 1 teaspoon caraway seeds
  Sweet-and-sour red cabbage
  Applesauce

PREP

Pat the pork loin dry. Mix together the garlic powder, onion powder, allspice, salt, and pepper. Apply the rub mixture to the pork. Set aside.

Select **SAUTÉ** on the Instant Pot® and adjust to **NORMAL**. When hot, add the oil. Season the potatoes and carrots with salt and pepper. Brown the potatoes and carrots in batches to add color. Remove and set aside. Sauté the red onions and garlic for a few minutes and set aside with the potatoes and carrots. Add more oil to the pot, if needed, and sear the pork well on all sides. Press **CANCEL**.

Place the sauerkraut and caraway seeds on top of the pork. Secure the lid on the pot. Close the pressure-release valve.

COOK

Select **MANUAL** and cook at high pressure for 12 minutes. When cooking is complete, use a quick release to depressurize. Add the potatoes, carrots, onions, and garlic on top. Select **MANUAL** and cook at low pressure for 6 minutes. When cooking is complete, use a quick release to depressurize.

SERVE

Serve pork with red cabbage and applesauce.

Jill Selkowitz blogs at ThisOldGal.com.

Super-Simple BBQ Pork Spareribs

You will be amazed at how incredibly tender these ribs get with just a few minutes of cooking time. A rib dinner doesn't have to be reserved only for the weekend!

PREP TIME	FUNCTION	CLOSED POT TIME	TOTAL TIME	RELEASE
10 minutes	Pressure/Manual (High)	50 minutes	1 hour + 10 minutes bake	Natural

SERVES: 2 to 4

- 1 onion, roughly chopped
- 2 teaspoons vanilla
- 1 cup apple cider or apple juice
- 1 teaspoon liquid smoke (optional)*
- ½ cup water
- 1 rack pork spareribs
- 1½ teaspoons kosher salt or smoked salt
- 1 teaspoon black pepper
- 1 cup barbecue sauce

PREP

Place the onion, vanilla, apple cider, liquid smoke, if using, and the water in the Instant Pot®. Cut the rack of ribs into three to four portions so they fit in the pot. Season with salt and pepper and place in the pot. Secure the lid on the pot. Close the pressure-release valve.

COOK

Select **MANUAL** and cook at high pressure for 15 to 20 minutes.** When cooking is complete, use a natural release to depressurize.

Place ribs on a baking sheet. Pour barbecue sauce over the ribs. Cook in the oven at 400°F for 10 minutes, flipping ribs halfway through. (You can also broil the ribs or finish cooking them on a grill.)

***TIP:** If finishing in the oven, use the liquid smoke and smoked salt.

****Baby back ribs take 15 minutes and St. Louis/spareribs take 20 minutes.

Braised Herb-Rubbed Pork Loin
with Parsnips & Carrots

If you've never cooked parsnips, give this creamy-white root vegetable a try in this autumnal dish. Parsnips look a bit like carrots and have a similar sweet taste that pairs very nicely with pork.

PREP TIME	FUNCTION	CLOSED POT	TOTAL TIME	RELEASE
35 minutes	Sauté (Normal); Meat/Stew (Less); Steam	40 minutes	1 hour 15 minutes + 10 minutes rest	Natural/Quick

SERVES: 6 to 8

- 2 teaspoons dried oregano, crushed
- 1 teaspoon dried rosemary, crushed
- 1 teaspoon garlic powder
- 1 teaspoon salt
- ½ teaspoon black pepper
- ½ teaspoon dried thyme, crushed
- ½ teaspoon dried sage, crushed
- 1 3-pound pork loin
- 2 tablespoons olive oil
- 4 large carrots, peeled and cut into 4-inch-long sticks
- 2 large parsnips, peeled and cut into 4-inch-long sticks
- ½ cup chicken broth
- ¼ cup apple cider
- 2 bay leaves
- 2 sprigs fresh rosemary

PREP
In a small bowl combine the oregano, rosemary, garlic powder, salt, pepper, thyme, and sage. Rub seasoning mixture all over the pork. Select **SAUTÉ** on the Instant Pot® and adjust to **NORMAL**. Add olive oil to pot. When oil is hot, add pork. Cook pork until browned, turning once, for about 5 minutes. Remove pork from the pot. Add the carrots and parsnips. Cook, stirring occasionally, for about 10 minutes or until the vegetables are lightly browned. Press **CANCEL**. Remove vegetables from pot.

Return pork to the pot. Add the chicken broth and apple cider. Place the bay leaves and rosemary over the pork. Secure the lid on the pot. Close the pressure-release valve.

COOK
Select **MEAT/STEW** and adjust to **LESS**. When cooking is complete, use a natural release to depressurize. Return carrots and parsnips to pot. Press **CANCEL.** Secure the lid on the pot. Close the pressure-release valve. Select **STEAM** and cook for 2 minutes. When cooking is complete, use a quick release to depressurize.

SERVE
Remove pork and let rest for 10 minutes before slicing. Remove and discard bay leaves and rosemary sprigs. Use a slotted spoon to transfer carrots and parsnips to a serving dish. Serve pork with carrots, parsnips, and cooking juices.

Moroccan Lamb Shanks with Dates

Pressure-cooking lamb shanks—a tough cut of meat—turns them meltingly tender and keeps them super juicy. The sauce has tremendous depth of flavor and complements the flavor of the lamb superbly.

PREP TIME	FUNCTION	CLOSED POT TIME	TOTAL TIME	RELEASE
35 minutes	Sauté (Normal); Meat/Stew (More)	1 hour 25 minutes	2 hours	Natural

SERVES: 3 to 4

- ½ teaspoon salt
- 1 tablespoon finely grated fresh ginger
- 1 tablespoon sweet paprika
- 2 teaspoons ground cumin
- 3 large lamb shanks (2 to 2½ pounds)
- 1 tablespoon olive oil
- ½ large yellow onion, thinly sliced
- 1 cup cherry tomatoes, halved
- ½ cup apple juice
- ½ cup chicken broth
- 1 tablespoon harissa*
- 1 3-inch-long cinnamon stick
- ¼ teaspoon black pepper
- ¼ teaspoon ground coriander
- ¼ cup chopped dates**
- Hot cooked couscous (optional)
- 15 large Medjool dates, pitted**
- ¼ cup golden raisins
- ¼ cup slivered dried apricots
- ⅓ cup pomegranate arils (seeds)
- ⅓ cup coarsely chopped fresh cilantro

PREP

Combine salt, ginger, paprika, and cumin; mix well. Rub mixture over lamb shanks; set aside.

Select **SAUTÉ** on the Instant Pot® and adjust to **NORMAL**. Add olive oil to pot. When oil is hot, add the onion and cook and stir until starting to soften for about 3 minutes. Press **CANCEL**. Add tomatoes. Cook and stir until tomatoes start to soften for about 3 minutes. Place seasoned shanks on top of tomato-onion mixture. Add the apple juice, chicken broth, harissa, cinnamon stick, pepper, coriander, and chopped dates. Secure the lid on the pot. Close the pressure-release valve.

COOK

Select **MEAT/STEW** and adjust to **MORE.** When cooking is complete, use a natural release to depressurize. Press **CANCEL**.

SERVE

If using, make a bed of couscous on a warm platter. Using a slotted spoon, transfer shanks from the pot to the platter. Select **SAUTÉ**. Add Medjool dates, raisins, and apricots. Cook and stir for 3 to 4 minutes. Press **CANCEL**.

Ladle date mixture over shanks. Sprinkle with pomegranate arils and cilantro.

*TIP: Harissa is a North African condiment made of chiles, garlic, caraway, spices, and olive oil. It can range from mild to fiery-hot. Choose one based on your personal taste.

**TIP: There are two types of dates called for in this recipe. Medjool dates are considered the "king of dates"—they are large, moist, soft, and creamy and have very little fibrous texture. They are added only at the end of cooking to warm through; they would completely break down if they were cooked with the lamb. The other type—more common and less expensive than the Medjool dates (often Deglet Noor dates)—are semidry and have more fiber, making them a little sturdier. They are cooked with the lamb to add flavor.

Poultry

Chicken Toscana

Setting the pressure-cook time for just 1 minute after the vegetables are added to the pot—and using a quick release to depressurize—ensures that they don't get overcooked (especially the delicate zucchini!).

PREP TIME	FUNCTION	CLOSED POT TIME	TOTAL TIME	RELEASE
35 minutes	Sauté (Normal); Poultry; Pressure/Manual (High)	35 minutes	1 hour 10 minutes	Quick

SERVES: 6

- 3 pounds bone-in chicken thighs, skin removed (about 6 thighs)
- ½ teaspoon salt
- ¼ teaspoon black pepper
- 2 tablespoons olive oil
- 1 sprig fresh rosemary
- 1 cup dry white wine
- 2 zucchini, cut into 1½-inch chunks
- 8 ounces button mushrooms, cleaned
- 1 6-ounce jar marinated artichoke hearts, drained
- 6 ounces chopped fire-roasted red peppers, drained
- 1 6-ounce jar pitted Kalamata olives, drained and halved
- 12 ounces pappardelle or other wide noodle, cooked according to package directions
- ⅓ cup finely chopped fresh flat-leaf parsley
- ¼ cup snipped fresh basil

PREP

Season chicken with salt and pepper. Select **SAUTÉ** on the Instant Pot® and adjust to **NORMAL**. Add the oil. When oil is hot, add rosemary sprig and stir until oil is very fragrant. Remove rosemary; discard. Working with half of the chicken at a time, brown chicken pieces on all sides in rosemary-infused oil about 5 minutes. Press **CANCEL**. Return all chicken to pot. Add wine to pot. Secure the lid on the pot. Close the pressure-release valve.

COOK

Select **POULTRY**. When cooking is complete, use a quick release to depressurize. Press **CANCEL**. Add zucchini, mushrooms, artichoke hearts, red peppers, and olives.

Secure the lid on the pot. Close the pressure-release valve. Select **MANUAL** and cook at high pressure for 1 minute. When cooking is complete, use a quick release to depressurize.

SERVE

Divide cooked pappardelle among six shallow pasta bowls. Using a slotted spoon, arrange chicken pieces and vegetables over pappardelle. Ladle a small amount of juices over each serving. Sprinkle with parsley and fresh basil.

Chicken Cacciatore with Porcini Mushrooms

Cacciatore means "hunter" in Italian. Dishes prepared "hunter-style" refer to a common set of ingredients—usually onions, mushrooms, herbs, wine, and tomatoes. The porcini mushrooms in this version of the Italian favorite add earthy, rich flavor to the dish.

PREP TIME	FUNCTION	CLOSED POT TIME	TOTAL TIME	RELEASE
35 minutes	Sauté (Normal/Less); Poultry	35 minutes	1 hour 10 minutes + 10 minutes simmer	Natural

SERVES: 4

- 1 tablespoon olive oil
- 2 pounds bone-in, skinned chicken thighs and/or drumsticks
- ½ teaspoon salt
- ¼ teaspoon black pepper
- ½ ounce dried porcini mushrooms, rinsed
- ½ cup boiling water
- 1 onion, coarsely chopped
- 1 red sweet pepper, coarsely chopped
- 2 cloves garlic, minced
- 1 cup dry red or white wine
- 1 28-ounce can whole tomatoes, undrained and coarsely cut up
- 1 teaspoon dried rosemary, crushed
- 1 teaspoon dried sage, crushed
- 1 bay leaf
- ½ cup black olives, halved
- ¼ cup chopped fresh flat-leaf parsley
- Cooked pasta, rice, or polenta

PREP

Select **SAUTÉ** on Instant Pot® and adjust to **NORMAL**. Add oil. Season chicken with salt and pepper. When oil is hot, add chicken. Cook chicken, half at a time, until browned, turning once, for about 7 to 8 minutes.

Meanwhile, place porcini mushrooms in a small bowl and add the boiling water. Let stand for 5 minutes. Drain, reserving liquid. Chop mushrooms.

Remove chicken from pot. Add onion, red sweet pepper, and garlic. Cook, stirring occasionally, until onion is softened, for about 2 minutes. Add wine. Simmer for 2 minutes. Press **CANCEL**. Add tomatoes, rosemary, sage, and the bay leaf. Stir in the mushrooms and the mushroom liquid. Return chicken to pot. Secure the lid on the pot.

COOK

Select **POULTRY**. When cooking is complete, use a natural release to depressurize. Press **CANCEL**.

SERVE

Transfer chicken to a platter; cover lightly with foil to keep warm. Skim fat from cooking liquid. Remove and discard bay leaf. Select **SAUTÉ** and adjust to **LESS**. Cook sauce for 10 minutes to reduce and slightly thicken. Press **CANCEL**.

Top chicken with sauce and vegetables, olives, and parsley. Serve with pasta, rice, or polenta.

Chicken Piccata

There is something irresistible about the combination of tangy lemon, briny capers, fresh herbs, and the rich flavor of butter—which is perhaps why this dish retains its popularity. Serve with pasta or rice and fresh steamed green beans or sautéed spinach.

PREP TIME	FUNCTION	CLOSED POT TIME	TOTAL TIME	RELEASE
20 minutes	Sauté (Normal); Manual/Pressure (High)	10 minutes	30 minutes + 5 minutes simmer	Quick

SERVES: 4

- 4 skinless, boneless chicken breasts (1½ to 1¾ pounds)
- ½ teaspoon salt
- ¼ teaspoon black pepper
- 1 tablespoon olive oil
- 1 cup chicken broth
- ¼ cup fresh lemon juice
- 2 tablespoons butter
- 2 tablespoons brined capers, drained
- 2 tablespoons chopped fresh flat-leaf parsley
- Hot cooked pasta or rice
- Lemon slices

PREP
Season the chicken with salt and pepper. Select **SAUTÉ** on the Instant Pot® and adjust to **NORMAL**. Heat oil in pot; add chicken and cook for 2 to 3 minutes per side until browned. Add broth. Press **CANCEL**. Secure the lid on the pot. Close the pressure-release valve.

COOK
Select **MANUAL** and cook at high pressure for 3 minutes. When cooking is complete, use a quick release to depressurize. Press **CANCEL**. Use tongs to remove chicken to a serving platter; cover to keep warm.

Add lemon juice to cooking liquid in pot. Select **SAUTÉ** and adjust to **NORMAL**. Bring to a simmer and cook for 5 minutes to reduce. Press **CANCEL**. Whisk butter into sauce; add capers and parsley.

SERVE
Pour sauce over chicken. Serve over pasta or rice. Serve with lemon slices.

Weeknight Chicken Marsala

Marsala is wine that has been fortified, or infused with a spirit such as brandy. It gives this dish its signature warm, smoky flavor.

PREP TIME	FUNCTION	CLOSED POT TIME	TOTAL TIME	RELEASE
30 minutes	Sauté (Normal); Poultry	30 minutes	1 hour + 8 minutes simmer	Natural

SERVES: 4

- 4 large bone-in chicken thighs (1¾ to 2 pounds total)
- ¼ teaspoon salt
- ¼ teaspoon black pepper
- 1 to 2 tablespoons olive oil
- 8 ounces fresh cremini mushrooms, thickly sliced
- 2 medium shallots, thinly sliced (about ⅔ cup)
- 2 cloves garlic, thinly sliced
- ½ cup reduced-sodium chicken broth
- ⅓ cup sweet Marsala wine
- ⅓ cup whipping cream
- ¼ cup chopped fresh flat-leaf parsley
- Cooked pasta (optional)

PREP

Select **SAUTÉ** on the Instant Pot® and adjust to **NORMAL**. Remove skin from chicken thighs. Sprinkle chicken with salt and pepper. Add 1 tablespoon oil to the hot pot. Add chicken thighs, bone sides up. Cook for 8 to 10 minutes or until meat is browned, flipping once halfway through cooking. Remove chicken from pot. Add mushrooms, shallots, and garlic to pot. If needed, add remaining 1 tablespoon oil. Cook for 5 to 7 minutes or until mushrooms are lightly browned, stirring occasionally. Press **CANCEL**.

Add chicken broth to mushroom mixture in the pot. Lay chicken thighs on top of the mushroom mixture. Secure the lid on the pot. Close the pressure-release valve.

COOK

Select **POULTRY** and adjust cook time to 10 minutes. When cooking is complete, use a natural release to depressurize. Press **CANCEL**. Transfer chicken thighs to a serving platter. Cover to keep warm.

Select **SAUTÉ** and adjust to **NORMAL**. Add wine to mushroom mixture in pot. Bring to boiling. Boil gently for 3 minutes. Stir in whipping cream. Cook for 5 minutes more or until sauce is slightly thickened, stirring occasionally. Press **CANCEL**.

SERVE

Serve mushroom sauce over chicken. Sprinkle with parsley. If desired, serve with cooked pasta.

Chicken Burrito Bowls

Bypass the restaurants that make these fast-food favorites out of ingredients that sit for hours in a steam table. The Instant Pot® allows you to make your own fresh and fast version at home for a lot less money.

PREP TIME	FUNCTION	CLOSED POT TIME	TOTAL TIME	RELEASE
15 minutes	Pressure/Manual (High)	1 hour 5 minutes	1 hour 20 minutes	Quick

SERVES: 6

- 1 **cup sour cream**
- 2 **tablespoons chipotle sauce (from a can of chipotle chiles in adobo)**
- 2 **tablespoons fresh lime juice**
- 1 **clove garlic, minced**
- ¼ **teaspoon salt**
- 2 **pounds skinless, boneless chicken breasts and/or thighs**
- 1 **28-ounce can diced tomatoes**
- 1 **tablespoon smoked paprika**
- 3 **cloves garlic, minced**
- 1 **cup chopped onion**
- 1 **teaspoon coarse salt**
- ½ **teaspoon black pepper**
- 1 **32-ounce container less-sodium chicken broth**
- 1 **14-ounce box instant whole grain brown rice**
- 2 **14-ounce cans black beans, rinsed and drained**
- 2 **cups shredded Colby jack cheese**
- **Snipped fresh cilantro**

PREP

For the chipotle sauce, in a small bowl combine the sour cream, 1 tablespoon of the chipotle sauce, lime juice, 1 clove minced garlic, and salt. Cover and refrigerate until serving.

Place the chicken, diced tomatoes, the remaining 1 tablespoon chipotle sauce, paprika, 3 cloves minced garlic, onion, coarse salt, black pepper, and 2 cups of the broth in the Instant Pot®. Secure the lid on the pot. Close the pressure-release valve.

COOK

Select **MANUAL** and cook at high pressure for 15 minutes. When cooking is complete, press **CANCEL** and use a quick release to depressurize. Remove the chicken from the cooking liquid.

Add the remaining broth, rice, and black beans to the cooking liquid. Secure the lid on the pot. Close the pressure-release valve. Select **MANUAL** and cook at high pressure for 5 minutes. When cooking is complete, use a quick release to depressurize.

SERVE

Meanwhile, use two forks to shred the chicken. Add the chicken to the pot; stir to combine with the rice-bean mixture.

Serve in bowls topped with cheese, chipotle sauce, and cilantro.

Shredded Chicken Tacos

Chipotle chiles in vinegary adobo sauce add heat and smoky flavor to the filling for these quick-to-fix tacos.

PREP TIME	FUNCTION	CLOSED POT TIME	TOTAL TIME	RELEASE
25 minutes	Sauté (Normal); Pressure/Manual (High)	20 minutes	45 minutes + 5 minutes simmer	Natural

SERVES: 6

- 1 14.5-ounce can fire-roasted diced tomatoes, undrained
- ½ cup chicken broth
- 1 to 2 canned chipotle chiles in adobo
- 2 cloves garlic, peeled
- 1 teaspoon ground cumin
- 2 pounds skinless, boneless chicken thighs
- ½ teaspoon salt
- ¼ teaspoon black pepper
- 1 tablespoon olive oil
- 12 6-inch corn tortillas, warmed
- ¾ cup crumbled queso fresco
- 2 tablespoons chopped fresh cilantro
- Lime wedges

PREP

In a blender combine tomatoes, broth, chipotle, garlic, and cumin. Cover and blend until smooth.

Season the chicken with salt and pepper. Select **SAUTÉ** on the Instant Pot® and adjust to **NORMAL**. Heat oil in pot; add chicken and cook for 2 to 3 minutes per side until browned. Add the blended tomato mixture. Press **CANCEL**. Secure the lid on the pot. Close the pressure-release valve.

COOK

Select **MANUAL** and cook at high pressure for 5 minutes. When cooking is complete, use a natural release to depressurize. Press **CANCEL**. Use tongs to remove chicken to a cutting board; shred chicken with a fork.

For a thicker sauce, select **SAUTÉ** and adjust to **NORMAL**. Bring sauce to a simmer. Cook for 5 minutes to reduce, stirring frequently. Add shredded chicken to pot; heat through. Press **CANCEL**.

SERVE

Serve chicken mixture in tortillas topped with queso fresco and cilantro. Serve with lime wedges.

Chicken Tamales

Steaming neat little packages of flavorful chicken filling surrounded by a rich masa dough is a perfect job for the Instant Pot®. Each bite is savory, toothsome, and absolutely delicious!

PREP TIME	FUNCTION	CLOSED POT TIME	TOTAL TIME	RELEASE
1 hour	Pressure/Manual (High)	35 minutes	2 hours 30 minutes + 1 hour soak	Quick

SERVES: 4 to 6

- 20 dried corn husks
- 3 cups masa harina
- 2 cups chicken broth
- 1 cup shortening or lard
- 1½ teaspoons salt
- 1 teaspoon baking powder
- 2½ cups shredded cooked chicken
- 1 cup salsa verde tomatillo salsa
- ¼ cup chopped fresh cilantro
- 1 serrano pepper, seeded and chopped
- 2 cloves garlic, minced
- 2 cups water
- Tamale sauce

PREP

Place corn husks in a large bowl. Cover with warm water and soak until soft and pliable for at least 1 hour.

For dough, in a medium bowl combine masa harina and broth. In a large bowl beat shortening, salt, and baking powder with an electric mixer until light and fluffy for about 1 minute. Add half of the masa mixture and beat until well blended. Add remaining masa mixture and beat until a soft dough forms. If needed, beat in additional broth, adding 1 tablespoon at a time.

For filling, in a medium bowl combine chicken, salsa, cilantro, serrano, and garlic.

Drain the corn husks and pat dry. Spread 3 to 4 tablespoons dough down center of a husk, leaving a 1-inch border on the sides. Spoon about 2 tablespoons chicken filling over dough. Fold sides of the husk, wrapping the dough around the filling and pressing gently to close. Fold the husk closed on both sides to make a neat package. Repeat with remaining husks, dough, and filling.

Place a vegetable steamer basket in the Instant Pot®. Add the water to pot and place tamales in steamer basket. Secure the lid on the pot. Close the pressure-release valve.

COOK

Select **MANUAL** and cook at high pressure for 25 minutes. When cooking is complete, use a quick release to depressurize.

SERVE

Serve with tamale sauce.

Easy Chicken Bouillabaisse

Traditional bouillabaisse is a French tomato-based seafood stew. Here, the same treatment is given to chicken. The toasted garlic bread is for sopping up the delicious broth flavored with fennel, thyme, white wine, orange juice, and garlic.

PREP TIME	FUNCTION	CLOSED POT TIME	TOTAL TIME	RELEASE
35 minutes	Sauté (More/Normal); Meat/Stew	50 minutes	1 hour 15 minutes	Natural

SERVES: 6

- 2 tablespoons olive oil
- 6 skinless, boneless chicken thighs (1½ pounds)
- 2 medium fennel bulbs, cut into wedges (reserve 2 tablespoons fronds)
- 1 large onion, halved and thinly sliced
- 2 bay leaves
- 1 large sprig fresh thyme
- ¼ teaspoon crushed red pepper
- 2 cups chicken broth
- 1 14.5-ounce can fire-roasted diced tomatoes
- 1 cup dry white wine
- ⅓ cup orange juice
- 2 cloves garlic, minced
- 1 tablespoon finely shredded orange zest
- Toasted garlic bread

PREP
Select **SAUTÉ** on the Instant Pot® and adjust to **MORE**. Add oil to pot. Cook chicken, half at a time, until golden brown, for about 10 minutes. Transfer chicken to a clean plate; set aside. Press **CANCEL**. Select **SAUTÉ** and adjust to **NORMAL**. Add fennel and onion to pot. Cook and stir until slightly softened for about 10 minutes. Return chicken to pot. Add bay leaves, thyme, crushed red pepper, chicken broth, tomatoes, wine, orange juice, and garlic. Press **CANCEL**. Secure lid on pot. Close the pressure-release valve.

COOK
Select **MEAT/STEW** and adjust cook time to 8 minutes. When cooking is complete, use a natural release to depressurize.

SERVE
Place 1 chicken thigh in each of six soup bowls. Remove and discard bay leaves. Ladle fennel, onion, and juices over the tops. Combine snipped reserved fennel fronds with orange zest and sprinkle over chicken.

Serve with toasted garlic bread.

Italian Summer Supper Salad with Chicken

Originally devised as a way to use up day-old bread, this bread and tomato salad—called *panzanella* in Italy—is best made with ripe, juicy summer tomatoes. It doesn't usually contain chicken, but adding it turns a side dish into a meal.

PREP TIME	FUNCTION	CLOSED POT TIME	TOTAL TIME	RELEASE
15 minutes	Poultry	1 hour 15 minutes	1 hour 30 minutes	Natural

SERVES: 6

- 1 whole 2½- to 3-pound chicken, skinned
- ¼ cup olive oil
- ½ teaspoon dried thyme
- ½ teaspoon dried sage
- 1 cup water
- 4 cups 1-inch cubes of Italian country bread, toasted*
- 3 medium heirloom tomatoes, cut into wedges
- 1 English cucumber, halved and cut into ½-inch-thick slices**
- ½ red onion, peeled, halved, and thinly sliced
- ¼ cup red wine vinegar
- 1 clove garlic, minced
- ⅔ cup extra virgin olive oil
- ½ teaspoon coarse salt
  Black pepper
- 20 large basil leaves, torn
  Parmesan shavings (optional)

PREP

Rub outside of chicken with the ¼ cup oil; sprinkle with thyme and sage. Place the trivet in the pot. Pour the water into the Instant Pot®. Place chicken on trivet. Secure the lid on the pot. Close the pressure-release valve.

COOK

Select **POULTRY** and adjust to 45 minutes cooking time. When cooking is complete, use a natural release to depressurize. Remove chicken from pot and allow to cool slightly.

SERVE

While chicken cooks, in a large salad bowl combine toasted bread cubes, tomatoes, cucumber, and red onion. In a jar with a tight-fitting lid combine vinegar, garlic, and the ⅓ cup olive oil.

When chicken is warm but not hot, use two forks to pull meat from bones into large bite-size pieces. Add chicken to bowl; toss gently. Shake dressing vigorously and drizzle over all ingredients in bowl. Season salad with the salt and pepper to taste. Toss gently.

Sprinkle basil over top of salad. If desired, top with Parmesan shavings. Enjoy salad warm or at room temperature.

*TIP: To toast the bread, toss the cubes with 2 tablespoons olive oil and spread in a single layer on a rimmed baking sheet. Toast in a 275°F oven for about 20 minutes or until very lightly browned. Let cool completely before using.

**TIP: Long, thin English cucumbers (also called hothouse cucumbers) are considered seedless and most often come wrapped in plastic to prevent them from drying out.

Peruvian Chicken Bowls with Green Sauce

This dish is suited to lovers of fiery food! The creamy avocado sauce cools it down a bit, but if you would prefer it less spicy, cut the amount of yellow pepper paste to 2 tablespoons.

PREP TIME	FUNCTION	CLOSED POT TIME	TOTAL TIME	RELEASE
35 minutes	Pressure/Manual (High)	40 minutes	1 hour 15 minutes	Quick

SERVES: 4

CHICKEN

- ¼ cup aji amarillo or aji mirasol (yellow hot pepper) paste*
- 1 tablespoon white vinegar
- 1 tablespoon olive oil
- 1½ pounds skinless, boneless chicken thighs, diced into 1½-inch pieces
- ¾ cup reduced-sodium chicken broth
- 1 pound small red potatoes (1½ to 2 inches in diameter), quartered
- 1 cup fresh or frozen corn kernels

SAUCE

- 1 cup avocado pulp
- Juice of 1 lime
- 1 cup fresh cilantro leaves
- 1 jalapeño pepper, coarsely chopped (seeds removed, optional)
- ¼ cup white vinegar
- ¼ cup crumbled cotija cheese or queso fresco
- ¼ cup water
- ¼ teaspoon salt

PREP

Combine pepper paste, vinegar, and oil in a bowl. Add chicken and toss to coat.

Pour ½ cup of the broth into the Instant Pot®. Layer in the chicken, potatoes, and corn. Pour remaining ¼ cup broth over all. Secure the lid on the pot. Close the pressure-release valve.

COOK

Select **MANUAL** and cook at high pressure for 10 minutes. When cooking is complete, use a quick release to depressurize.

While chicken is cooking, make the sauce: Process avocado, lime juice, cilantro, jalapeño, vinegar, cheese, and the water in a food processor or blender until smooth. Taste and season with desired amount of salt. Refrigerate until ready to use.

SERVE

Divide chicken, potatoes, and corn among bowls. Drizzle with green sauce. If desired, sprinkle with additional cilantro and cheese.

*TIP: Aji amarillo and aji mirasol are both types of Peruvian hot peppers. If you can't find the jarred paste in the Mexican section of your supermarket, try a Hispanic market. They are also both widely available online.

Moroccan Chicken Tagine

This savory North African stew is named for its traditional cooking pot—the tagine—that is an earthenware utensil with a concave conical lid. Its unusual lid shape allows aromatic steam to condense and flow back into the food, adding flavor. The Instant Pot® performs the same vital task.

PREP TIME	FUNCTION	CLOSED POT TIME	TOTAL TIME	RELEASE
30 minutes	Sauté (Normal); Meat/Stew (Less)	1 hour	1 hour 30 minutes	Natural

SERVES: 6 to 8

- 2 teaspoons ground turmeric
- 2 teaspoons ground cumin
- 1 teaspoon ground coriander
- 1 teaspoon salt
- ½ teaspoon black pepper
- 8 skinless, boneless chicken thighs
- 2 tablespoons olive oil
- 1 medium red onion, peeled and thinly sliced
- 3 cloves garlic, minced
- 1½ cups dried brown lentils
- ½ cup chopped, pitted Medjool dates
- ½ cup halved pitted green olives
- 2 cinnamon sticks
- ¼ cup dry white wine
- 2 cups chicken broth
- 1 bunch fresh cilantro, tied together with kitchen string

  Snipped cilantro

  Lemon wedges

PREP
In a small bowl combine the turmeric, cumin, coriander, salt, and pepper. Mix well. Sprinkle chicken thighs evenly with spice mixture.

Add oil to the Instant Pot®. Select **SAUTÉ** and adjust to **NORMAL**. Working two at a time, brown thighs on both sides. Transfer thighs to a plate; set aside.

Add onion to the oil remaining in the pot; cook and stir for 2 minutes. Add garlic; cook and stir for 1 minute more. Add lentils, dates, olives, cinnamon sticks, wine, chicken broth, and chicken. Place cilantro bundle on top of chicken. Press **CANCEL**.

Secure the lid on the pot. Close the pressure-release valve.

COOK
Select **MEAT/STEW** and adjust cook time to **LESS**. When cooking is complete, use a natural release to depressurize.

SERVE
Remove cilantro bundle and discard.

Transfer cooked chicken to a plate. Spoon lentil mixture into a shallow bowl or onto plates; arrange thighs on top of lentils. Sprinkle with cilantro and serve with lemon wedges.

Thai Green Curry Chicken

Craving curry? Skip the carryout and make it yourself in just a little more than 30 minutes.

PREP TIME	FUNCTION	CLOSED POT TIME	TOTAL TIME	RELEASE
15 minutes	Sauté (Normal); Pressure/Manual (High)	20 minutes	35 minutes	Quick

SERVES: 4

- 1 tablespoon coconut oil
- 1 shallot, thinly sliced
- 1 tablespoon minced fresh ginger
- 1 serrano pepper, seeded and minced
- 1 pound skinless, boneless chicken breast, thinly sliced*
- ½ teaspoon salt
- 1 14-ounce can coconut milk, shaken
- ¼ cup Thai green chile paste
- 2 carrots, thinly sliced
- 8 ounces green beans, trimmed
- 1 medium yellow or red sweet pepper, cut into strips
- Hot cooked jasmine rice
- 4 lime wedges
- ¼ cup chopped fresh cilantro leaves
- ¼ cup thinly sliced fresh basil leaves
- ¼ cup coarsely chopped roasted and salted cashews

PREP
Select **SAUTÉ** on the Instant Pot® and adjust to **NORMAL**. Add oil to pot. When oil is hot, add shallot, ginger, and pepper. Cook and stir until aromatics are slightly wilted for about 2 minutes. Add chicken to pot. Season with salt. Cook and stir just until no longer pink for about 3 minutes. Press **CANCEL**.

Add coconut milk and chile paste to pot. Stir until combined. Stir in carrots, green beans, and sweet pepper. Secure the lid on the pot. Close the pressure-release valve.

COOK
Select **MANUAL** and cook at high pressure for 4 minutes. When cooking is complete, use a quick release to depressurize.

SERVE
Serve over hot cooked jasmine rice with lime wedges for squeezing. Top with cilantro, basil, and cashews.

***TIP:** Place chicken breast in freezer for 30 minutes prior to slicing to cut thin, evenly sized pieces.

Carla Bushey blogs at AdventuresofaNurse.com.

General Tso's Chicken

This intensely flavored sweet-and-spicy dish tastes just like the one with the same name from your favorite Chinese restaurant.

PREP TIME	FUNCTION	CLOSED POT TIME	TOTAL TIME	RELEASE
25 minutes	Sauté (Normal); Pressure/Manual (High)	20 minutes	45 minutes	Quick

SERVES: 6

- 1 teaspoon sesame oil
- 1½ pounds skinless, boneless chicken breast and/or thighs, cubed
- 6 tablespoons rice vinegar
- 6 tablespoons soy sauce
- 1 clove garlic, chopped
- ¼ teaspoon ground ginger
- ¼ teaspoon crushed red pepper
- ¾ cup hoisin sauce
- 4 tablespoons brown sugar
- 2 tablespoons cornstarch
- 2 cups cooked white rice
- 1 green onion, chopped
- Sesame seeds

PREP

Pour the sesame oil in the Instant Pot®. Select **SAUTÉ** and adjust to **NORMAL**. Add chicken to the pot. Cook and stir for 5 minutes or until chicken is white (does not need to be cooked all the way through). Press **CANCEL**.

In a separate bowl mix together the rice vinegar, soy sauce, garlic, ginger, crushed red pepper, hoisin sauce, and brown sugar. Pour the mixture over the chicken in the pot. Secure the lid on the pot. Close the pressure-release valve.

COOK

Select **MANUAL** and cook at high pressure for 10 minutes. When cooking is complete, use a quick release to depressurize. Press **CANCEL**.

Select **SAUTÉ** and adjust to **NORMAL**. Bring to a slight boil. Whisk in the cornstarch until mixture turns thick and bubbly for about 2 minutes. Press **CANCEL**.

SERVE

Serve the chicken over rice. Sprinkle with green onions and sesame seeds.

Barbara Schieving is the creator of the blog PressureCookingToday.com.

Chicken Lazone

This decadent dish of chicken in a slightly spicy cream sauce served over spaghetti originated at Brennan's, the famed New Orleans restaurant. Some versions include cayenne—add a little bit to the spice mixture for the chicken if you like.

PREP TIME	FUNCTION	CLOSED POT TIME	TOTAL TIME	RELEASE
20 minutes	Sauté (Normal); Pressure/Manual (High)	15 minutes	35 minutes	Quick

SERVES: 6

- 2 teaspoons garlic powder
- 1 teaspoon onion powder
- 1 teaspoon chili powder
- 1 teaspoon paprika
- 1 teaspoon salt
- ½ teaspoon black pepper
- 2 pounds chicken tenders
- 2 tablespoons butter
- 2 tablespoons vegetable oil
- ½ cup chicken broth
- 2 tablespoons cornstarch
- 2 tablespoons water
- 2 cups heavy cream
- 10 to 12 ounces spaghetti, prepared according to package directions
- 2 tablespoons finely chopped fresh flat-leaf parsley

PREP
In a bowl combine garlic powder, onion powder, chili powder, paprika, salt, and pepper. Add the chicken; toss with your hands to coat the chicken with spices.

COOK
Select **SAUTÉ** on the Instant Pot® and adjust to **NORMAL**. When hot, add the butter and oil. Stir until butter is melted. Briefly sauté the chicken, a few pieces at a time, on both sides and remove to a plate.

When all the chicken has been sautéed, press **CANCEL** and add the chicken broth and chicken to the pot. Secure the lid on the pot. Close the pressure-release valve. Select **MANUAL** and cook at high pressure for 3 minutes. When cooking is complete, use a quick release to depressurize. Press **CANCEL**.

In a small bowl dissolve the cornstarch in the 2 tablespoons water. Push the chicken to one side of the pot and add cornstarch mixture. Stir to combine. Select **SAUTÉ** and constantly stir until sauce thickens. Press **CANCEL** and gradually stir in heavy cream.

SERVE
Serve chicken and sauce over spaghetti. Sprinkle with parsley.

Jill Selkowitz blogs at ThisOldGal.com.

One-Pot Chicken & Rice

Five-spice powder—a Chinese spice blend of cinnamon, cloves, fennel seed, star anise, and Szechuan peppercorns—gives this simple dish its distinctive Asian flavor.

PREP TIME	FUNCTION	CLOSED POT TIME	TOTAL TIME	RELEASE
10 minutes	Sauté; Pressure/Manual (High)	20 minutes	30 minutes + 30 minutes marinate	Natural

SERVES: 4 to 6

- 1½ **pounds skinless, boneless chicken thighs, cut into 1½-inch pieces**
- 3 **tablespoons black soy sauce***
- 3 **tablespoons low-sodium soy sauce**
- 1 **teaspoon seasoned rice vinegar**
- ¼ **teaspoon five-spice powder**
- 2 **teaspoons grated fresh ginger**
- 1 **teaspoon toasted sesame oil**
- 2 **teaspoons vegetable oil**
- 1½ **cups jasmine or other white rice**
- 3 **cups chicken broth**
- 8 **ounces cremini mushrooms, washed, stem ends trimmed, and cut in half**
- **Sliced green onions**

PREP

Place chicken in a 1-gallon resealable plastic bag. Whisk together the black soy sauce, soy sauce, rice vinegar, five-spice powder, and ginger. Pour over the chicken. Seal the bag and marinate at room temperature for 30 minutes or in the refrigerator up to overnight.

Using a slotted spoon, remove chicken from marinade. Select **SAUTÉ** on the Instant Pot®. Add sesame oil and vegetable oil to the pot. When oil is hot, brown chicken in two batches in the pot.

Press **CANCEL**. Combine rice, broth, and mushrooms in the pot. Add browned chicken to pot; stir to combine. Secure the lid on the pot. Close the pressure-release valve.

COOK

Select **MANUAL** and cook at high pressure for 3 minutes. When cooking is complete, use a natural release to depressurize.

SERVE

Stir to evenly distribute chicken throughout rice. Serve chicken and rice topped with sliced green onions.

*TIP: Black soy sauce—used in Thai cooking—is made by fermenting soy sauce with sugar or molasses. As its name implies, it is black in color and has the consistency of a light syrup. It adds sweetness and saltiness to foods. Look for it in the Asian section of your supermarket or at an Asian market.

Spanish Arroz con Pollo

This creamy one-pot rice-and-chicken dish gets its pungent flavor, aroma, and sunny yellow color from saffron—the stems of a type of crocus flower. It's a very pricey spice, so if you want to skip it, you can—but it won't be quite the same.

PREP TIME	FUNCTION	CLOSED POT TIME	TOTAL TIME	RELEASE
35 minutes	Sauté (Normal); Pressure/Manual (High)	55 minutes	1 hour 30 minutes + 5 minutes stand	Natural

SERVES: 4 to 6

½ teaspoon saffron threads, crushed (optional)

3 tablespoons warm water (optional)

2½ pounds chicken breasts, thighs, and/or drumsticks (bone-in, skin removed)

½ teaspoon salt

¼ teaspoon black pepper

2 tablespoons olive oil

1 cup chopped yellow onion

1 medium red sweet pepper, sliced

3 cloves garlic, minced

1 14.5-ounce can diced tomatoes, undrained

1½ teaspoons paprika

1½ teaspoons dried oregano, crushed

⅛ teaspoon crushed red pepper

¾ cup dry white wine or chicken broth

1½ cups water or chicken broth

1 cup short grain white rice

½ cup fresh or frozen peas

½ cup pimiento-stuffed green olives, sliced

PREP
If using, in a small bowl combine the saffron and the warm water. Set aside.

Season the chicken with the salt and black pepper. Select **SAUTÉ** on the Instant Pot and adjust to **NORMAL**. Add oil to pot. When the oil is hot, working with half the chicken at a time, brown chicken pieces on all sides. Remove the chicken to a plate. Add the onion, sweet pepper, and garlic to the pot. Cook for 3 to 5 minutes or until crisp-tender. Press **CANCEL**. Add the chicken, tomatoes, paprika, oregano, crushed red pepper, wine, the 1½ cups water, rice, and, if using, saffron. Secure the lid on the pot. Close the pressure-release valve.

COOK
Select **MANUAL** and cook at high pressure for 15 minutes. When cooking is complete, use a natural release to depressurize.

SERVE
Fluff the rice with a fork. Add the peas to the pot and let stand for 5 minutes to warm through. Sprinkle servings with the sliced olives.

Cheesy Chicken Instant Mac with Veggies

Make this from-scratch mac and cheese in your Instant Pot® and you will never make it any other way again! The whole family will gobble it up—veggies and all.

PREP TIME	FUNCTION	CLOSED POT TIME	TOTAL TIME	RELEASE
25 minutes	Pressure/Manual (High); Sauté (Less)	35 minutes	1 hour	Quick

SERVES: 6

- 12 ounces skinless, boneless chicken breast halves (2 small)
- ½ teaspoon salt
- ¼ teaspoon black pepper
- ½ cup water
- 8 ounces dried elbow macaroni
- 2 carrots, thinly sliced
- 1 small onion, chopped
- 3 cloves garlic, minced
- 1 tablespoon butter
- 3 cups water
- 2 cups shredded cheddar cheese (8 ounces)
- 4 ounces cream cheese, cut into cubes
- ¾ cup half-and-half
- 2 cups coarsely torn fresh spinach (optional)

PREP

Sprinkle chicken with ¼ teaspoon of the salt and the pepper. Place the trivet in the bottom of the Instant Pot®. Add the ½ cup water to the pot. Place chicken on trivet in a single layer. Secure the lid on the pot. Close the pressure-release valve.

COOK

Select **MANUAL** and cook at high pressure for 7 minutes. When cooking is complete, use a quick release to depressurize. Transfer chicken to a cutting board; set aside. Remove trivet from pot. Discard liquid. Add macaroni, carrots, onion, garlic, butter, and remaining ¼ teaspoon salt to pot. Pour the 3 cups water over all in pot. Secure the lid on the pot. Close the pressure-release valve.

Select **MANUAL** and cook at high pressure for 2 minutes. When cooking is complete, use a natural release to depressurize. Press **CANCEL**. Do not drain off liquid.

Add cheddar cheese, cream cheese, and half-and-half to macaroni mixture in pot. Select **SAUTÉ** and adjust to **LESS**. Cook and stir for 2 to 3 minutes or until cheese is melted and mixture is well combined. Press **CANCEL**.

SERVE

Chop the chicken. Stir into hot macaroni and cheese. If desired, stir in spinach just before serving.

HAM & PEAS CHEESY CHICKEN INSTANT MAC WITH VEGGIES: Prepare as directed except add 1 to 2 tablespoons Dijon mustard with the half-and-half. Stir in ¾ cup chopped cooked ham and ¾ cup frozen (thawed) shelled green peas with the chicken. Continue to cook for 2 minutes to heat through, stirring frequently.

CHEESY CHICKEN INSTANT MAC WITH SALSA: Prepare as directed except stir in ¾ cup jarred salsa with the chicken at the end.

Indian Butter Chicken

This dish of juicy chicken thighs served in a slightly spicy, luxuriously rich tomato cream sauce will be a hit with even the least adventurous eaters in your family.

PREP TIME	FUNCTION	CLOSED POT TIME	TOTAL TIME	RELEASE
35 minutes	Sauté (Normal); Poultry	45 minutes	1 hour 20 minutes	Natural

SERVES: 4

- 8 skinless, boneless chicken thighs
- 2 tablespoons garam masala
- 1 teaspoon salt
- 1 teaspoon black pepper
- 4 tablespoons butter
- 1 onion, chopped
- 1 jalapeño pepper, seeded and finely chopped
- 4 cloves garlic, minced
- 1 tablespoon minced fresh ginger
- 1 teaspoon ground cumin
- ½ teaspoon ground turmeric
- 1 14.5-ounce can diced tomatoes
- 1 8-ounce can tomato sauce
- ½ cup chicken broth
- ½ cup heavy cream
- ½ cup chopped fresh cilantro
  Cooked white rice

PREP

Sprinkle the chicken thighs with 1 tablespoon of the garam masala, the salt, and black pepper; rub into chicken with fingers. Select **SAUTÉ** on the Instant Pot® and adjust to **NORMAL**. Add 2 tablespoons of the butter. When the butter is melted, add half the chicken. Cook chicken until browned, turning once, for about 10 minutes. Remove chicken from pot. Repeat with remaining chicken.

Add onion and the remaining 2 tablespoons butter. Cook, stirring occasionally, until onions are lightly browned, for about 5 minutes. Add the jalapeño, garlic, and ginger. Cook and stir for 2 minutes more. Add the remaining 1 tablespoon garam masala, the cumin, and turmeric. Cook and stir for 1 minute. Press **CANCEL**. Stir in the diced tomatoes, tomato sauce, and chicken broth. Place the chicken on sauce. Secure the lid on the pot. Close the pressure-release valve.

COOK

Select **POULTRY**. When cooking is complete, use a natural release to depressurize.

SERVE

Stir in heavy cream and cilantro. Serve over cooked white rice.

Chicken, Broccoli & Carrots with Curry Peanut Sauce

The sauce in this Thai-inspired one-pot dish has a little kick, but it's still very family-friendly—perfect for those busy weeknights!

PREP TIME	FUNCTION	CLOSED POT TIME	TOTAL TIME
35 minutes	Sauté (Normal); Slow Cook (More)	2 hours 25 minutes	2 hours 30 minutes

SERVES: 6

- 1 tablespoon olive oil
- ½ cup chopped green onions (half bunch)
- 4 cloves garlic, minced
- 1 2-inch piece fresh ginger, peeled and minced
- 2 to 2½ pounds skinless, boneless chicken thighs, cut into 1½-inch pieces
- 1 teaspoon kosher salt
- 2 cups low-sodium chicken broth
- ½ cup smooth peanut butter
- 2 tablespoons soy sauce
- 1 tablespoon fish sauce
- 2 tablespoons red curry paste
- 3 cups broccoli florets
- 1 cup bias-sliced carrots
- 1 tablespoon cornstarch
- 2 tablespoons cold water
- Hot cooked rice
- Chopped fresh cilantro
- ¼ cup chopped green onions
- Chopped roasted peanuts (optional)
- Sriracha sauce

PREP
Select **SAUTÉ** on the Instant Pot® and adjust to **NORMAL**. Add the oil. When hot, add the scallions, garlic, and ginger; cook for 1 minute. Press **CANCEL**. Add the chicken to the pot and sprinkle with salt. Add the broth, peanut butter, soy sauce, fish sauce, and curry paste; stir to combine. Secure the lid on the pot. Open the pressure-release valve.

COOK
Select **SLOW COOK** and adjust to **MORE**. Cook for 2 hours or until chicken is cooked through. Stir in the broccoli and carrots. Cook, covered, for 25 to 30 minutes or until the vegetables are crisp-tender. Press **CANCEL**.

Combine cornstarch and the cold water in a small bowl. Stir into pot. Select **SAUTÉ** and adjust to **NORMAL**. Cook and stir for 2 to 3 minutes or until sauce is slightly thickened. Press **CANCEL**.

SERVE
Serve the chicken, vegetables, and sauce over hot cooked rice. Top with cilantro, onions, and, if desired, peanuts. Pass the sriracha.

Light Chicken Stroganoff

Love the rich flavor of beef stroganoff but trying to lighten things up? Try this version made with chicken thighs in a yogurt-based sauce served over whole grain noodles.

PREP TIME	FUNCTION	CLOSED POT TIME	TOTAL TIME	RELEASE
30 minutes	Sauté (Normal); Manual/Pressure (High)	15 minutes	45 minutes	Quick

SERVES: 6

- 1 **12-ounce package whole grain wide noodles**
- 2 **tablespoons olive oil**
- 2 **skinless, boneless chicken breasts, cut into bite-size pieces**
- 4 **skinless, boneless chicken thighs, cut into bite-size pieces**
- 3 **large leeks, cleaned and thinly sliced (white parts only)**
- 16 **ounces button mushrooms, stems and caps thickly sliced**
- 2 **teaspoons fresh thyme leaves**
- ½ **cup dry white wine**
- 1 **tablespoon Worcestershire sauce**
- ½ **teaspoon salt**
- ¼ **teaspoon black pepper**
- 2 **teaspoons Dijon mustard**
- 2 **cups plain low-fat yogurt**
- 2 **tablespoons all-purpose flour**
- 1 **teaspoon paprika**
- ¼ **cup chopped fresh flat-leaf parsley**

PREP

In a large pot of boiling salted water cook noodles according to package directions.

While noodles cook, select **SAUTÉ** on the Instant Pot® and adjust to **NORMAL**. Add olive oil to pot. Brown chicken pieces in oil for about 10 minutes. Add leeks and mushrooms; continue to cook and stir for 2 to 3 minutes or until leeks soften.

Stir in thyme, wine, Worcestershire sauce, salt, and pepper. Press **CANCEL**. Secure the lid on the pot. Close the pressure-release valve.

COOK

Select **MANUAL** and cook at high pressure for 5 minutes. When cooking is complete, use a quick release to depressurize. Press **CANCEL**. In a small bowl stir together mustard, yogurt, and flour. Add to pot. Press **SAUTÉ** and adjust to **NORMAL**. Cook and stir for 2 minutes or until slightly thickened. Press **CANCEL**.

SERVE

Spoon stroganoff over noodles. Sprinkle lightly with paprika and chopped parsley.

Teriyaki Turkey Tenderloins

Sure, you can use the bottled stuff, but it's so easy to stir up a homemade teriyaki sauce, and the flavor is so much better and fresher.

PREP TIME	FUNCTION	CLOSED POT TIME	TOTAL TIME	RELEASE
15 minutes	Sauté (Normal); Poultry	30 minutes	45 minutes	Natural

SERVES: 4

- 1 tablespoon vegetable oil
- 1 to 1½ pounds turkey tenderloins (about 2 tenderloins)
- ¾ cup ponzu or soy sauce
- ¼ cup mirin or white wine
- ¼ cup brown sugar
- 1 tablespoon minced fresh ginger
- 3 cloves garlic, minced
- ¼ teaspoon ground white pepper
  Dash cayenne pepper
- 1 tablespoon cornstarch mixed with 2 tablespoons cold water

PREP

Select **SAUTÉ** on the Instant Pot® and adjust to **NORMAL**. When hot, add the oil to the pot. Add the turkey and cook for 8 to 10 minutes or until evenly browned. Press **CANCEL**. Drain fat.

Combine ponzu, mirin, brown sugar, ginger, garlic, white pepper, and cayenne pepper in a bowl. Mix well. Pour over the turkey. Secure the lid on the pot. Close the pressure-release valve.

COOK

Select **POULTRY** and adjust cook time to 8 minutes. When cooking is complete, use a natural release to depressurize. Press **CANCEL**. Remove turkey to a serving plate. Let rest for 5 minutes, then slice.

Select **SAUTÉ** on the pot and adjust to **NORMAL**. When the cooking juices come to a boil, whisk in the cornstarch mixture and cook for 1 minute. Press **CANCEL**.

SERVE

Pour sauce over the turkey or serve on the side.

Turkey Tikka Masala

Chicken tikka masala is often the first Indian dish many people try—and then they're hooked. This version swaps turkey tenderloin for the chicken, but the other flavor elements are all there—particularly the gingery tomato-coconut milk sauce. Serve it over aromatic, nutty-flavored basmati rice.

PREP TIME	FUNCTION	CLOSED POT TIME	TOTAL TIME	RELEASE
15 minutes	Sauté (Normal); Pressure/Manual (High)	25 minutes	40 minutes + 4 hours marinating	Quick

SERVES: 6

- ¾ cup plain yogurt
- 1 tablespoon freshly squeezed lemon juice
- 2 teaspoons black pepper
- 1 tablespoon cumin
- 1 teaspoon crushed red pepper
- 1 teaspoon ground cinnamon
- 1 teaspoon salt
- 1 2-inch piece fresh ginger, peeled and grated
- 2 turkey tenderloins (1½ pounds), patted dry
- 2 tablespoons vegetable oil
- 1 medium onion, coarsely chopped
- 3 cloves garlic, minced
- 1 14.5-ounce can fire-roasted diced tomatoes, undrained
- ½ cup coconut milk
- Hot cooked basmati rice
- ⅓ cup chopped fresh basil leaves
- ⅓ cup chopped fresh cilantro

PREP

Combine yogurt, lemon juice, black pepper, cumin, crushed red pepper, cinnamon, salt, and half of the ginger in a 1-gallon resealable plastic bag. Massage to combine. Add turkey; press to immerse in marinade. Seal bag tightly. Refrigerate for at least 4 hours or overnight.

Select **SAUTÉ** on the Instant Pot® and adjust to **NORMAL**. Add oil to pot. When hot, add onion, garlic, and remaining ginger. Cook, stirring constantly, for 3 to 4 minutes or until paste forms. Press **CANCEL**. Stir in tomatoes and turkey. Secure the lid on the pot. Close the pressure-release valve.

COOK

Select **MANUAL** and cook at high pressure for 8 minutes. Once cooking is complete, use a quick release to depressurize.

SERVE

Remove turkey from pot and transfer to a cutting board. Using two forks, pull tenderloins into bite-size pieces. Return turkey to pot. Add coconut milk. Stir to combine. Serve over basmati rice. Sprinkle with basil and cilantro.

Bacon-Cheddar Turkey Meatloaf with Caramelized Onions

Serve this yummy meatloaf with mashed potatoes and steamed green beans.

PREP TIME	FUNCTION	CLOSED POT TIME	TOTAL TIME	RELEASE
30 minutes	Sauté (Normal); Meat/Stew	1 hour 10 minutes	1 hour 40 minutes + 5 minutes stand	Natural

SERVES: 6

- 8 ounces sliced bacon, chopped
- 1 medium onion, chopped
- 1 cup water
- 1 egg
- 2 tablespoons barbecue sauce
- 1 tablespoon chili powder
- 2 cloves garlic, minced
- ¼ teaspoon black pepper
- 1 cup shredded cheddar cheese
- ½ cup quick-cooking oats
- 1 to 1¼ pounds ground turkey
- ¼ cup barbecue sauce
- Sour cream (optional)
- Fresh chives, snipped (optional)

PREP
Select **SAUTÉ** on the Instant Pot® and adjust to **NORMAL**. When hot, add bacon and onion. Cook until bacon is crisp and onion is tender and browned, stirring occasionally, for 4 to 5 minutes. Press **CANCEL**. Transfer bacon and onion to a small bowl using a slotted spoon. Carefully pour bacon grease from pot and discard. Place trivet in pot. Add the water to pot.

For meatloaf, in a large bowl whisk together egg, the 2 tablespoons barbecue sauce, chili powder, garlic, and pepper. Stir in half the cheese and all the oats. Add turkey and the bacon mixture; mix well. On a 12×8-inch piece of heavy foil shape meat mixture into an 8-inch-long loaf in the center of the foil. Holding the ends of the foil, lower the meatloaf down into the pot until it rests on the trivet. Tuck foil into pot as needed to allow the lid to go on. Secure the lid on the pot. Close the pressure-release valve.

COOK
Select **MEAT/STEW**. When cooking is complete, use a natural release to depressurize.

SERVE
Carefully remove meatloaf from the pot by lifting the ends of foil. Transfer meatloaf to a platter. Spoon the ¼ cup barbecue sauce over the top of the meatloaf. Sprinkle with remaining ½ cup cheese. Let stand for 5 minutes before serving. If desired, serve with sour cream sprinkled with chives.

Fish & Shellfish

Lemony Steamed Salmon with Dill-Caper Mayonnaise

Serve this Scandinavian-style salmon warm or chill it in the refrigerator for a few hours and serve it cold.

PREP TIME	FUNCTION	CLOSED POT TIME	TOTAL TIME	RELEASE
20 minutes	Pressure/Manual (High)	10 minutes	30 minutes	Quick

SERVES: 4

DILL-CAPER MAYONNAISE

- ½ cup olive-oil mayonnaise
- ½ cup plain Greek yogurt
- 2 tablespoons minced red onion
- 2 tablespoons capers, rinsed and drained
- 1 tablespoon freshly squeezed lemon juice
- 1 tablespoon finely chopped fresh dill

SALMON

- Juice of 2 large lemons (½ cup)
- 1 cup dry white wine
- 2 cloves garlic, smashed
- 3 stems of parsley
- 4 4-ounce fresh salmon fillets, about ¾ inch thick
- 2 teaspoons finely shredded lemon zest

PREP

For Dill-Caper Mayonnaise, combine mayonnaise, yogurt, red onion, capers, 1 tablespoon lemon juice, and the dill in a small bowl. Mix well. Cover. Sauce may be made 1 day ahead and refrigerated.

For the fish, combine lemon juice (and juiced lemon shells), wine, garlic, and parsley in the Instant Pot®. Place trivet in pot. Fold thin sides of salmon fillets under thick sides; arrange folded fillets on trivet. Sprinkle fillets with lemon zest. Secure the lid on the pot. Close the pressure-release valve.

COOK

Select **MANUAL** and cook at high pressure for 2 minutes. When cooking is complete, use a quick release to depressurize.

SERVE

Serve salmon with Dill-Caper Mayonnaise.

Salmon with Miso Butter

Miso gives the butter a savory, pleasantly salty, umami flavor. You can use any type of miso. From mildest to most pungent, they are white, yellow, and red.

PREP TIME	FUNCTION	CLOSED POT TIME	TOTAL TIME	RELEASE
35 minutes	Manual (Pressure/Low)	10 minutes	45 minutes	Quick

SERVES: 4

- 1 **cup water**
- 1 **lemon, halved**
- 4 **4- to 5-ounce salmon fillets**
- ¼ **teaspoon salt**
- ⅛ **teaspoon black pepper**
- ¼ **cup butter, softened**
- 4 **teaspoons miso paste**
- ⅛ **teaspoon crushed red pepper**
- 1 **tablespoon chopped fresh chives**
- **Romaine Slaw**

PREP

Place trivet in Instant Pot®. Add the water to pot. Squeeze one half of the lemon into the water. Place salmon fillets in steamer basket; squeeze other half of lemon over the fish. Sprinkle with salt and black pepper. Secure the lid on the pot. Close the pressure-release valve.

COOK

Select **MANUAL** and cook at low pressure for 2 minutes. When cooking is complete, use a quick release to depressurize.

SERVE

Meanwhile, for miso butter, in a small bowl combine butter, miso, and crushed red pepper; mix well. Stir in chives.

Serve salmon with miso butter and the Romaine Slaw.

ROMAINE SLAW: In a large bowl combine 2 small romaine hearts, shredded; 4 radishes, halved and thinly sliced; 2 English cucumbers, halved and thinly sliced; 2 green onions, sliced; and 1 tablespoon chopped fresh cilantro. In a small bowl combine 2 tablespoons natural rice vinegar, 1 teaspoon toasted sesame oil, 1 teaspoon soy sauce, ½ teaspoon sugar, and a dash of red pepper flakes. While whisking, drizzle in ¼ cup olive oil until it thickens slightly. Pour dressing over romaine mixture; toss to coat.

Balsamic-Glazed Salmon over Spinach

Cook the spinach until it's just wilted to maintain its fresh flavor and bright green color. You'll need to do it in two batches.

PREP TIME	FUNCTION	CLOSED POT TIME	TOTAL TIME	RELEASE
10 minutes	Pressure/Manual (High); Sauté (Normal)	10 minutes	20 minutes + 10 minutes sauté	Quick

SERVES: 4

- 1 to 1½ pounds wild-caught Pacific salmon
- ¼ cup balsamic vinegar
- 1½ teaspoons herbes de Provence
- 1½ teaspoons sea salt
- ½ teaspoon black pepper
- 1 cup water
- 3 tablespoons butter
- 2 cloves garlic, minced
- 2 pounds baby spinach (four 8-ounce bags)

PREP

Preheat the broiler on your oven. Move rack to 6 inches below broiler.

Cut the salmon in two pieces to fit in the Instant Pot® if necessary. Drizzle 1 tablespoon of the vinegar, the herbes de Provence, 1 teaspoon of the salt, and the pepper over the flesh side of the salmon.

Pour the water in the pot. Place the trivet in the bottom of the pot. Place fish, flesh side up, on the trivet. Secure the lid on the pot. Close the pressure-release valve.

COOK

Select **MANUAL** and cook at high pressure for 2 minutes. When cooking is complete, use a quick release to depressurize. Press **CANCEL**. Gently lift out the trivet with the fish. Place fish on rimmed baking sheet.

Place 1 tablespoon of the butter on top of the fish (divide between pieces). Broil the fish for 1 minute or until herbs are lightly browned.

Meanwhile, pour liquid from pot. Select **SAUTÉ** and adjust to **NORMAL**. Add 1 tablespoon of the remaining butter to the pot. When melted, add half of the garlic, half of the spinach, and ¼ teaspoon of the salt. Cook, stirring, until the spinach is just wilted. Use tongs or a slotted spoon to remove spinach from pot and arrange on a platter. Repeat with remaining butter, garlic, spinach, and salt. Use tongs or a slotted spoon to remove spinach from pot and add to platter.

Add the remaining 3 tablespoons vinegar to the pot and reduce until a glaze that coats the back of a spoon is formed for about 2 minutes.

SERVE

Arrange salmon on spinach. Drizzle the glaze on the salmon and serve immediately.

Braised Salmon in Tomato-Caper Sauce

Serve this Mediterranean-style salmon with cooked rice or polenta and a crisp green salad.

PREP TIME	FUNCTION	CLOSED POT TIME	TOTAL TIME	RELEASE
25 minutes	Sauté (Normal); Pressure/Manual (High)	20 minutes	45 minutes	Quick

SERVES: 4

- 1 tablespoon olive oil
- 2 shallots, finely chopped
- 1 red sweet pepper, chopped
- ½ cup white wine
- 1 28-ounce can whole tomatoes, undrained and cut up
- 1 tablespoon capers
- 1 teaspoon dried oregano, crushed
- ½ teaspoon dried thyme, crushed
- ½ teaspoon crushed red pepper
- 4 4-ounce salmon fillets
- ¼ teaspoon salt
- ¼ teaspoon black pepper
- Cooked rice (optional)
- ¼ cup chopped fresh flat-leaf parsley

PREP

Select **SAUTÉ** on the Instant Pot® and adjust to **NORMAL**. Add olive oil to pot. When the oil is hot, add shallots and red sweet pepper. Cook, stirring occasionally, until shallots and pepper are just softened for about 3 minutes. Add white wine. Simmer for 2 minutes. Stir in tomatoes, capers, oregano, thyme, and crushed red pepper. Press **CANCEL**. Place salmon fillets in sauce. Sprinkle with salt and pepper. Secure the lid on the pot. Close the pressure-release valve.

COOK

Select **MANUAL** and cook at high pressure for 3 minutes. When cooking is complete, use a quick release to depressurize.

SERVE

If desired, serve with cooked rice. Top with parsley before serving.

Sole en Papillote

Cooking *en papillote*, or in parchment, is a classic French technique. It is particularly suited to delicate foods such as fish and vegetables. It's a wonderful way to infuse foods with flavor, retaining natural juices.

PREP TIME	FUNCTION	CLOSED POT TIME	TOTAL TIME	RELEASE
20 minutes	Pressure/Manual (Low)	15 minutes	35 minutes	Quick

SERVES: 2

- 1 **cup water**
- 1 **cup matchstick-cut zucchini**
- ½ **cup matchstick-cut yellow sweet pepper**
- ¼ **cup chopped tomatoes**
- 1 **clove garlic, minced**
- 2 **teaspoons olive oil**
- ¼ **teaspoon salt**
- ⅛ **teaspoon crushed red pepper**
- 2 **4- to 5-ounce fresh sole or tilapia fillets**
- 2 **sprigs fresh thyme**
- 1 **tablespoon butter**
- ½ **teaspoon lemon zest**
- 2 **tablespoons dry white wine**
  Lemon wedges

PREP
Place trivet in Instant Pot®. Add the water to the pot.

In a medium bowl combine zucchini, yellow sweet pepper, tomatoes, garlic, olive oil, ⅛ teaspoon of the salt, and the crushed red pepper. Divide zucchini mixture between two 14-inch squares of parchment paper, placing mixture to one side of parchment; top with fillets. Sprinkle fish with remaining ⅛ teaspoon salt.

Top each fillet with a sprig of thyme, half of the butter, ¼ teaspoon of the lemon zest, and 1 tablespoon of the wine. For each packet, fold parchment over fish and vegetables; fold the open sides in several times to secure, curving the edge into a circular pattern to seal. Place packets on trivet. Secure the lid on the pot. Close the pressure-release valve.

COOK
Select **MANUAL** and cook on low pressure for 7 minutes. When cooking is complete, use a quick release to depressurize.

SERVE
Place each packet on a serving plate. Cut open with kitchen shears. Serve with lemon wedges.

Asian-Style Steamed Fish & Vegetables

You can use any white fish you like—tilapia, cod, halibut, or sea bass—in this super light and healthful veggie-packed dish.

PREP TIME	FUNCTION	CLOSED POT TIME	TOTAL TIME	RELEASE
40 minutes	Rice; Steam	30 minutes	1 hour 10 minutes	Quick

SERVES: 4

- 1 pound fresh or frozen skinless tilapia, cod, or other thin white fish fillets (about ½ inch thick)
- 1 cup raw jasmine or basmati rice
- 1 cup water
- ½ teaspoon salt
- 2 green onions
- ⅓ cup water
- 3 tablespoons reduced-sodium soy sauce
- 1 tablespoon minced fresh ginger
- 2 teaspoons fish sauce (optional)
- 1 teaspoon sriracha sauce
- ¼ teaspoon black pepper
- 2 heads baby bok choy, halved lengthwise
- 1½ cups matchstick-cut carrots
- 1 tablespoon toasted sesame oil
- 1 tablespoon honey
- 2 teaspoons white and/or black sesame seeds, lightly toasted

PREP

Thaw fish, if frozen; set aside. Add rice, the 1 cup water, and ¼ teaspoon of the salt to the Instant Pot®. Secure the lid on the pot. Close the pressure-release valve. Select **RICE**. When cooking is complete, use a quick release to depressurize. Transfer rice to a medium bowl; cover to keep warm.

Meanwhile, thinly slice green onions, keeping white bottoms separate from green tops. In a small bowl whisk together the water, soy sauce, ginger, fish sauce (if using), and sriracha. Stir in sliced white bottoms of green onions. Reserve green tops.

Add ginger mixture to the pot after removing the rice. Press **CANCEL**. Place the trivet in the bottom of the pot. If necessary, cut fish into four serving-size pieces. Rinse fish; pat dry with paper towels. Sprinkle fish with remaining ¼ teaspoon salt and the pepper. Stack fish fillets in even layers on trivet in the pot. Top with bok choy and carrots. Secure the lid on the pot. Close the pressure-release valve.

COOK

Select **STEAM** and cook for 3 minutes. When cooking is complete, use a quick release to depressurize.

SERVE

Transfer carrots and bok choy to a platter. Lift trivet from the pot; transfer fish to the platter. Cover to keep warm. Add oil and honey to liquid in pot. Whisk until well combined.

Stir green onion tops and sesame seeds into cooked rice. Divide rice, fish, and vegetables among plates. Drizzle all with cooking liquid from pot.

Citrus Fish Soup with Pistou

Pistou is essentially the French version of Italian pesto—but without nuts. The aromatic condiment infuses this light and fresh fish soup with terrific flavor.

PREP TIME	FUNCTION	CLOSED POT TIME	TOTAL TIME	RELEASE
20 minutes	Sauté (Normal); Pressure/Manual (High)	15 minutes	35 minutes	Quick

SERVES: 4

PISTOU

- 2 **cloves garlic, peeled**
- 3 **cups packed fresh basil leaves**
- ¼ **teaspoon salt**
- ⅓ **cup olive oil**
- ½ **cup grated Asiago or Romano cheese**

SOUP

- 2 **tablespoons olive oil**
- 2 **medium fennel bulbs, trimmed and coarsely chopped**
- 1 **cup coarsely chopped red sweet pepper**
- 2 **cloves garlic, chopped**
- 4 **cups chicken broth**
- 1 **14.5-ounce can diced tomatoes, undrained**
- 2 **teaspoons Old Bay seafood seasoning**
- 1 **pound cod fillets or other white fish, cut into 1-inch pieces**
- 2 **teaspoons orange zest**
- 2 **tablespoons fresh orange juice**
- 1 **teaspoon lemon zest**
- 1 **tablespoon fresh lemon juice**

PREP

For the Pistou, in a food processor combine garlic, basil, salt, oil, and cheese. Process until well blended. Transfer to a bowl; cover and set aside until serving.

For the soup, select **SAUTÉ** on the Instant Pot® and adjust to **NORMAL**. Add the olive oil to the pot. When hot, add fennel, red sweet pepper, and garlic. Sauté for 3 minutes, stirring frequently. Press **CANCEL**. Add broth, tomatoes, seasoning, and fish. Secure the lid on the pot. Close the pressure-release valve.

COOK

Select **MANUAL** and cook at high pressure for 2 minutes. When cooking is complete, use a quick release to depressurize.

SERVE

Stir in the orange juice and zest and lemon zest and juice. Divide soup among bowls. Top each serving with a spoonful of the Pistou.

Ratatouille-Style Tuna

Serve this saucy, Provençal-style dish with crusty slices of warmed French bread for sopping up the delicious cooking juices.

PREP TIME	FUNCTION	CLOSED POT TIME	TOTAL TIME	RELEASE
25 minutes	Sauté (Normal); Pressure/Manual (High)	15 minutes	40 minutes	Quick

SERVES: 4

- 2 tablespoons olive oil
- 3 garlic cloves, minced
- 2 cups 1-inch cubes eggplant
- ½ onion, diced
- ½ green sweet pepper, diced
- ½ teaspoon dried basil
- ¼ teaspoon dried oregano
- ½ teaspoon salt
- 1 zucchini, quartered and cut into ½-inch slices
- 4 roma tomatoes, seeded and diced
- 4 tuna steaks, about 1 inch thick
- Salt and black pepper
- Lemon wedges (optional)

PREP

Select **SAUTÉ** on the Instant Pot® and adjust to **NORMAL**. Add oil to pot. When oil is hot, add garlic, eggplant, onion, green sweet pepper, basil, oregano, and salt to the pot. Cook and stir for 2 to 3 minutes or until vegetables are barely tender. Press **CANCEL**.

Secure the lid on the pot. Select **MANUAL** and cook at **HIGH** pressure for 4 minutes. Once cooking is complete, use a quick release to depressurize.

Stir zucchini and tomatoes into vegetable mixture. Season tuna steaks with salt and black pepper to taste. Nestle tuna into mixture, trying not to overlap. Secure the lid on the pot. Close the pressure-release valve.

COOK

Select **MANUAL** and cook at high pressure for 1 minute. Once cooking is complete, use a quick release to depressurize.

PREP

Remove tuna to a serving platter. Stir the ratatouille and pour over the tuna. If desired, serve with fresh lemon wedges.

Carla Bushey blogs at AdventuresofaNurse.com.

Super-Quick Tuna & Noodles

Sometimes you just want rich, cheesy comfort food. Maybe it's a cold, rainy day—or maybe it's just been a not-very-good day. This family favorite will make everything good again.

PREP TIME	FUNCTION	CLOSED POT TIME	TOTAL TIME	RELEASE
5 minutes	Pressure/Manual (High)	25 minutes	30 minutes	Quick

SERVES: 6

1 16-ounce package egg noodles

3 cups water

1 12-ounce can tuna, drained

1 cup frozen peas

3 10½-ounce cans cream of mushroom soup

1 cup shredded cheddar cheese

¼ cup bread crumbs (optional)

PREP

Place the noodles in the Instant Pot® and cover with the water. Place the tuna, peas, and soup on top of the pasta. Secure the lid on the pot. Close the pressure-release valve.

COOK

Select **MANUAL** and cook at high pressure for 4 minutes. When cooking is complete, use a quick release to depressurize.

SERVE

Stir in the cheese. If desired, place the mixture in a baking dish and cover with bread crumbs. Place under the broiler for 2 to 3 minutes.

Citrus Prawns with Orange-Cashew Rice

Prawns look a bit like a cross between a shrimp and a lobster and have sweet, delicately flavored meat. If you can't find them, jumbo shrimp will work perfectly well in this dish.

PREP TIME	FUNCTION	CLOSED POT TIME	TOTAL TIME	RELEASE
40 minutes	Rice; Pressure/Manual (High)	40 minutes	30 minutes + 1 hour marinate	Natural/Quick

SERVES: 4

PRAWNS

¼ cup vegetable oil

1 tablespoon Dijon mustard

3 cloves garlic, minced

Juice from 1 lemon (3 to 4 tablespoons)

Juice from 1 lime (2 to 3 tablespoons)

Juice from 2 oranges (about ½ cup)

20 large prawns or jumbo shrimp, peeled and deveined

ORANGE-CASHEW RICE

1½ cups long grain rice

2 cups water

2 teaspoons orange zest

Juice from 1 orange (about ¼ cup)

¼ teaspoon salt

¾ cup roasted salted cashew halves

PREP

For prawns, in a resealable plastic bag combine oil, mustard, garlic, lemon juice, lime juice, and orange juice. Shake well to mix. Add prawns; gently shake bag to coat all prawns with marinade. Transfer bag to refrigerator; let prawns marinate for 1 hour.

When prawns have marinated for about 25 minutes, prepare Orange-Cashew Rice: Combine rice, the water, orange zest, orange juice, and salt in the Instant Pot®. Secure the lid on the pot. Close the pressure-release valve.

COOK

Select **RICE**. When cooking is complete, use a natural release to depressurize. Transfer cooked rice to a bowl. Stir in cashews. Cover to keep warm.

Place the trivet in the pot. Arrange prawns on trivet. Pour the marinade in the pot up to, but not touching, the prawns; discard extra marinade. Secure the lid on the pot. Close the pressure-release valve. Press **CANCEL**.

Select **MANUAL** and cook at high pressure for 1 minute. When cooking is complete, use a quick release to depressurize.

SERVE

Serve prawns on top of Orange-Cashew Rice; drizzle with hot marinade from pot.

Spicy Shrimp with Grits & Bacon

The jalapeño contributes most of the heat to this dish. Poblano peppers are generally fairly mild—although they can vary a bit in their heat level—and have a mellow, fruity flavor.

PREP TIME	FUNCTION	CLOSED POT TIME	TOTAL TIME	RELEASE
30 minutes	Pressure/Manual (High); Sauté (Normal)	30 minutes	1 hour	Natural

SERVES: 4

- 1 **pound fresh or frozen peeled and deveined jumbo shrimp (15 shrimp)**
- ¾ **cup water**
- ¾ **cup coarsely ground cornmeal**
- 1 **cup reduced-sodium chicken broth**
- 1 **cup whipping cream**
- 3 **cloves garlic, minced**
- ¼ **teaspoon salt**
- ⅛ **teaspoon black pepper**
- 1 **cup water**
- 4 **slices bacon, chopped**
- 1 **medium poblano pepper, cut into thin bite-size strips**
- ½ **cup chopped red onion**
- 1 **small jalapeño pepper, finely chopped**
- 1 **tablespoon cider vinegar (optional)**

PREP

Thaw shrimp if frozen. Set aside. For grits, in a 1½-quart round ceramic or glass round casserole (make sure the dish will fit down into the Instant Pot® first), stir together the ¾ cup water, cornmeal, broth, cream, garlic, salt, and black pepper. Tear an 18-inch-long sheet of foil. Fold the sheet lengthwise into thirds to make a long, narrow sling.

Place the trivet in bottom of the pot. Add the 1 cup water. Place filled casserole in the center of the foil sling. Use the sling to lower the casserole into the pot until it sits on the trivet. Tuck foil into pot so the lid will go on. Secure the lid on the pot. Close the pressure-release valve.

COOK

Select **MANUAL** and cook at high pressure for 10 minutes. When cooking is complete, use a natural release to depressurize. Press **CANCEL**. Lift the casserole out of the pot using the foil sling. Cover casserole loosely to keep warm.

Meanwhile, rinse shrimp with cold water; pat dry with paper towels. Carefully remove the trivet from pot and pour out the water. Select **SAUTÉ** and adjust to **NORMAL**. When hot, add bacon. Cook for 3 to 4 minutes. Add poblano pepper, onion, and jalapeño. Cook for 5 to 7 minutes or until bacon is browned and vegetables are just tender, stirring occasionally. Using a slotted spoon, transfer bacon mixture to a medium bowl; set aside.

Cook shrimp in bacon drippings in pot for 4 minutes or until shrimp are opaque, turning once halfway through cooking. If desired, add vinegar to bacon mixture; toss to coat. Add all shrimp and the bacon mixture to the pot; toss gently to combine. Press **CANCEL**.

SERVE

To serve, divide grits among shallow bowls. Top evenly with shrimp mixture.

Spicy Scallops with Tomatoes over Couscous

Israeli couscous is also called pearl couscous. It is larger than fine-grained Moroccan-style couscous and has a wonderfully toothsome, chewy texture when cooked.

PREP TIME	FUNCTION	CLOSED POT TIME	TOTAL TIME	RELEASE
20 minutes	Sauté (Normal); Pressure/Manual (High)	10 minutes	30 minutes	Quick

SERVES: 4

- 1 **pound sea scallops**
- **Kosher salt**
- **Black pepper**
- 2 **tablespoons olive oil**
- 2 **cloves garlic, minced**
- 1 **10-ounce can diced tomatoes with green chiles**
- 1 **8-ounce can tomato sauce**
- 2 **tablespoons fresh lime juice**
- 4 **cups hot cooked Israeli couscous**
- 1 **jalapeño pepper, thinly sliced**
- 2 **tablespoons chopped fresh cilantro**
- 2 **tablespoons sliced green onion**

PREP

Pat the scallops dry and lightly season with salt and black pepper.

Select **SAUTÉ** on the Instant Pot® and adjust to **NORMAL**. Add olive oil. When oil is hot, add scallops and garlic. Cook scallops, without moving, for 1 minute or just until golden brown on bottom. Turn scallops over and repeat. (The scallops will not be cooked through at this point.) Press **CANCEL**.

Add the tomatoes and tomato sauce to the pot. Secure the lid on the pot. Close the pressure-release valve.

COOK

Select **MANUAL** and cook at high pressure for 1 minute. When cooking is complete, use a quick release to depressurize.

SERVE

Stir in lime juice. Serve the scallops and cooking liquid over the couscous. Top with jalapeño slices, cilantro, and green onion.

Beer-Buzzed Mussels

Mussels are tender and taste delightfully of the sea, but the real draw is the flavorful cooking liquid—which is drizzled over the mussels and sopped up with toasted baguette. Yum!

PREP TIME	FUNCTION	CLOSED POT TIME	TOTAL TIME	RELEASE
30 minutes	Sauté (Normal); Steam	20 minutes	50 minutes	Quick

SERVES: 2 or 3 as a main dish; 4 to 6 as an appetizer

- 2 **tablespoons butter**
- 1 **tablespoon minced garlic**
- ½ **teaspoon crushed red pepper**
- ½ **teaspoon black pepper**
- 2 **sprigs fresh thyme**
- 1 **bay leaf**
- 1 **12-ounce bottle wheat beer**
- 2 **pounds green-lip or black mussels, scrubbed and debearded***
- ½ **cup chopped flat-leaf parsley**
  Lemon wedges (optional)
  Toasted baguette slices (optional)

PREP
Select **SAUTÉ** on the Instant Pot® and adjust to **NORMAL**. Add butter to pot. When butter is melted, add garlic and crushed red pepper. Cook and stir over medium heat for 1 minute or until garlic is fragrant but not browned. Press **CANCEL**. Add black pepper, thyme, bay leaf, and beer; stir to combine. Add mussels to pot. Secure the lid on the pot. Close the pressure-release valve.

COOK
Select **STEAM** and cook for 3 minutes. When cooking is complete, use a quick release to depressurize.

SERVE
Transfer mussels to serving bowls. Remove and discard bay leaf. Ladle with steaming liquid. Sprinkle with chopped parsley. If desired, garnish with lemon wedges and serve with toasted baguette slices for dipping.

*****TIP:** Cook mussels the day they are purchased. If using wild-harvested mussels, soak in a bowl of cold water for 20 minutes to help flush out grit and sand. (This is not necessary for farm-raised mussels.) Using a stiff brush, scrub mussels, one at a time, under cold running water. Debeard mussels about 10 to 15 minutes before cooking. The beard is the small cluster of fibers that emerges from the shell. To remove the beards, grasp the string between your thumb and forefinger and pull toward the hinge. You can also use pliers or fish tweezers. Be sure that the shell of each mussel is tightly closed. If any shells are open, tap them gently. Discard any mussels that don't close within a few minutes. Discard any mussels with cracked or damaged shells.

Mussels Frites

It doesn't get more French than this bistro-style favorite—mussels steamed in garlic-infused white wine and served with herbed fries and flavored mayonnaise for dipping.

PREP TIME	FUNCTION	CLOSED POT TIME	TOTAL TIME	RELEASE
30 minutes	Manual/Pressure (High)	20 minutes	50 minutes	Quick

SERVES: 4 to 6

FRITES

- 1 tablespoon chopped fresh rosemary
- 1½ teaspoons garlic powder
- 1 teaspoon salt
- ¾ teaspoon black pepper
- 1½ pounds russet or gold potatoes, cut into ½-inch-thick sticks
- 3 tablespoons olive oil

MUSSELS

- 1 cup white wine
- 3 roma tomatoes, seeded and chopped
- 2 cloves garlic, minced
- 1 bay leaf
- 2 pounds mussels, scrubbed and debearded (see Tip, page 147)
- ½ cup chopped fresh flat-leaf parsley

DIPPING SAUCE

- ⅓ cup mayonnaise
- 2 tablespoons minced roasted red pepper
- 1 clove garlic, minced

PREP

Preheat oven to 450°F. In a small bowl combine rosemary, garlic powder, salt, and pepper. On a large baking sheet or roasting pan toss the potatoes with the olive oil and spice mixture. Roast for 25 to 30 minutes or until tender and browned, stirring once.

Combine the wine, tomatoes, garlic, and bay leaf in the Instant Pot®. Top with the mussels. Secure the lid on the pot. Close the pressure-release valve.

COOK

Select **MANUAL** and cook at high pressure for 3 minutes. When cooking is complete, use a quick release to depressurize.

SERVE

Meanwhile, for the dipping sauce, in a small bowl combine the mayonnaise, roasted red pepper, and garlic.

Top mussels with parsley. Serve the frites with the dipping sauce alongside the mussels.

Steamed Lobster Tail with Meunière Sauce

Rich, meaty lobster tail doesn't need a lot of embellishment. This classic French sauce of browned butter, lemon, parsley, and capers is just right.

PREP TIME	FUNCTION	CLOSED POT TIME	TOTAL TIME	RELEASE
10 minutes	Steam	10 minutes	20 minutes	Quick

SERVES: 2

½ cup water

½ cup white wine

1 to 2 fresh thyme sprig(s)

2 garlic cloves, sliced

2 small (4-ounce) lobster tails, cut in half from top to tail

¼ cup unsalted butter

2 tablespoons fresh lemon juice

2 tablespoons chopped fresh flat-leaf parsley

1 tablespoon capers, drained and minced

PREP

Place the trivet in the pot. Place the water, wine, thyme, and garlic in the Instant Pot®. Place tails, shell sides down, on trivet. Secure the lid on the pot. Close the pressure-release valve.

COOK

Select **STEAM** and cook for 2 minutes. When cooking is complete, use a quick release to depressurize.

SERVE

While tails are steaming, heat butter over medium-high heat in a skillet until golden brown for about 3 to 5 minutes. Remove from heat and carefully stir in lemon juice, parsley, and capers. (Careful—hot butter may splatter.) Keep warm until tails are ready.

Drizzle sauce over tails or pour in a dish for dipping.

Beans & Grains

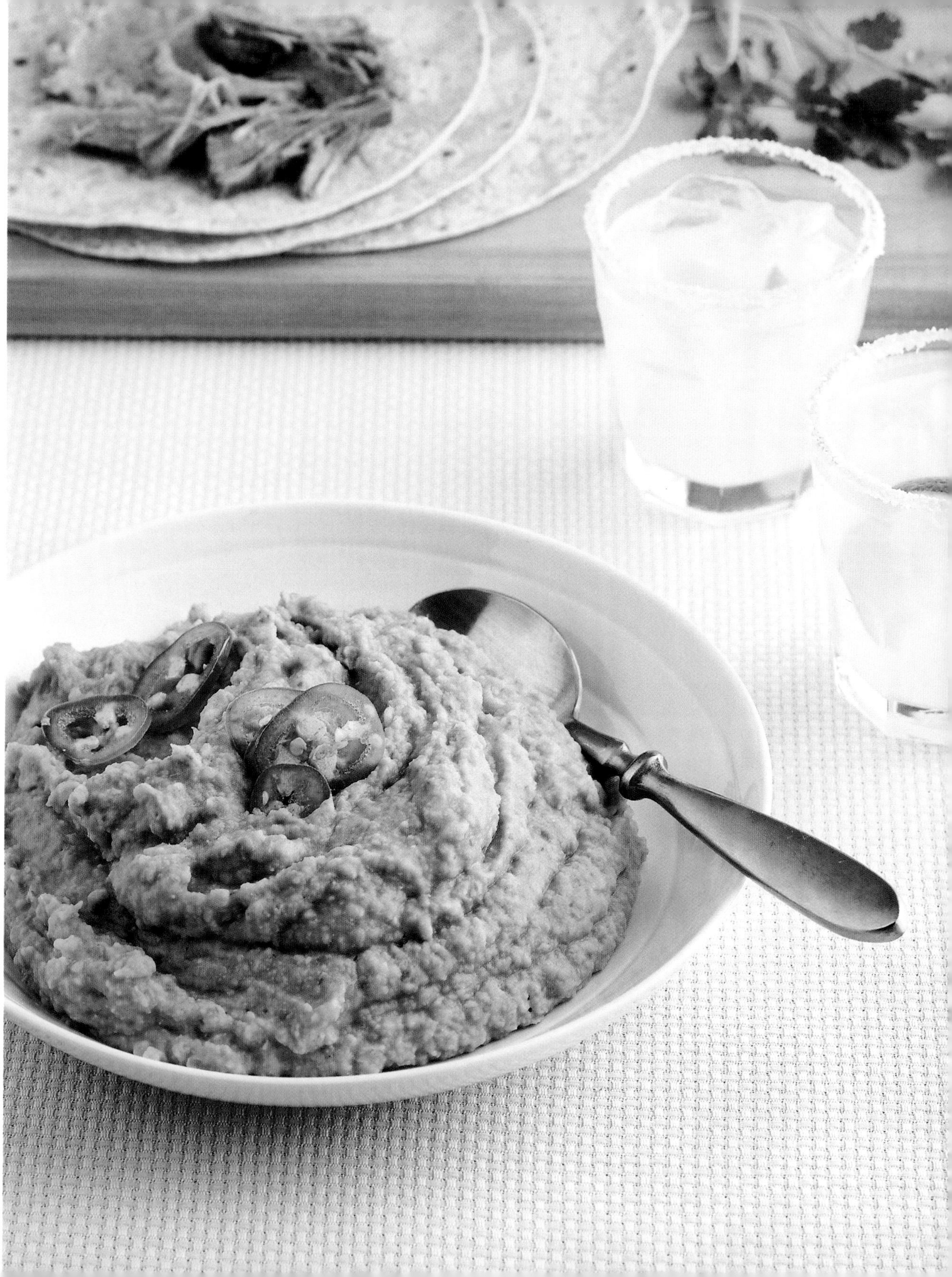

No-Fry Refried Beans

There's no frying—and no soaking—required to make these creamy, Mexican-style pinto beans. Serve them as a side to tacos, burritos, or quesadillas or with hot cooked rice as a main dish.

PREP TIME	FUNCTION	CLOSED POT TIME	TOTAL TIME	RELEASE
20 minutes	Pressure/Manual (High); Sauté (Normal)	1 hour 20 minutes	1 hour 40 minutes	Natural

SERVES: 6 to 8

- 1½ cups dried pinto beans
- 5 cups reduced-sodium chicken broth
- 4 to 6 sprigs fresh cilantro
- ¾ teaspoon ground cumin
- 1 bay leaf (optional)
- 1 tablespoon vegetable oil
- ½ cup chopped onion
- 1 small jalapeño pepper, finely chopped
- 3 cloves garlic, minced
- 2 tablespoons chopped fresh cilantro
- 1 teaspoon chopped fresh oregano or ¼ teaspoon dried oregano, crushed
- Salt and freshly ground black pepper

PREP

Rinse beans with cold water and pick through the beans to remove any pebbles or discolored or shriveled beans. Add the beans to the Instant Pot®. Add broth, cilantro, ½ teaspoon of the cumin, and, if desired, the bay leaf. Secure the lid on the pot. Close the pressure-release valve.

COOK

Select **MANUAL** and cook on high pressure for 40 minutes. When cooking is complete, use a natural release to depressurize. Press **CANCEL**.

Pour beans into a heatproof colander set over a large bowl to catch the cooking liquid. Remove and discard bay leaf (if using) and cilantro sprigs. Set beans and liquid aside.

Select **SAUTÉ** on the pot and adjust to **NORMAL**. When hot, add the oil to the pot. Add the onion, jalapeño, and garlic. Cook for 3 minutes or until tender, stirring occasionally. Press **CANCEL**. Stir in remaining ¼ teaspoon cumin. Return drained beans to pot with onion mixture. Add 1½ cups of the reserved bean cooking liquid.

SERVE

Using a potato masher or immersion blender, mash or blend beans to desired consistency, adding additional bean cooking liquid as needed. Stir in chopped cilantro and oregano.

Season to taste with salt and black pepper.

Cajun Red Beans & Rice

Rice and beans is a hearty, filling—and highly economical—combo enjoyed all over the world. With the switch of the type of legume, the seasonings, and other ingredients, it becomes a completely different dish.

PREP TIME	FUNCTION	CLOSED POT TIME	TOTAL TIME	RELEASE
25 minutes	Sauté (Normal); Bean/Chili (Normal)	1 hour 25 minutes	1 hour 50 minutes + overnight soak	Natural

SERVES: 6 to 8

- 1 pound dried red kidney beans
- 2 tablespoons olive oil
- 1 pound andouille sausage, sliced
- 1 onion, chopped
- 1 green sweet pepper, chopped
- 2 stalks celery, chopped
- 1 jalapeño pepper, seeded (if desired) and finely chopped
- 3 cloves garlic, minced
- 4 cups reduced-sodium chicken broth
- 2 bay leaves
- 2 teaspoons Cajun seasoning
- ½ teaspoon black pepper
- ½ teaspoon dried thyme, crushed
- ½ teaspoon dried sage, crushed
- Cooked white rice

PREP

Soak beans in water to cover overnight. Rinse and drain.

Select **SAUTÉ** on the Instant Pot® and adjust to **NORMAL**. Add olive oil. When oil is hot, add the sausage and cook for 5 minutes or until browned. Add the onion, sweet pepper, celery, jalapeño, and garlic. Cook and stir until vegetables are softened for about 3 minutes. Press **CANCEL**.

Add the beans, broth, bay leaves, Cajun seasoning, black pepper, thyme, and sage. Secure the lid on the pot. Close the pressure-release valve.

COOK

Select **BEAN/CHILI*** and adjust to **NORMAL**. When cooking is complete, use a natural release to depressurize.

SERVE

Remove and discard bay leaves. Serve with cooked white rice.

*TIP: If your Instant Pot® doesn't have a **BEAN/CHILI** button, select **MANUAL** and cook for 30 minutes at high pressure.

Caribbean Rice & Beans

In this island-inspired dish, the rice and beans are stirred together. To make it vegetarian (even vegan!), use vegetable broth in place of the chicken broth.

PREP TIME	FUNCTION	CLOSED POT TIME	TOTAL TIME	RELEASE
15 minutes	Sauté (Normal); Rice	35 minutes	50 minutes	Natural

SERVES: 4 as a main dish; 8 as a side dish

- 2 tablespoons vegetable oil
- 1 onion, chopped
- 3 cloves garlic, minced
- 1 tablespoon minced fresh ginger
- 2 cups reduced-sodium chicken broth
- 2 cups cooked black beans or red beans or two 15-ounce cans black beans or red beans, drained and rinsed
- 1½ cups long grain white rice, rinsed and drained
- 1 cup canned coconut milk (full fat)
- 1 whole scotch bonnet or habanero pepper, pricked with a fork
- 2 sprigs fresh thyme or ½ teaspoon dried thyme, crushed
- ½ teaspoon salt
- ¼ teaspoon ground allspice
- ¼ cup chopped fresh cilantro or parsley

PREP
Select **SAUTÉ** on the Instant Pot® and adjust to **NORMAL**. Add oil to pot. When oil is hot, add the onion. Cook and stir until onion is softened for about 3 minutes. Add garlic and ginger. Cook for 2 minutes more, stirring occasionally. Press **CANCEL**. Stir in chicken broth, beans, rice, coconut milk, scotch bonnet, thyme, salt, and allspice. Secure the lid on the pot. Close the pressure-release valve.

COOK
Select **RICE**. When cooking is complete, use a natural release to depressurize.

SERVE
Remove and discard whole scotch bonnet pepper and, if using, thyme sprigs. Top each serving with chopped cilantro.

Cuban Black Beans & Rice

If you forgot to soak the beans overnight, you can use the quick-soak method: Place beans in a large pot and cover with water by 2 inches. Bring to a boil and let boil for 1 minute. Remove from heat and let the beans stand, covered, for 1 hour. Drain, rinse, and proceed with the recipe.

PREP TIME	FUNCTION	CLOSED POT TIME	TOTAL TIME	RELEASE
25 minutes	Sauté (Normal); Pressure/Manual (High)	1 hour 35 minutes	2 hours + overnight soak	Natural

SERVES: 6 to 8

- 1 pound dried black beans
- 2 tablespoons olive oil
- 1 large onion, chopped
- 1 red sweet pepper, chopped
- 1 green sweet pepper, chopped
- 1 jalapeño pepper, seeded (if desired) and finely chopped
- 2 cloves garlic, minced
- 4 cups chicken broth
- 1 large smoked ham hock or 2 small smoked ham hocks
- 2 roma tomatoes, seeded and chopped
- 2 bay leaves
- 1 teaspoon dried oregano
- 1 teaspoon ground cumin
- 1 teaspoon paprika
- 1 teaspoon salt
- ½ teaspoon black pepper
- Lime wedges
- Cooked white rice
- Fresh cilantro leaves

PREP
Soak beans in water to cover overnight. Rinse and drain.

Select **SAUTÉ** on the Instant Pot® and adjust to **NORMAL**. Add olive oil. When oil is hot, add the onion, sweet peppers, jalapeño, and garlic. Cook and stir until vegetables are softened for about 5 minutes. Press **CANCEL**. Add the beans, broth, ham hock(s), tomatoes, bay leaves, oregano, cumin, paprika, salt, and black pepper. Secure the lid on the pot. Close the pressure-release valve.

COOK
Select **MANUAL** and cook at high pressure for 45 minutes. When cooking is complete, use a natural release to depressurize.

Remove ham hock(s); let cool slightly. Remove and discard bay leaves. Mash bean mixture with a potato masher to desired consistency. When the ham hock is cool enough to handle, remove meat; chop. Stir the meat into the beans.

SERVE
Serve with lime wedges over cooked white rice. Top with cilantro.

Cowboy Beans

You can use a bag of the mixed beans for soup in this recipe, but it's also a good way to use up all the dibs and dabs of beans in your pantry. No need to soak the beans for this recipe.

PREP TIME	FUNCTION	CLOSED POT TIME	TOTAL TIME	RELEASE
20 minutes	Sauté (Normal); Pressure/Manual (High)	2 hours 5 minutes	2 hours 25 minutes + 10 minutes simmer	Natural

SERVES: 8

- 4 slices bacon, diced
- 1 medium onion, diced
- 1 pound mixed dried beans, washed
- 1 15-ounce can tomato sauce
- ½ cup brown sugar
- 1 tablespoon dry mustard
- Dash cinnamon
- 3 cups water

PREP

Select **SAUTÉ** on the Instant Pot® and adjust to **NORMAL**. When hot, cook bacon, stirring occasionally, until cooked through, for about 5 minutes. Remove bacon to a paper towel lined plate. Add onion to the bacon fat and cook for 1 to 2 minutes, just until tender. Press **CANCEL**.

Add beans, tomato sauce, brown sugar, dry mustard, cinnamon, and cooked bacon to pot. Add the water, making sure that beans are completely covered with liquid. Stir to combine. Secure the lid on the pot. Close the pressure-release valve.

COOK

Select **MANUAL** and cook at high pressure for 90 minutes. When cooking is complete, use a natural release to depressurize. Press **CANCEL**.

SERVE

Select **SAUTÉ** and adjust to **NORMAL**. Cook for 10 minutes or until liquid is desired consistency. Press **CANCEL**.

Kathy Hester is the creator of HealthySlowCooking.com and author of
The Ultimate Vegan Cookbook for Your Instant Pot®.

Vegan Creamy Black-Eyed Peas

Nutritional yeast—not the same type used for baking bread—is added to many vegan recipes to give them a savory, cheesy flavor. Look for it in the health foods section of your supermarket.

PREP TIME	FUNCTION	CLOSED POT TIME	TOTAL TIME	RELEASE
10 minutes	Sauté (Normal); Pressure/Manual (High)	45 minutes	55 minutes	Natural

SERVES: 4

- 1 tablespoon olive oil
- ½ cup minced onion
- 1 teaspoon minced garlic
- ½ teaspoon smoked paprika
- ¼ teaspoon liquid smoke
- 1½ cups dried black-eyed peas
- 3 cups water
- 2 tablespoons nutritional yeast
- Salt and black pepper

PREP
Select **SAUTÉ** on the Instant Pot® and adjust to **NORMAL**. When hot, add the oil to the pot.

Add the onion and cook, stirring, until softened, for about 2 to 3 minutes. Add the garlic, paprika, and liquid smoke. **SAUTÉ** for 1 minute more. Add the black-eyed peas and the water. Press **CANCEL**. Secure the lid on the pot. Close the pressure-release valve.

COOK
Select **MANUAL** and cook at high pressure for 25 minutes. When cooking is complete, use a natural release to depressurize.

SERVE
Stir in the yeast and salt and pepper to taste.

Ham & Sweet Corn Risotto

This recipe may call for high-starch Arborio rice—the standard for the Italian dish—but the ingredients and flavorings are all-American. Try it with fresh corn during sweet corn season.

PREP TIME	FUNCTION	CLOSED POT TIME	TOTAL TIME	RELEASE
20 minutes	Sauté (Normal); Manual/Pressure (High)	25 minutes	45 minutes + 10 minutes stand	Quick

SERVES: 6

- 2 tablespoons olive oil
- 1 large shallot, finely chopped
- 1½ cups Arborio rice
- 2 cloves garlic, minced
- 1 cup dry white wine
- ½ teaspoon salt
- ¼ teaspoon freshly ground black pepper
- 5 cups chicken broth
- 2 cups fresh sweet corn kernels or 2 cups frozen corn, thawed
- 1 cup chopped ham
- 1 cup shredded pepper Jack cheese
- 2 tablespoons snipped fresh dill

PREP
Select **SAUTÉ** on the Instant Pot® and adjust to **NORMAL**. Add oil to pot. When oil is hot, add shallot and rice. Cook and stir for 5 minutes or until rice looks translucent. Stir in garlic and wine; cook and stir 2 to 3 minutes or until wine is absorbed. Press **CANCEL**.

Add salt, pepper, broth, corn, and ham. Secure the lid on the pot. Close the pressure-release valve.

COOK
Select **MANUAL** and cook at high pressure for 8 minutes. When cooking is complete, use a quick release to depressurize.

SERVE
Stir the risotto until any surface liquid disappears, then stir in cheese. Let stand for 10 minutes before serving. Garnish each serving with dill.

Mushroom & Spinach Risotto

The traditional cooking method for risotto involves standing at the stove and stirring almost constantly to achieve the signature creamy texture of the dish. The Instant Pot® eliminates that, turning out luscious risotto with the touch of a button.

PREP TIME	FUNCTION	CLOSED POT TIME	TOTAL TIME	RELEASE
25 minutes	Sauté (Normal); Pressure/Manual (High)	20 minutes	45 minutes	Quick

SERVES: 4

- 2 tablespoons olive oil
- ⅓ cup chopped shallots
- 1 8-ounce package cremini mushrooms, sliced
- ¼ teaspoon salt
- ⅛ teaspoon crushed red pepper
- 2 cloves garlic, minced
- 2 cups chicken or vegetable broth
- 1 cup Arborio rice
- ¼ teaspoon dried thyme
- 1 tablespoon butter
- 2 cups baby spinach
- ⅓ cup freshly grated Parmesan cheese

PREP

Select **SAUTÉ** on the Instant Pot® and adjust to **NORMAL**. Add oil to pot. When oil is hot, add shallots and cook for 2 minutes to soften, stirring occasionally. Add mushrooms, salt, and crushed red pepper; cook for 4 minutes or until mushrooms are tender, stirring frequently. Add garlic; cook and stir for 1 minute more. Press **CANCEL**. Add broth, rice, and thyme. Secure the lid on the pot. Close the pressure-release valve.

COOK

Select **MANUAL** and cook at high pressure for 6 minutes. When cooking is complete, use a quick release to depressurize.

SERVE

Add butter and spinach to rice mixture; stir to wilt spinach. Stir in Parmesan cheese.

Wild Rice-Blueberry Pilaf

Two Northwoods ingredients come together in this earthy pilaf. Try it with roast turkey or chicken.

PREP TIME	FUNCTION	CLOSED POT TIME	TOTAL TIME	RELEASE
15 minutes	Sauté (Normal); Pressure/Manual (High)	45 minutes	1 hour	Natural

SERVES: 6 to 8

- 3 tablespoons butter
- ⅓ cup finely chopped red onion
- 1 cup wild rice
- 1 cup long grain brown rice
- 3 cups chicken broth
- 2 teaspoons fresh thyme leaves
- ½ teaspoon salt
- ¼ teaspoon black pepper
- ⅓ cup toasted, coarsely chopped pecans
- ½ cup dried blueberries
- ¼ cup chopped fresh flat-leaf parsley

PREP

Select **SAUTÉ** on the Instant Pot® and adjust to **NORMAL**. Add butter to pot. When melted, add onion. Cook onion, stirring constantly until softened for about 2 to 3 minutes. Add wild rice and brown rice; cook and stir for 4 to 5 minutes or until rice toasts. Press **CANCEL**. Add broth, thyme, salt, and pepper.

Secure the lid on the pot. Close the pressure-release valve.

COOK

Select **MANUAL** and cook at high pressure for 25 minutes. When cooking is complete, use a natural release to depressurize.

SERVE

Add pecans, blueberries, and parsley; toss well. Serve immediately.

Greek Quinoa, Chickpea & Lettuce Wraps

Although most quinoa is sold prerinsed, it's not a bad idea to rinse it again, just in case. In their natural state, the grains are coated with a bitter substance called saponin that is thought to ward off birds and other creatures that might want to munch on them.

PREP TIME	FUNCTION	CLOSED POT TIME	TOTAL TIME	RELEASE
30 minutes	Pressure/Manual (High)	15 minutes	45 minutes + 5 minutes cool	Quick

SERVES: 4

- 1 **cup water**
- ¾ **cup dried tricolor quinoa, rinsed and drained**
- ½ **teaspoon salt**
- 1 **15-ounce can garbanzo beans, rinsed and drained**
- 1 **cup thinly sliced English cucumber**
- 1 **small red sweet pepper, cut into thin strips**
- ½ **cup thinly sliced green onions**
- ⅓ **cup olive oil**
- ⅓ **cup lemon juice**
- ⅓ **cup chopped fresh mint**
- ¼ **teaspoon freshly ground black pepper**
- 12 **Bibb lettuce leaves**
- ½ **cup crumbled feta cheese**
- ⅓ **cup pine nuts, toasted**

PREP
Combine the water, quinoa, and salt in the Instant Pot®; stir to combine. Secure the lid on the pot. Close the pressure-release valve.

COOK
Select **MANUAL** and cook at high pressure for 2 minutes. Once cooking is complete, use a quick release to depressurize.

Drain off liquid if needed. Spread cooked quinoa in a shallow pan and let cool for 5 minutes before using.

SERVE
Transfer cooled quinoa to a large bowl. Add beans, cucumber, sweet pepper, and green onions.

In a small bowl whisk together oil, lemon juice, mint, and black pepper. Pour over quinoa mixture; toss gently until well combined.

Divide lettuce leaves among four plates, placing them bowl sides up. Spoon quinoa mixture evenly onto lettuce leaves. Sprinkle with feta cheese and pine nuts.

Wheat Berry Pilaf with Kalamata Olives

Wheat berries have a delightfully chewy texture and nutty flavor. Tossed with garlic, sautéed mushrooms, soy sauce, white wine, herbs, lemon, and meaty Kalamata olives, they become a savory side to beef or lamb.

PREP TIME	FUNCTION	CLOSED POT TIME	TOTAL TIME	RELEASE
5 minutes	Pressure/Manual (High); Sauté (Normal)	1 hour 10 minutes	1 hour 15 minutes + 10 minutes sauté	Natural

SERVES: 4 to 6

- 1 cup uncooked wheat berries
- 4 cups water
- 1 tablespoon olive oil
- 1 small onion, chopped
- ½ teaspoon salt
- 1 tablespoon butter
- 4 cloves garlic, minced
- 8 ounces mushrooms, sliced
- 1 tablespoon soy sauce
- ¼ cup dry white wine
- ¼ cup chicken broth
- ½ teaspoon snipped fresh thyme
- 1 teaspoon snipped fresh rosemary
- 1 teaspoon lemon zest
- ⅓ cup pitted Kalamata olives, sliced
- Black pepper

PREP
Combine wheat berries and the water in the Instant Pot®. Secure the lid on the pot. Close the pressure-release valve.

COOK
Select **MANUAL** and cook at high pressure for 35 minutes. When cooking is complete, use a natural release to depressurize. Press **CANCEL**.

Drain wheat berries in a fine-mesh strainer and set aside. Wipe inner pot dry and replace.

Select **SAUTÉ** and adjust to **NORMAL**. Add oil to pot. When oil is hot, add onion and salt. Cook and stir until onion is softened for about 4 to 5 minutes. Add butter, garlic, mushrooms, and soy sauce and continue cooking for 5 to 7 minutes until mushrooms release their liquid. Add wine and chicken broth and simmer for about 3 minutes until liquid begins to evaporate. Add cooked wheat berries, thyme, rosemary, lemon zest, and olives. Heat through, stirring occasionally. Press **CANCEL**.

SERVE
Season to taste with pepper and additional salt.

Kale, Farro & Feta

Farro is the Italian name for emmer wheat, an ancient variety of hard wheat. It comes whole, semi-pearled, and pearled. Whole farro retains all of the bran. It has the most fiber but takes the longest time to cook. Semi-pearled has some of the bran removed, and pearled has all of it removed. It cooks the most quickly—especially in the Instant Pot®.

PREP TIME	FUNCTION	CLOSED POT TIME	TOTAL TIME	RELEASE
10 minutes	Sauté (Normal); Pressure/Manual (High)	40 minutes	50 minutes	Natural

SERVES: 6 to 8

- 1 **cup pearled farro**
- 1 **tablespoon olive oil**
- 8 **cups chopped kale (about 1 large bunch)**
- 1½ **cups reduced-sodium chicken broth or vegetable broth**
- 1 **tablespoon fresh lemon juice**
- ¼ **teaspoon salt**
- ¼ **teaspoon black pepper**
- ⅓ **cup crumbled feta cheese**
- ¼ **cup toasted almond slices**

PREP
Rinse farro under running water. Set aside. Select **SAUTÉ** on the Instant Pot® and adjust to **NORMAL**. When hot, add the oil and chopped kale. Cook for 2 minutes, stirring often. Press **CANCEL**. Place farro and broth in the pot. Secure the lid on the pot. Close the pressure-release valve.

COOK
Select **MANUAL** and cook at high pressure for 25 minutes. When cooking is complete, use a natural release to depressurize.

SERVE
Stir in lemon juice, salt, and pepper. Spoon mixture into a serving bowl. Top with feta and almonds. Serve immediately.

Thai Quinoa Salad

While the quinoa is cooking and cooling, prep the rest of the ingredients for this fresh and light veggie-packed salad that can be on the table in 30 minutes.

PREP TIME	FUNCTION	CLOSED POT TIME	TOTAL TIME	RELEASE
5 minutes	Pressure/Manual (High)	15 minutes	30 minutes + 5 minutes cool	Quick

SERVES: 4 to 6

- 1½ cups quinoa, rinsed and drained
- 2 cups water
- ⅛ teaspoon salt
- ¼ cup fresh lime juice
- ¼ cup untoasted sesame oil
- 1 tablespoon soy sauce
- 1 teaspoon sugar
- ⅛ to ¼ teaspoon crushed red pepper
- 1 small clove garlic, minced
- 2 tablespoons chopped green onions (green part only)
- 2 cups lightly packed green leaf lettuce or baby spinach leaves
- 1 medium seedless cucumber, thinly bias-sliced
- 2 medium carrots, thinly bias-sliced
- 2 cups leftover shredded chicken
- ½ cup fresh loosely packed basil leaves
- ⅓ cup loosely packed fresh mint leaves
- ½ cups peanuts, coarsely chopped
- Lime wedges

PREP
Combine quinoa, the water, and salt in the Instant Pot®. Secure the lid on the pot. Close the pressure-release valve.

COOK
Select **MANUAL** and cook at high pressure for 2 minutes. When cooking is complete, use a quick release to depressurize.

While quinoa is cooking, make the dressing: Combine lime juice, sesame oil, soy sauce, sugar, crushed red pepper, garlic, and green onions in a small bowl. Whisk until the sugar dissolves.

Spread cooked quinoa in a shallow pan and let cool for 5 minutes before using.

SERVE
In a large bowl combine quinoa, lettuce, cucumber, carrots, and chicken. Drizzle with the dressing. Toss gently to coat. Top with basil, mint leaves, and peanuts. Serve with lime wedges.

Laura Pazzaglia blogs at HipPressureCooking.com.

1-Minute Golden Pressure-Cooker Pilaf

Turmeric—prized by cooks for its earthy, pungent flavor and by naturopaths for its proven anti-inflammatory properties—gives this simple pilaf its beautiful golden color.

PREP TIME	FUNCTION	CLOSED POT TIME	TOTAL TIME	RELEASE
5 minutes	Sauté (Normal); Pressure/Manual (High)	10 minutes	15 minutes	Natural

SERVES: 6

- 2 cups quinoa, rinsed and drained*
- 2 tablespoons olive oil
- 2 garlic cloves, smashed
- 2 teaspoons turmeric
- 2 teaspoons cumin
- 1 teaspoon salt
- 3 cups water

  Chopped fresh mint, cilantro, or curly-leaf parsley, for garnish (optional)

PREP
Select **SAUTÉ** on the Instant Pot® and adjust to **NORMAL**. When hot, add the oil and garlic. **SAUTÉ** for about 30 seconds. Press **CANCEL**. Stir in the turmeric, cumin, and salt. Add the water and quinoa to the pot. Secure the lid on the pot. Close the pressure-release valve.

COOK
Select **MANUAL** and cook at high pressure for 1 minute. When cooking is complete, use a natural release to depressurize.

SERVE
Transfer quinoa to a serving bowl. Fluff with a fork. If desired, garnish with fresh herbs before serving.

*****TIP:** Although most quinoa is prerinsed, it's a good step to take to ensure that the bitter natural coating called saponin is fully rinsed and rubbed off of the grains.

Mexican Quinoa

Quinoa is high in protein and low in carbohydrate—making it an ideal health food. When it's combined with black beans, vegetables, and Mexican seasonings—and topped with a little salty cheese—you won't even think about the fact that it's good for you.

PREP TIME	FUNCTION	CLOSED POT TIME	TOTAL TIME	RELEASE
25 minutes	Sauté (Normal); Pressure/Manual (High)	15 minutes	40 minutes	Quick

SERVES: 4

- 2 tablespoons olive oil
- ½ cup coarsely chopped onion
- ½ cup coarsely chopped yellow sweet pepper
- 1 medium jalapeño pepper, seeded and finely chopped
- 2 cloves garlic, minced
- ½ teaspoon salt
- 1¾ cups chicken or vegetable broth
- 1 cup uncooked white quinoa, rinsed and drained
- 1 15-ounce can black beans, rinsed and drained
- 1 cup coarsely chopped fresh tomato
- 1 tablespoon chili powder
- 2 tablespoons chopped fresh cilantro
- ½ cup crumbled queso fresco
  Lime wedges

PREP
Select **SAUTÉ** on the Instant Pot® and adjust to **NORMAL**. Heat oil in pot; add onion, sweet pepper, jalapeño, garlic, and salt. Cook for 3 to 5 minutes or until softened, stirring frequently. Press **CANCEL**. Add broth, quinoa, beans, tomato, and chili powder. Secure the lid on the pot. Close the pressure-release valve.

COOK
Select **MANUAL** and cook at high pressure for 2 minutes. When cooking is complete, use a quick release to depressurize.

SERVE
Stir cilantro into quinoa mixture. Top with queso fresco and serve with lime wedges.

Jill Nussinow blogs at TheVeggieQueen.com and is the author of *Vegan Under Pressure*.

Chickpea-Broccoli Salad

This colorful blend of chickpeas, broccoli, red onion, and Kalamata olives dressed in a classic Dijon vinaigrette is the perfect dish to take on a picnic.

PREP TIME	FUNCTION	CLOSED POT TIME	TOTAL TIME	RELEASE
25 minutes	Pressure/Manual (High, Low)	35 minutes	1 hour	Natural/Quick

SERVES: 4

- ¾ **cup dried chickpeas, soaked overnight and drained**
- 3 **cloves garlic, minced**
- 1 **cup vegetable stock**
- ½ **pound broccoli florets or broccolini**
- ½ **cup sliced red onion**
- ¼ **cup chopped fresh flat-leaf parsley**
- 3 **tablespoons chopped Kalamata olives (optional)**
- ¼ **to ½ teaspoon crushed red pepper**

DRESSING

- 1 **tablespoon fresh lemon juice**
- 1 **tablespoon red wine vinegar**
- 2 **teaspoon Dijon mustard**
- 1 **teaspoon minced fresh garlic**
- 1 **tablespoon extra virgin olive oil**

PREP
Combine chickpeas, garlic, and stock in the Instant Pot®. Secure the lid on the pot. Close the pressure-release valve.

COOK
Select **MANUAL** and cook at high pressure for 13 minutes. When cooking is complete, use a natural release to depressurize.

While the chickpeas cook, make the dressing: Whisk lemon juice, vinegar, mustard, garlic, and olive oil in a medium bowl; set aside.

Add the broccoli to the pot. Secure the lid on the pot. Close the pressure-release valve. Select **MANUAL** and cook at low pressure for 1 minute. When cooking is complete, use a quick release to depressurize. (Alternatively, stir in the broccoli, secure the lid, and let sit until the broccoli becomes tender.)

SERVE
Using a slotted spoon, transfer the contents to a serving bowl.

Combine the dressing with the beans and broccoli. Add the onion, parsley, olives (if using), and crushed red pepper; toss to coat.

Serve salad warm or chilled.

Vegetables

Light & Fluffy Mashed Potatoes

Go classic or with one of the fun variations—Cheesy Garlic or Sriracha-Ranch.

PREP TIME	FUNCTION	CLOSED POT TIME	TOTAL TIME	RELEASE
20 minutes	Pressure/Manual (High); Sauté (Less)	30 minutes	50 minutes	Natural

SERVES: 6 to 8

- **2 pounds russet or Yukon gold potatoes, peeled and cut into 2- to 3-inch pieces**
- **2 cups reduced-sodium chicken broth or water***
- **¼ teaspoon black pepper**
- **½ cup milk**
- **2 tablespoons butter**
- **Salt**
- **Chopped fresh chives (optional)**
- **Freshly ground black pepper (optional)**

PREP

Combine potatoes, broth, and pepper in the Instant Pot®. Secure the lid on the pot. Close the pressure-release valve.

COOK

Select **MANUAL** and cook at high pressure for 6 minutes. When cooking is complete, use a natural release to depressurize. Press **CANCEL**.

Carefully pour most of the liquid from the pot into a medium bowl; set aside. Add milk and butter to the potatoes in pot. Select **SAUTÉ** and adjust to **LESS**. Use a potato masher to mash potatoes to desired texture. Add reserved cooking liquid as needed to reach desired consistency. Season to taste with salt. Press **CANCEL**.

SERVE

Spoon potatoes into a serving bowl; if desired, sprinkle with chives and/or pepper.

*TIP: If cooking potatoes in water, add ½ teaspoon salt to the potatoes before cooking.

CHEESY GARLIC MASHED POTATOES: Prepare as above except add 4 cloves garlic, minced, to the potatoes before cooking and substitute ½ cup sour cream, ⅓ cup shredded cheddar cheese, and ¼ cup finely shredded Parmesan cheese for the milk and butter.

SRIRACHA-RANCH MASHED POTATOES: Prepare as above except decrease milk to ¼ cup and substitute ⅓ cup bottled ranch dressing and 1 to 2 teaspoons bottled sriracha sauce for the butter.

Green Beans with Shallots & Pecans

While your turkey roasts in the oven, use the Instant Pot® to make this quick and delicious side dish.

PREP TIME	FUNCTION	CLOSED POT TIME	TOTAL TIME	RELEASE
15 minutes	Sauté (Normal); Steam	15 minutes	30 minutes + 5 minutes sauté	Quick

SERVES: 8

- ½ cup pecan halves and pieces, coarsely chopped
- 1 cup water
- 1½ pounds fresh green beans, stem ends trimmed
- ¼ cup unsalted butter
- ⅓ cup finely chopped shallot
- ¼ cup packed brown sugar
- 1 teaspoon kosher salt
- ½ teaspoon coarsely ground black pepper

PREP

Select **SAUTÉ** on the Instant Pot® and adjust to **NORMAL**. Add the pecans and cook for 2 to 3 minutes or until lightly toasted, stirring often. Remove from the pot and set aside. Press **CANCEL**.

Fill a large bowl with water and ice; set aside. Add the 1 cup water and a vegetable steamer basket with legs to the pot.* Add the green beans to the steamer basket. Secure the lid on the pot. Close the pressure-release valve.

COOK

Select **STEAM** and adjust to 2 minutes. When cooking is complete, use a quick release to depressurize. Press **CANCEL**.

Carefully remove the steamer basket and transfer the beans to the ice water for 1 minute to stop the cooking. Transfer the beans to paper towels to dry. (Make sure the beans are dry before adding them to the pot in the next step.)

Thoroughly dry the inner pot. Select **SAUTÉ** and adjust to **NORMAL**. Add the butter to the pot. When butter is hot, add the shallot and cook for 2 to 3 minutes or until golden. Add the sugar, stirring constantly, until dissolved. Add the pecans and cook for 1 minute, stirring constantly. Add the green beans, salt, and pepper, tossing to coat.

Cook for 2 to 3 minutes or until the beans are heated through, tossing occasionally. Press **CANCEL**.

SERVE

Season to taste with pepper and additional salt.

*__TIP:__ If your steamer basket doesn't have legs, place the trivet in the pot first, then place steamer basket on top of it.

Garlic Broccoli with Lemon & Olives

Steaming broccoli helps retain nutrients and its beautiful bright green color. Its pleasing, cabbagey flavor is just right accented with lemon, garlic, and olives.

PREP TIME	FUNCTION	CLOSED POT TIME	TOTAL TIME	RELEASE
10 minutes	Steam; Sauté (Normal)	10 minutes	20 minutes + 5 minutes sauté	Quick

SERVES: 4

- 1 cup water
- 4 cups broccoli florets
- 1 tablespoon olive oil
- 3 cloves garlic, minced
- ¼ cup sliced Kalamata olives
- 2 teaspoons lemon zest
- 1 tablespoon fresh lemon juice
- ¼ teaspoon kosher salt
- ¼ teaspoon coarsely ground black pepper

PREP
Pour the water in the Instant Pot®. Place a steamer with legs in the pot.*
Add the broccoli to the steamer basket. Secure the lid on the pot. Close the pressure-release valve.

COOK
Select **STEAM** and adjust to 2 minutes. When cooking is complete, use a quick release to depressurize. Press **CANCEL**.

Carefully remove the steamer basket and transfer the broccoli to a bowl.

Thoroughly dry the inner pot. Select **SAUTÉ** and adjust to **NORMAL**. Add the oil. When the oil is hot, add the garlic, olives, lemon zest and juice, and broccoli to the pot. Toss to combine. Cook and stir for 2 to 3 minutes or until the broccoli is heated through, tossing occasionally. Press **CANCEL**.

SERVE
Season the broccoli with salt and pepper.

*TIP: If your steamer basket doesn't have legs, place the trivet in the pot first, then place steamer basket on top of it.

Corn on the Cob with Herb Butter

Swap out the chives and flat-leaf parsley with different herbs if you like. Any soft-leaf herb such as basil, oregano, marjoram, tarragon, or dill will do.

PREP TIME	FUNCTION	CLOSED POT TIME	TOTAL TIME	RELEASE
10 minutes	Steam (Less)	15 minutes	25 minutes	Quick

SERVES: 4

- 1 cup water
- 4 ears corn, shucked
- ¼ cup butter, softened
- 2 teaspoons chopped fresh chives
- 2 teaspoons chopped fresh flat-leaf parsley
- ⅛ teaspoon salt
- Dash cayenne pepper

PREP
Place the trivet in the Instant Pot®. Add the water to the pot and place corn on the trivet. Secure the lid on the pot. Close the pressure-release valve.

COOK
Select **STEAM** and adjust to **LESS**. When cooking is complete, use a quick release to depressurize.

SERVE
While corn is steaming, for herb butter, combine butter, chives, parsley, salt, and cayenne; mix well. Serve corn with herb butter.

Collards with Smoked Ham Hocks & Sweet Onions

Collards can be quickly sautéed so they stay slightly firm or slow-simmered until they're very soft. Here, they're cooked to a perfect in-between stage and classically flavored with smoked ham and sweet onions.

PREP TIME	FUNCTION	CLOSED POT TIME	TOTAL TIME	RELEASE
30 minutes	Sauté (Normal); Steam	15 minutes	45 minutes	Quick

SERVES: 6 to 8

- 6 slices hickory-smoked bacon, chopped
- 8 ounces smoked ham, diced
- 2 large Vidalia or other sweet onions, peeled, quartered, and thinly sliced (3 cups)
- ⅓ cup apple cider vinegar
- 1 tablespoon brown sugar
- 1 teaspoon salt
- ¼ teaspoon black pepper
- 1 teaspoon hot pepper sauce
- 2 to 2½ pounds fresh collard greens, washed, dried, and coarsely chopped (16 cups)

PREP

Select **SAUTÉ** on the Instant Pot® and adjust to **NORMAL**. Add chopped bacon to pot. Cook and stir bacon for 5 to 10 minutes or until crisp. Using a slotted spoon, transfer crisp bacon to paper towel-lined plate to drain.

Add ham and onions to the pot; cook and stir for 5 to 6 minutes or until onions are limp and ham is browned. Press **CANCEL**; cool slightly. Add vinegar, sugar, salt, pepper, and hot pepper sauce; mix well. Select **SAUTÉ** and adjust to **NORMAL**. Push collards into pot a batch at a time, waiting until one batch wilts down before adding another. Press **CANCEL**. When all collards are in the pot, secure the lid on the pot. Close the pressure-release valve.

COOK

Select **STEAM** and adjust cook time to 8 minutes. Once cooking is complete, use a quick release to depressurize.

SERVE

Using a slotted spoon, transfer collards to a serving dish; sprinkle with reserved crisp bacon bits.

Steamed Cauliflower with Cayenne & Parmesan

Just a few simple ingredients give this vegetable side wonderful flavor. Try it with a grilled steak.

PREP TIME	FUNCTION		CLOSED POT TIME	TOTAL TIME	RELEASE
10 minutes	Steam		15 minutes	25 minutes	Quick

SERVES: 4

- 1 **cup water**
- 6 **cups large cauliflower florets**
- 2 **tablespoons butter, melted**
- 1 **tablespoon fresh lemon juice**
- ¼ **teaspoon salt**
-   **Dash cayenne pepper**
- ⅓ **cup finely shredded Parmesan cheese**
- 1 **tablespoon chopped fresh flat-leaf parsley**

PREP
Place a vegetable steamer basket with legs in the Instant Pot®.* Add the water to pot and place cauliflower in basket. Secure the lid on pot. Close the pressure-release valve.

COOK
Select **STEAM** and adjust cook time to 1 minute. When cooking is complete, use a quick release to depressurize.

SERVE
Meanwhile, in a medium bowl combine butter, lemon juice, salt, and cayenne. Add cooked cauliflower to butter mixture; stir gently to coat. Top with Parmesan and parsley.

*TIP: If your steamer basket doesn't have legs, place the trivet in the pot first, then place steamer basket on top of it.

Bacon-Basil Succotash

This Southern favorite gets gussied up with bacon, basil, jalapeño, and garlic. It's just the thing to serve with a smoky ham steak.

PREP TIME	FUNCTION	CLOSED POT TIME	TOTAL TIME	RELEASE
25 minutes	Sauté (Normal); Steam	20 minutes	45 minutes	Quick

SERVES: 6 to 8

- 4 slices bacon, chopped
- 1 cup coarsely chopped red sweet pepper
- ½ cup chopped red onion
- 1 jalapeño pepper, seeded and finely chopped
- 2 cloves garlic, minced
- 1 16-ounce package frozen corn kernels
- 2 cups frozen baby lima beans
- ½ cup chicken broth
- ½ cup chopped fresh basil
- Salt and black pepper

PREP

Select **SAUTÉ** on the Instant Pot® and adjust to **NORMAL**. Add bacon to pot. Cook, stirring occasionally, until bacon is crisp for about 5 minutes. Transfer bacon to a bowl, leaving drippings in pot. Add sweet pepper, onion, jalapeño, and garlic to pot. Cook, stirring occasionally, until softened for about 3 minutes. Press **CANCEL**.

Stir in corn, lima beans, and chicken broth. Secure the lid on the pot. Close the pressure-release valve.

COOK

Select **STEAM** and adjust cook time to 6 minutes. When cooking is complete, use a quick release to depressurize.

SERVE

Stir in the bacon and basil. Season to taste with salt and black pepper.

Brussels Sprouts with Bacon & Balsamic

After being steamed to tender perfection, the sprouts are browned with the bacon until they get a crisp, golden edge. A drizzle of balsamic vinegar adds a hint of sweetness.

PREP TIME	FUNCTION	CLOSED POT TIME	TOTAL TIME	RELEASE
20 minutes	Pressure/Manual (High); Sauté (Normal)	20 minutes	40 minutes	Quick

SERVES: 4

- **2 cups water**
- **12 ounces fresh Brussels sprouts, trimmed and halved**
- **5 slices bacon, chopped**
- **2 tablespoons chopped fresh chives**
- **2 tablespoons balsamic vinegar**
- **¼ teaspoon black pepper**
- **⅛ teaspoon salt**

PREP
Place a vegetable steamer basket with legs in the Instant Pot®.* Add the water to the pot. Add Brussels sprouts to pot, arranging evenly in the steamer basket. Secure the lid on the pot. Close the pressure-release valve.

COOK
Select **MANUAL** and cook at high pressure for 2 minutes. When cooking is complete, use a quick release to depressurize. Press **CANCEL**. Transfer Brussels sprouts to a medium bowl. Remove steamer basket from pot; pour water from the pot. Wipe pot dry.

Select **SAUTÉ** and adjust to **NORMAL**. Add half of the Brussels sprouts and half of the bacon to the pot. Cook for 5 to 7 minutes or until sprouts are browned and bacon is crisp, stirring occasionally. Transfer sprouts and bacon to a serving dish; cover to keep warm. Repeat with remaining sprouts and bacon. Add to serving dish with first half of sprouts and bacon. Press **CANCEL**.

SERVE
Sprinkle sprouts with chives and drizzle with vinegar; sprinkle with pepper and salt. Toss quickly to coat. Serve immediately.

*TIP: If your steamer basket doesn't have legs, place the trivet in the pot first, then place steamer basket on top of it.

Spicy Indian Savoy Cabbage

Deep green, crinkly-leaved savoy cabbage has a mild, earthy flavor that takes beautifully to the Indian spices. The flavor of this dish is so complex and delicious you'll be tempted to eat it as your main course!

PREP TIME	FUNCTION		CLOSED POT TIME	TOTAL TIME	RELEASE
20 minutes	Sauté (Normal); Pressure/Manual (High)		5 minutes	25 minutes	Quick

SERVES: 4 to 6

- 1   **2-inch piece fresh ginger, peeled and cut into ½-inch slices**
- 4   **cloves garlic, chopped**
- 1   **large jalapeño pepper, stemmed, halved, and seeded**
- 2   **teaspoons garam masala**
- 1   **teaspoon ground turmeric**
- ½   **cup chicken broth**
- 3   **tablespoons coconut oil**
- 1   **tablespoon black mustard seeds**
- 1   **teaspoon coriander seeds**
- 1   **teaspoon cumin seeds**
- 1   **3-inch cinnamon stick**
- 1   **whole jalapeño pepper**
- 2   **cups thinly sliced yellow onions**
- ½   **teaspoon salt**
- 10   **cups thinly sliced, cored savoy cabbage (about 1½ pounds)**
- ½   **cup snipped fresh cilantro**

PREP

In a food processor combine ginger, garlic, jalapeño, garam masala, turmeric, and ¼ cup of the broth. Cover and process until a coarse paste forms; set aside.

Select **SAUTÉ** on the Instant Pot® and adjust to **NORMAL**. Add the oil. When hot, add the mustard seeds, coriander seeds, cumin seeds, cinnamon stick, and whole jalapeño. Cook, stirring frequently, for 2 minutes. (The mustard seeds will pop and spatter as they cook.) Add onions and cook for 4 to 5 minutes or until lightly browned. Add the ginger mixture and salt. Cook for 3 minutes, stirring often. Add the cabbage and remaining broth. Stir to combine from the bottom up. Press **CANCEL**.

Secure the lid on the pot. Close the pressure-release valve.

COOK

Select **MANUAL** and cook at high pressure for 3 minutes. When cooking is complete, use a quick release to depressurize.

SERVE

Remove and discard the cinnamon stick and whole jalapeño.

Sprinkle with cilantro.

Jill Nussinow blogs at TheVeggieQueen.com and is the author of *Vegan Under Pressure*.

Maple-Vinegar-Braised Parsnips

Balsamic vinegar adds tanginess and maple syrup a bit of sweetness to this simple root-vegetable dish. Be sure to use real maple syrup for the best flavor.

PREP TIME	FUNCTION	CLOSED POT TIME	TOTAL TIME	RELEASE
15 minutes	Pressure/Manual (High)	10 minutes	25 minutes	Quick

SERVES: 4

- 1½ pounds parsnips, peeled and cut into ½-inch slices on the diagonal
- ¼ cup vegetable stock
- 3 tablespoons balsamic vinegar
- 2 tablespoons maple syrup
- Salt and black pepper

PREP
Combine the parsnips, stock, and vinegar in the Instant Pot®.

Secure the lid on the pot. Close the pressure-release valve.

COOK
Select **MANUAL** and cook at high pressure for 4 minutes. When cooking is complete, use a quick release to depressurize.

Stir in the maple syrup. Season to taste with salt and pepper.

SERVE
Transfer to a bowl and serve.

Mashed Sweet Potatoes with Streusel Topping

We love this trick: The streusel topping is browned on Sauté in the Instant Pot® before being removed and set aside to cool, so it stays crunchy even after it's sprinkled on the cooked sweet potatoes right before serving.

PREP TIME	FUNCTION	CLOSED POT TIME	TOTAL TIME
20 minutes	Sauté (Normal); Slow Cook (More)	3 hours 30 minutes	3 hours 50 minutes

SERVES: 8

STREUSEL TOPPING

- 1 tablespoon butter
- ¼ cup rolled oats
- 2 tablespoons flaked coconut
- 2 tablespoons chopped pecans
- 2 tablespoons brown sugar
- Dash cinnamon

SWEET POTATOES

- 2 pounds sweet potatoes, peeled and cut into 2-inch chunks
- ¾ cup orange juice
- Zest of 1 orange (1 tablespoon)

PREP

For the streusel topping, select **SAUTÉ** on Instant Pot® and adjust to **NORMAL**. When hot, add the butter to the pot. When melted, add the oats, coconut, and pecans. Cook for about 5 minutes until lightly toasted, stirring frequently. Stir in brown sugar and cinnamon. Press **CANCEL**. Pour onto a plate to cool.

Add sweet potatoes to the pot. Pour orange juice over the sweet potatoes and toss so that all sides of the potatoes have been coated with orange juice. Secure the lid on the pot. Open the pressure-release valve.

COOK

Select **SLOW COOK** and adjust to **MORE**. Cook for 3½ hours until potatoes are very tender.

SERVE

Add orange zest to undrained potatoes and mash until smooth. Transfer to a serving bowl. Sprinkle with streusel topping.

Orange-Honey Beets with Parsley

Beets are one of the best vegetables to cook in the Instant Pot®. Their dense texture usually requires a long cook time, but they cook quickly under pressure—and they turn out fork-tender, never mushy.

PREP TIME	FUNCTION	CLOSED POT TIME	TOTAL TIME	RELEASE
25 minutes	Manual/Pressure (High)	35 minutes	1 hour	Natural

SERVES: 4

- 2 tablespoons olive oil
- 2 shallots, chopped
- 3 pounds beets (with tops), trimmed, peeled, and cut into 2-inch chunks
- ½ cup freshly squeezed orange juice
- 3 tablespoons red wine vinegar
- 3 tablespoons honey
- ½ teaspoon salt
- ½ teaspoon black pepper
- ½ cup chopped fresh flat-leaf parsley
- 1 teaspoon orange zest

PREP
Select **SAUTÉ** on the Instant Pot® and adjust to **NORMAL**. Add olive oil and shallots. Cook, stirring often, until shallots are softened for about 3 minutes. Press **CANCEL**. Stir in the beets, orange juice, vinegar, honey, salt, and pepper. Secure the lid on the pot. Close the pressure-release valve.

COOK
Select **MANUAL** and cook at high pressure for 13 minutes. When cooking is complete, use a natural release to depressurize.

SERVE
Stir in parsley and orange zest.

Artichoke "Nests" with Garlic Clove Eggs

As pretty to look at as they are delicious to eat, these make a fitting first course for a fancy dinner party in the spring, when artichokes are in season. Your guests will be so impressed!

PREP TIME	FUNCTION	CLOSED POT TIME	TOTAL TIME	RELEASE
35 minutes	Steam; Sauté (Normal)	20 minutes	55 minutes	Quick

SERVES: 4

- ½ cup olive oil
- ¼ cup freshly squeezed lemon juice
- 1 teaspoon honey
- 2½ cups chicken broth
- 2 medium artichokes (about 8 ounces each)
- 12 whole cloves garlic, peeled
- 1 tablespoon snipped fresh dill
- 1 teaspoon salt
- ½ teaspoon black pepper
- 1 bay leaf

PREP

Combine the oil, lemon juice, honey, and chicken broth in the Instant Pot®. Mix well.

Use kitchen shears to snip the thorny tips of each of the leaves on the artichokes. Cut artichokes in half lengthwise. Using a serrated spoon or paring knife, carefully remove the artichokes' thorny centers. Place artichokes in the pot, turning each to coat with liquid. Turn artichokes so cut sides are above oil mixture, packed tightly together. Place 3 garlic cloves in the indentation of each artichoke half. Sprinkle artichokes with dill, salt, and pepper. Drop bay leaf into pot. Secure the lid on the pot. Close the pressure-release valve.

COOK

Select **STEAM** and adjust cook time to 9 minutes. When cooking is complete, use a quick release to depressurize. Press **CANCEL**.

Using a slotted spoon, remove artichokes and transfer to serving plates.

Select **SAUTÉ** and adjust to **NORMAL**. Let liquid boil for 5 minutes or until slightly reduced. Remove and discard bay leaf. Skim fat from top of liquid. Press **CANCEL**.

SERVE

Spoon liquid over artichokes. Serve warm or at room temperature.

Soups, Stews & Chili

Beef Burgundy

Chuck—a tough cut of meat—gets butter-knife-tender after slow cooking in a blend of dry red wine and beef broth flavored with bacon, pearl onions, and herbs. Look for fines herbes in the spice aisle of your supermarket. The classic blend is chervil, chives, parsley, and tarragon.

PREP TIME	FUNCTION	CLOSED POT TIME	TOTAL TIME
35 minutes	Sauté (Normal); Slow Cook (More)	4 hours	4 hours 35 minutes

SERVES: 6

- ¼ **cup all-purpose flour**
- ½ **teaspoon salt**
- ¼ **teaspoon black pepper**
- 2 **tablespoons butter**
- 4 **slices bacon, chopped**
- 2 **pounds beef chuck, trimmed of excess fat and cut into 1-inch cubes**
- 1 **14.4-ounce bag frozen pearl onions, thawed**
- 8 **ounces button mushrooms, cleaned and cut in halves**
- 1 **teaspoon fines herbes**
- 1 **cup burgundy wine or dry red wine blend**
- 1½ **cups beef broth**
- 8 **ounces egg noodles, cooked according to package directions**
- ¼ **cup chopped fresh flat-leaf parsley**

PREP

Combine flour, salt, and pepper in a resealable plastic bag. Close bag; shake to mix well. Set aside.

Add bacon to the Instant Pot®. Select **SAUTÉ** on the Instant Pot® and adjust to **NORMAL**. Cook and stir bacon for 5 to 7 minutes or until crisp. Remove crisp bacon with a slotted spoon; transfer to paper towels to drain. Chill until serving time.

Press **CANCEL**. Carefully remove inner pot; pour bacon fat into another container. Replace pot. Add butter; select **SAUTÉ** and adjust to **NORMAL**. Add beef cubes to flour mixture in bag. Shake to coat cubes with flour. Brown beef cubes, half at a time, in butter on all sides. Transfer to a bowl. Add onions to pot. Cook and stir for 1 minute. Add onions to reserved beef cubes.

Add mushrooms to pot, adding more butter if necessary. Cook and stir until golden. Press **CANCEL**. Return reserved beef cubes, onions, and fines herbes to the pot. Stir in wine and beef broth; mix gently. Secure the lid on the pot. Open the pressure-release valve.

COOK

Select **SLOW COOK** and adjust to **MORE**. Cook for 4 hours.

SERVE

When cooking is complete, spoon beef burgundy over hot cooked noodles. Sprinkle with parsley and reserved bacon.

Greek Beef Stifado

This classic stew is flavored with aromatic spices—whole allspice and whole cloves. They infuse the dish with a warm, slightly sweet flavor—a lovely balance to the acidity of the tomatoes and red wine. They soften enough in the marinating and cooking time that you won't mind eating them whole.

PREP TIME	FUNCTION	CLOSED POT TIME	TOTAL TIME	RELEASE
1 hour	Sauté (Normal); Meat/Stew (Normal)	1 hour 5 minutes	2 hours 5 minutes + 6 hours marinate	Natural

SERVES: 8

- 1   3- to 3½-pound beef chuck roast or rump roast, cut into ¾-inch cubes
- 4   cloves garlic, minced
- 2   bay leaves
- 15   whole allspice berries, bruised
- 10   whole cloves
- 1   teaspoon dried oregano
- ⅔   cup dry red wine
- ¼   cup red wine vinegar
- 3   tablespoons olive oil
- 1   16-ounce package frozen white pearl onions, thawed and patted dry
- 4   large ripe tomatoes, peeled and chopped
- ¼   cup tomato puree
    Salt and black pepper
- 16   ounces orzo, cooked according to package directions
- ½   cup shredded Pecorino cheese

PREP
Place cubed beef in a large nonmetal container. Add garlic, bay leaves, allspice, cloves, oregano, red wine, and red wine vinegar. Mix well. Cover and refrigerate for at least 6 hours or up to overnight.

Drain beef cubes, reserving marinade. Pour olive oil into Instant Pot®. Select **SAUTÉ** and adjust to **NORMAL**. Working in small batches, brown beef cubes in oil until browned on all sides. Transfer browned meat to a plate. Working in small batches, brown onions in oil. Transfer browned onions to a plate. Press **CANCEL**.

Return beef cubes, accumulated juices, and onions to the pot. Add reserved marinade, tomatoes, and tomato puree. Stir gently.

Secure the lid on the pot. Close the pressure-release valve.

COOK
Select **MEAT/STEW** and adjust to **NORMAL**. When cooking is complete, use a natural release to depressurize.

SERVE
Remove and discard bay leaves. Season with salt and pepper to taste. Serve stew over cooked orzo. Top with cheese.

Beef Chili

While the chili cooks in the Instant Pot®, bake a batch of corn bread in the oven. Everything will be ready at the same time.

PREP TIME	FUNCTION	CLOSED POT TIME	TOTAL TIME	RELEASE
20 minutes	Sauté (Normal); Pressure/Manual (High)	1 hour	1 hour 20 minutes	Natural

SERVES: 8

1½ **pounds ground beef**

1 **cup chopped onion**

4 **cloves garlic, minced**

1 **15-ounce can tomato sauce**

2 **15- to 16-ounce cans kidney beans, drained**

1 **cup beef broth**

2 **14.5-ounce cans diced tomatoes, undrained**

2 **tablespoons chili powder**

½ **teaspoon black pepper**

1 **4.5-ounce can diced green chiles, undrained (optional)**

Hot sauce (optional)

Shredded cheddar cheese, sour cream, and/or sliced green onions

PREP
Select **SAUTÉ** on the Instant Pot® and adjust to **NORMAL**. Cook ground beef, onion, and garlic for about 10 minutes or until the meat is browned and onion is tender. Press **CANCEL**. Add tomato sauce, beans, broth, tomatoes, chili powder, black pepper, and green chiles (if using). Secure the lid on the pot. Close the pressure-release valve.

COOK
Select **MANUAL** and cook at high pressure for 10 minutes. When cooking is complete, use a natural release to depressurize.

SERVE
Serve chili with hot sauce (if using), cheese, sour cream, and/or green onions.

French Pork Stew

This hearty, garlicky stew (12 cloves!) of pork, sausage, dried lima beans (also called butter beans), and vegetables will warm you up on the coldest winter night.

PREP TIME	FUNCTION	CLOSED POT TIME	TOTAL TIME
1 hour 10 minutes	Sauté (Normal); Slow Cook (More)	7 hours	8 hours 10 minutes

SERVES: 6 to 8

- ¼ cup all-purpose flour
- 1 teaspoon salt
- ½ teaspoon black pepper
- 1 pound pork shoulder, cut into ¾-inch cubes
- 4 slices thick-cut bacon, chopped
- 1 large onion, chopped
- 2 carrots, peeled and bias-cut into ¼-inch-thick slices
- 12 cloves garlic, smashed and peeled
- ½ cup tomato paste
- 1½ cups dry white wine
- ½ pound dried large lima beans, soaked overnight in water to cover and drained
- 5 cups chicken broth
- 2 14.5-ounce cans fire-roasted tomatoes
- 2 tablespoons apple brandy, brandy, or apple cider (optional)
- 1 pound andouille or other garlic sausage, bias-cut into 1-inch chunks
- Bouquet garni*
- Fresh curly-leaf parsley, chopped, for garnish
- Sliced baguette, for serving

PREP

Combine flour, salt, and pepper in a large bowl. Add cubed pork and toss to coat; set aside.

Select **SAUTÉ** on the Instant Pot® and adjust to **NORMAL**. Cook bacon until crisp for 5 to 7 minutes. Press **CANCEL**. Remove from pot with a slotted spoon and drain on a paper towel-lined plate. Refrigerate until serving time. Reserve 3 tablespoons of the bacon fat in the pot; set remainder aside.

Brown half of the pork in the bacon fat. Remove from pot; repeat with remaining pork. Cook onion, carrots, and garlic for 4 to 5 minutes or until vegetables are lightly browned, adding more bacon fat if needed.

Add tomato paste and cook for 1 minute, stirring constantly. Add wine, stirring constantly. Add browned pork, drained beans, chicken broth, tomatoes and their liquid, brandy, sausage, and bouquet garni. Press **CANCEL**. Secure the lid on the pot. Open the pressure-release valve.

COOK

Select **SLOW COOK** and adjust to **MORE**. Cook for 7 to 8 hours or until pork and beans are tender.

SERVE

Divide stew among serving bowls; sprinkle with chopped parsley and reserved crisp bacon. Serve with baguette slices.

*TIP: Bouquet garni is a French term for a bundle of fresh herbs wrapped in cheesecloth (for easy removal) that is added to stews and braises to add flavor. The herbs included in the bouquet garni vary from dish to dish. For this stew, place 8 sprigs curly-leaf parsley, 2 sprigs fresh thyme, and 1 bay leaf in the center of a square of cheesecloth. Bring up the corners and tie with kitchen string.

Pork Chile Verde

It takes just a few minutes to prep the vegetables for the homemade green salsa—and the result is so much fresher tasting than the jarred stuff.

PREP TIME	FUNCTION	CLOSED POT TIME	TOTAL TIME	RELEASE
40 minutes	Sauté (Normal); Meat/Stew (More)	1 hour 25 minutes	2 hours 5 minutes	Natural

SERVES: 6

- 2 to 2½ pounds boneless pork shoulder, trimmed and cut into 2-inch cubes
- 1 teaspoon kosher salt
- 1 tablespoon olive oil
- 6 to 8 tomatillos, husked, rinsed, and quartered
- 2 to 3 poblano peppers, seeded and roughly chopped
- 2 Anaheim or cubanelle peppers, seeded and roughly chopped
- 1 serrano or jalapeño pepper, roughly chopped
- 1 cup chopped white onion
- 3 cloves garlic, peeled
- 2 teaspoons cumin seeds, toasted*
- 1 teaspoon dried Mexican oregano
- 1 cup chicken broth
- 1 cup loosely packed cilantro
  Flour tortillas, warmed
  Lime wedges

PREP

Season the pork with the salt. Select **SAUTÉ** on the Instant Pot® and adjust to **NORMAL**. Add the oil to the pot. When the oil is hot, add the pork (in small batches) and cook for 3 to 4 minutes or until browned on all sides. As pork is browned, remove to a bowl with a slotted spoon.

Press **CANCEL**. Remove most of the fat from the pot. Add the tomatillos, chile peppers, onion, garlic, cumin seeds, oregano, and chicken broth to the pot. Secure the lid on the pot. Close the pressure-release valve.

COOK

Select **MEAT** and adjust to **MORE**. When cooking is complete, use a natural release to depressurize.

Use a slotted spoon to transfer cooked pork to a bowl. Add the cilantro to the pot. Use an immersion blender to blend the salsa (do not overprocess). Taste the salsa and season to taste with additional salt. Return the pork to the salsa and stir to combine.

SERVE

Serve with tortillas and lime wedges.

*****TIP:** Toast cumin seeds in a small dry skillet over medium heat until lightly browned and fragrant, stirring constantly, for about 3 to 4 minutes.

Pork Posole Rojo

Posole is a classic Mexican stew featuring meat and chewy hominy (dried and rehydrated corn) in a chile-laced broth. Toppings such as radish, shredded cabbage, onion, cilantro, and avocado give it a fresh touch.

PREP TIME	FUNCTION	CLOSED POT TIME	TOTAL TIME	RELEASE
15 minutes	Sauté (More); Meat/Stew	1 hour 20 minutes	1 hour 35 minutes	Natural

SERVES: 6

- 2 tablespoons olive oil
- 2 pounds country-style pork ribs
- 1 small yellow onion, peeled and quartered
- 6 garlic cloves, peeled
- 2 tablespoons ancho chile powder
- 2 cups water
- 1 teaspoon salt
- 4 cups chicken broth
- 1 teaspoon oregano
- 2 15-ounce cans white hominy, drained

OPTIONAL TOPPINGS

Thinly sliced radishes

Shredded cabbage

Coarsely chopped fresh cilantro

Thinly sliced red onion

Cubed ripe avocado

Lime wedges for squeezing

PREP
Select **SAUTÉ** on the Instant Pot® and adjust to **MORE**. Add oil to pot. When oil is hot, brown ribs in batches until browned on all sides for about 5 minutes per batch. Add all ribs back to pot. Press **CANCEL**.

In a blender container combine onion, garlic, chile powder, the water, and salt. Blend until smooth. Add onion-chile mixture to pot. Add chicken broth, oregano, hominy, and pork ribs to pot. Secure the lid on the pot. Close the pressure-release valve.

COOK
Select **MEAT/STEW**. When cooking time is complete, use a natural release to depressurize.

SERVE
Remove ribs from the pot and coarsely shred meat. Return shredded meat to pot. Divide posole among serving bowls and top with desired toppings.

Neapolitan Pork-Pumpkin Stew

In most of Italy, pumpkin is a much-loved autumn vegetable savored in fancy restaurants as well as in simple country fare like this stew.

PREP TIME	FUNCTION	CLOSED POT TIME	TOTAL TIME	RELEASE
45 minutes	Sauté (Normal/More); Pressure/Manual (High)	20 minutes	1 hour 5 minutes	Quick

SERVES: 6

- 6 slices bacon, chopped
- 1 pound pork tenderloin, trimmed and cut into bite-size pieces
- 5 cloves garlic, minced
- 6 cups chicken broth
- 2 fennel bulbs, trimmed and coarsely chopped, fronds reserved
- 4 cups 1½-inch cubes of culinary pumpkin* or butternut squash
- 1 cup dry ditalini pasta, macaroni, or mini penne
- ¼ teaspoon crushed red pepper (optional)
- ¼ teaspoon salt
- ⅛ teaspoon black pepper

PREP

Select **SAUTÉ** and adjust to **NORMAL**. Add bacon to pot. Cook and stir until bacon is crispy, about 6 to 8 minutes. Press **CANCEL**. Remove bacon to a paper towel-lined plate to drain. Remove all but about 1 tablespoon bacon fat from the pot.

Select **SAUTÉ** and adjust to **MORE**. Brown pork cubes, half at a time, on all sides in the drippings. As pork cubes brown, remove to a plate with a slotted spoon and set aside.

When all pork is browned, add garlic to the pot. Cook, stirring constantly, for 1 minute or until golden. Press **CANCEL**. Add ¼ cup of the chicken broth. Scrape bottom and sides of pot to loosen browned bits.

Add remaining chicken broth, fennel, pumpkin, and pasta to pot. Stir in the reserved pork and accumulated juices, crushed red pepper (if using), salt, and black pepper. Secure the lid on the pot. Close the pressure-release valve.

COOK

Select **MANUAL** and cook at high pressure for 1 minute. When cooking is complete, use a quick release to depressurize (there may be some spattering out of the top of the pot).

SERVE

Let stew stand for 3 to 4 minutes before serving. Top with coarsely chopped fennel fronds and crisped bacon.

*****TIP:** Culinary pumpkins are smaller than decorative pumpkins and have sweet, dense flesh. You'll find them in the produce section of the supermarket—not in bins outside of the store.

Dutch Brown Bean Stew

This hearty stew of brown beans, sausage, onions, carrots, red-skin potatoes, and apples has fall written all over it. If you can't find brown beans, pinto beans make a perfectly fine substitute.

PREP TIME	FUNCTION	CLOSED POT TIME	TOTAL TIME	RELEASE
25 minutes	Sauté (Normal); Pressure/Manual (High)	1 hour 25 minutes	1 hour 50 minutes	Natural/Quick

SERVES: 6 to 8

- 8 ounces bacon, sliced crosswise into ¼-inch strips
- 12 to 14 ounces kielbasa or other smoked sausage, cut into ½-inch rounds
- 1 cup dried brown beans or pinto beans, picked over and rinsed
- 4 cups chicken broth
- 2 medium yellow onions, peeled, halved, and sliced ¼ inch thick
- 1 teaspoon salt
- 1 16-ounce bag baby carrots
- 2 medium Granny Smith apples, peeled, cored, and cut into 8 wedges each
- 1¼ pounds B-size red-skin potatoes, quartered
- Black pepper
- ¼ cup finely chopped fresh flat-leaf parsley

PREP

Select **SAUTÉ** on the Instant Pot® and adjust to **NORMAL**. Add bacon and kielbasa to pot. Cook, stirring frequently, for 6 to 7 minutes or until bacon edges are brown and crisp. Press **CANCEL**. Using a small ladle or spoon, remove excess fat from the pot and discard. Add beans, broth, onions, and salt to pot. Stir to combine.

Secure the lid on the pot. Close the pressure-release valve.

COOK

Select **MANUAL** and cook at high pressure for 30 minutes. When cooking is complete, use a natural release to depressurize. Press **CANCEL**.

Add carrots, apples, and potatoes to pot. Secure the lid on the pot. Select **MANUAL** and cook at high pressure for 3 minutes. When cooking is complete, use a quick release to depressurize.

SERVE

Season to taste with black pepper. Ladle stew into bowls. Sprinkle with parsley.

Chicken Noodle Soup

This tastes just like the chicken noodle soup your grandmother made—with the addition of red sweet pepper and baby spinach.

PREP TIME	FUNCTION	CLOSED POT TIME	TOTAL TIME	RELEASE
15 minutes	Poultry (More); Pressure/Manual (High); Sauté (Normal)	2 hours	2 hours 15 minutes	Natural/Quick

SERVES: 8

- 1 3½- to 4-pound whole chicken
- 1 large red onion
- 3 stalks celery
- 1 bay leaf
- 6 cups chicken broth
- 2 medium carrots, thinly sliced
- 1 medium red sweet pepper, coarsely chopped
- 2 cups dried wide egg noodles
- 4 cloves garlic, minced
- 1 teaspoon salt
- ½ teaspoon dried thyme
- ½ teaspoon sage
- ½ teaspoon black pepper
- 3 cups fresh baby spinach leaves
   Juice of 1 lemon (3 to 4 tablespoons)

PREP
Place chicken in the Instant Pot®. Cut onion in half; set half aside. Cut remaining half into wedges; place on top of chicken. Cut 1 stalk of celery in half; add to pot with chicken. Add bay leaf to pot. Slowly pour broth over all in the pot.

COOK
Secure the lid on the pot. Close the pressure-release valve. Select **POULTRY** and adjust to **MORE**. When cooking is complete, use a natural release to depressurize. Press **CANCEL**.

Meanwhile, chop reserved red onion half. Thinly slice remaining 2 stalks celery. Set aside. Once pressure is released from the pot, transfer the chicken to a large cutting board; set aside. Use a slotted spoon to remove and discard onion wedges, celery stalk, and bay leaf from liquid in pot. If desired, strain liquid in pot through a fine-mesh sieve; return liquid to pot if strained. Skim fat from top of liquid in pot if desired.

Add chopped onion, sliced celery, carrots, sweet pepper, noodles, garlic, salt, thyme, sage, and black pepper to pot. Secure the lid on the pot. Close the pressure-release valve.

Select **MANUAL** and cook at high pressure for 2 minutes. When cooking is complete, use a quick release to depressurize. Press **CANCEL**.

SERVE
When chicken is cool enough to handle, remove meat from bones. Discard bones and skin. Cut meat into bite-size pieces. Add chicken to soup in the pot. Select **SAUTÉ** and adjust to **NORMAL**. Cook, uncovered, for 1 to 2 minutes or until soup is heated through. Press **CANCEL**. Stir in spinach and lemon juice just before serving.

ASIAN-STYLE CHICKEN NOODLE SOUP: Prepare as directed except substitute 8 ounces rice noodles for the egg noodles, substitute 2 tablespoons reduced-sodium soy sauce for the salt, substitute 3 to 4 tablespoons rice vinegar for the lemon juice, substitute shredded napa cabbage for the spinach, and substitute 2 tablespoons finely chopped fresh ginger for the dried thyme.

Chicken Pho

Pho [fuh] has taken the country by storm—and it's no wonder. This Vietnamese version of chicken noodle soup features chicken and rice noodles in an aromatic broth that is topped with bean sprouts and fresh herbs.

PREP TIME	FUNCTION	CLOSED POT TIME	TOTAL TIME
35 minutes	Sauté (Normal); Slow Cook (More)	4 hours	4 hours 35 minutes

SERVES: 4 to 6

- 1 tablespoon vegetable oil
- 6 bone-in chicken thighs, skinned
- ½ teaspoon salt
- ¼ teaspoon black pepper
- 2 large shallots, finely chopped
- ½ teaspoon sugar
- 8 ounces shiitake mushrooms, stemmed and sliced
- 4 cups chicken broth
- 2 cups water
- 2 teaspoons fish sauce
- 1 2-inch piece fresh ginger, thinly sliced
- 1 cinnamon stick, broken in half
- 3 whole cloves
- 1 star anise
- 1 8- to 12-ounce package rice noodles, cooked according to package directions
- 1 bunch cilantro, chopped
- 1 bunch Thai basil or sweet basil, chopped
- 2 cups bean sprouts
- ½ cup sliced scallions
- 2 jalapeño peppers, sliced
- 1 lime, cut into small wedges
- Hoisin sauce (optional)

PREP
Select **SAUTÉ** and adjust to **NORMAL**. Add oil to pot. Season chicken with salt and black pepper. When oil is hot, add half of the chicken to pot. Cook chicken until browned, turning once, for about 12 minutes. Remove chicken from pot. Repeat with remaining chicken. Add shallots and sugar. Cook and stir until shallots are softened and lightly browned for about 3 minutes. Add mushrooms; cook and stir for 2 minutes more. Press **CANCEL**. Add chicken broth, the water, and fish sauce. Return all chicken to pot.

Prepare spice bag: Place ginger, cinnamon stick, cloves, and star anise on a double-thick, 6-inch square of 100%-cotton cheesecloth. Bring up corners and tie closed with 100%-cotton string. Add to pot. Secure the lid on the pot. Open the pressure-release valve.

COOK
Select **SLOW COOK** and adjust to **MORE**. Cook for 4 to 4½ hours or until chicken is tender. Press **CANCEL**.

SERVE
Carefully remove chicken and spice bag from pot. Discard spice bag. When chicken is cool enough to handle, remove the meat; return meat to pot. Discard bones.

Serve soup in large bowls. Add desired amount of rice noodles to each bowl. Top with cilantro, basil, bean sprouts, scallions, and jalapeños as desired. Serve with lime wedges and hoisin sauce (if using).

Chicken & Shrimp Gumbo

Okra is a traditional component of gumbo, not only because it was a vegetable familiar to the African-American cooks who created the dish but also because it has a natural thickening agent.

PREP TIME	FUNCTION	CLOSED POT TIME	TOTAL TIME	RELEASE
45 minutes	Sauté (Normal); Pressure/Manual (High)	35 minutes	1 hour 20 minutes	Quick

SERVES: 8

- 1 tablespoon vegetable oil
- 1 pound skinless, boneless chicken thighs, cut into 2-inch pieces
- ¼ cup vegetable oil
- ½ cup all-purpose flour
- 1 tablespoon Cajun seasoning
- 1 tablespoon dried thyme
- 1 teaspoon smoked paprika
- ½ teaspoon kosher salt
- 1 cup chopped onion
- 1 cup chopped green sweet pepper
- 2 stalks celery, chopped
- 4 cloves garlic, minced
- 4 cups chicken broth
- 1 14.5-ounce can diced tomatoes, undrained
- 1 pound medium shrimp, peeled and deveined
- 2 cups frozen sliced okra
- 4 to 5 cups hot cooked rice
- Chopped fresh flat-leaf parsley

PREP

Select **SAUTÉ** on the Instant Pot® and adjust to **NORMAL**. Add the 1 tablespoon oil to the pot. When hot, add the chicken. Cook for 5 to 6 minutes or until browned. Using a slotted spoon, transfer the chicken to a bowl, leaving any fat in the pot.

Add the ¼ cup oil, flour, Cajun seasoning, thyme, paprika, and salt to the pot. Cook, stirring constantly, for 5 minutes. Add the onion, pepper, celery, and garlic to the pot. Cook, stirring constantly, for 3 to 5 minutes or until the vegetables are softened. Press **CANCEL**. Add the chicken and any juices in the bowl, broth, and tomatoes to the pot. Secure the lid on the pot. Close the pressure-release valve.

COOK

Select **MANUAL** and cook at high pressure for 10 minutes. When cooking is complete, use a quick release to depressurize. Press **CANCEL**.

Select **SAUTÉ** and adjust to **NORMAL**. Add the shrimp and okra to the pot and cook for 5 minutes or until okra is crisp-tender and shrimp are cooked through. Press **CANCEL**.

SERVE

Ladle the gumbo over the hot cooked rice and sprinkle with parsley.

Chicken & Wild Rice Soup

This soup gets its richness from a combination of whipping cream and cream cheese. The sherry cuts through the richness and adds a depth of flavor but isn't a necessity.

PREP TIME	FUNCTION	CLOSED POT TIME	TOTAL TIME	RELEASE
30 minutes	Pressure/Manual (High); Sauté (Normal)	1 hour 35 minutes	2 hours 5 minutes	Natural

SERVES: 6

- 2 pounds bone-in chicken breast halves, skinned
- ¾ cup dried wild rice, rinsed and drained
- 5 cups reduced-sodium chicken broth
- 2 medium carrots, thinly sliced
- 1 cup sliced fresh button mushrooms
- 1 stalk celery, thinly sliced
- ½ cup chopped onion
- ¼ cup dry long grain white rice
- 3 cloves garlic, minced
- 1 teaspoon dried thyme
- ¾ cup whipping cream or half-and-half
- 4 ounces cream cheese, softened and cut into cubes
- ¼ cup dry sherry (optional)
- ⅓ cup chopped fresh flat-leaf parsley

PREP
Place chicken and wild rice in the Instant Pot®. Pour broth over all. Secure the lid on the pot. Close the pressure-release valve.

COOK
Select **MANUAL** and cook at high pressure for 10 minutes. When cooking is complete, use a natural release to depressurize. Press **CANCEL**.

Transfer chicken to a cutting board; set aside. Add carrots, mushrooms, celery, onion, white rice, garlic, and thyme to rice mixture in pot.

Secure the lid on the pot. Close the pressure-release valve. Select **MANUAL** and cook at high pressure for 5 minutes. When cooking is complete, use a natural release to depressurize. Press **CANCEL**.

Meanwhile, remove chicken from bones; discard bones. Cut chicken into bite-size pieces. Add chicken, whipping cream, cream cheese, and sherry (if using) to the pot. Select **SAUTÉ** and adjust to **NORMAL**. Cook and stir for 1 to 2 minutes or until heated through and cream cheese is completely melted and smooth. Press **CANCEL**.

SERVE
Ladle soup into bowls. Sprinkle with parsley.

Brazilian Black Bean Soup

This filling and nutritious soup is considered the national dish of Brazil. To make your own *feijoada* [fay-SHWA-da] truly tango, serve it over hot cooked rice with stewed collards on the side.

PREP TIME	FUNCTION	CLOSED POT TIME	TOTAL TIME	RELEASE
25 minutes	Pressure/Manual (High)	1 hour 5 minutes	1 hour 30 minutes	Natural

SERVES: 6

- 1½ cups chopped onions
- ½ cup thinly sliced green onions
- 2 cloves garlic
- 12 ounces dried black beans (2 cups)
- 1 smoked pork hock
- 2 bay leaves
- 2 teaspoons ground coriander
- Stems of 1 bunch cilantro, tied with kitchen string
- 2 teaspoons finely shredded orange zest
- Juice of one large orange
- 1½ cups chicken broth
- Hot cooked rice (optional)
- 2 oranges, peeled and sectioned*
- ½ cup chopped fresh cilantro or flat-leaf parsley

PREP
Combine onions, green onions, garlic, black beans, pork hock, bay leaves, coriander, cilantro stems, orange zest, orange juice, and chicken broth in the Instant Pot®. Secure the lid on the pot. Close the pressure-release valve.

COOK
Select **MANUAL** and cook on high pressure for 40 minutes. When cooking is complete, use a natural release to depressurize.

SERVE
Remove cilantro stems and bay leaves and discard. Remove pork hock and transfer to a cutting board. Using two forks, shred meat and return to pot; mix well.

Serve as a soup or, if desired, over cooked white rice. Garnish with orange sections; sprinkle with chopped cilantro.

*TIP: To section an orange, cut a thin slice off of the stem end and bottom of the orange to expose the fruit. Stand the fruit upright on a cutting board. Cut sections of peel off the orange from top to bottom, following the curve of the fruit. To release the sections, insert a small thin knife on either side of each one, cutting from the outside of the fruit toward the center.

Black Bean & Mushroom Chili

With cumin, oregano, and a double dose of smoke from both smoked paprika and chipotle powder, this flavorful vegan chili doesn't need added salt.

PREP TIME	FUNCTION	CLOSED POT TIME	TOTAL TIME	RELEASE
20 minutes	Pressure/Manual (High)	20 minutes	40 minutes	Quick

SERVES: 8

- 3 cups chopped onion
- 8 cloves garlic, minced
- 2 pounds mushrooms, sliced
- 2 14.5-ounce cans salt-free diced tomatoes, undrained
- 3 15-ounce cans salt-free black beans, undrained
- 1 tablespoon cumin
- 1 tablespoon oregano
- ½ tablespoon smoked paprika
- ½ teaspoon chipotle powder
- 1 pound frozen corn, defrosted

    Baked potato or cooked brown rice (optional)

    Enlightened Faux Parmesan

PREP

Combine onions, garlic, mushrooms, tomatoes, black beans, cumin, oregano, smoked paprika, and chipotle powder in the Instant Pot®. Secure the lid on the pot. Close the pressure-release valve.

COOK

Select **MANUAL** and cook at high pressure for 6 minutes. When cooking is complete, use a quick release to depressurize. Stir in the corn.

SERVE

Sprinkle with Enlightened Faux Parmesan. If desired, serve over a baked potato or brown rice.

ENLIGHTENED FAUX PARMESAN: In a food processor or blender combine 1 cup rolled oats, 1 cup nutritional yeast, and 1 tablespoon salt-free seasoning. Blend until powdery.

TIP: If desired, use the **SAUTÉ** function and sauté the onion, garlic, and mushrooms first.

Indian-Style Lentil Soup

Some brands of garam masala contain salt. If the brand you are using doesn't contain salt, you may need to add salt to taste to the finished soup. Toasting the spice blend briefly intensifies its flavor.

PREP TIME	FUNCTION	CLOSED POT TIME	TOTAL TIME
20 minutes	Sauté (Normal); Slow Cook (More)	3 hours 30 minutes	3 hours 50 minutes

SERVES: 6

1 tablespoon butter

1 medium onion, chopped

3 cloves garlic, finely chopped

1 tablespoon chopped fresh ginger

1 jalapeño pepper, seeded and finely chopped

2 teaspoons garam masala

1 pound dried lentils, rinsed

8 cups vegetable or chicken broth

1 tablespoon fresh lemon juice

Plain yogurt (optional)

Chopped fresh cilantro (optional)

PREP

Select **SAUTÉ** on the Instant Pot® and adjust to **NORMAL**. When hot, add butter to pot. Add onion, garlic, ginger, and jalapeño. Cook for 1 minute. Add garam masala and cook for an additional 1 minute. Add lentils and broth. Stir to combine. Press **CANCEL**. Secure the lid on the pot. Open the pressure-release valve.

COOK

Select **SLOW COOK** and adjust to **MORE**. Cook for 3½ to 4½ hours until lentils are very tender.

SERVE

Add lemon juice to pot. (Soup can be served as is or, for a creamier version, use an immersion blender for 30 seconds to puree some of the lentils.)

Ladle into soup bowls. If desired, garnish with plain yogurt and cilantro.

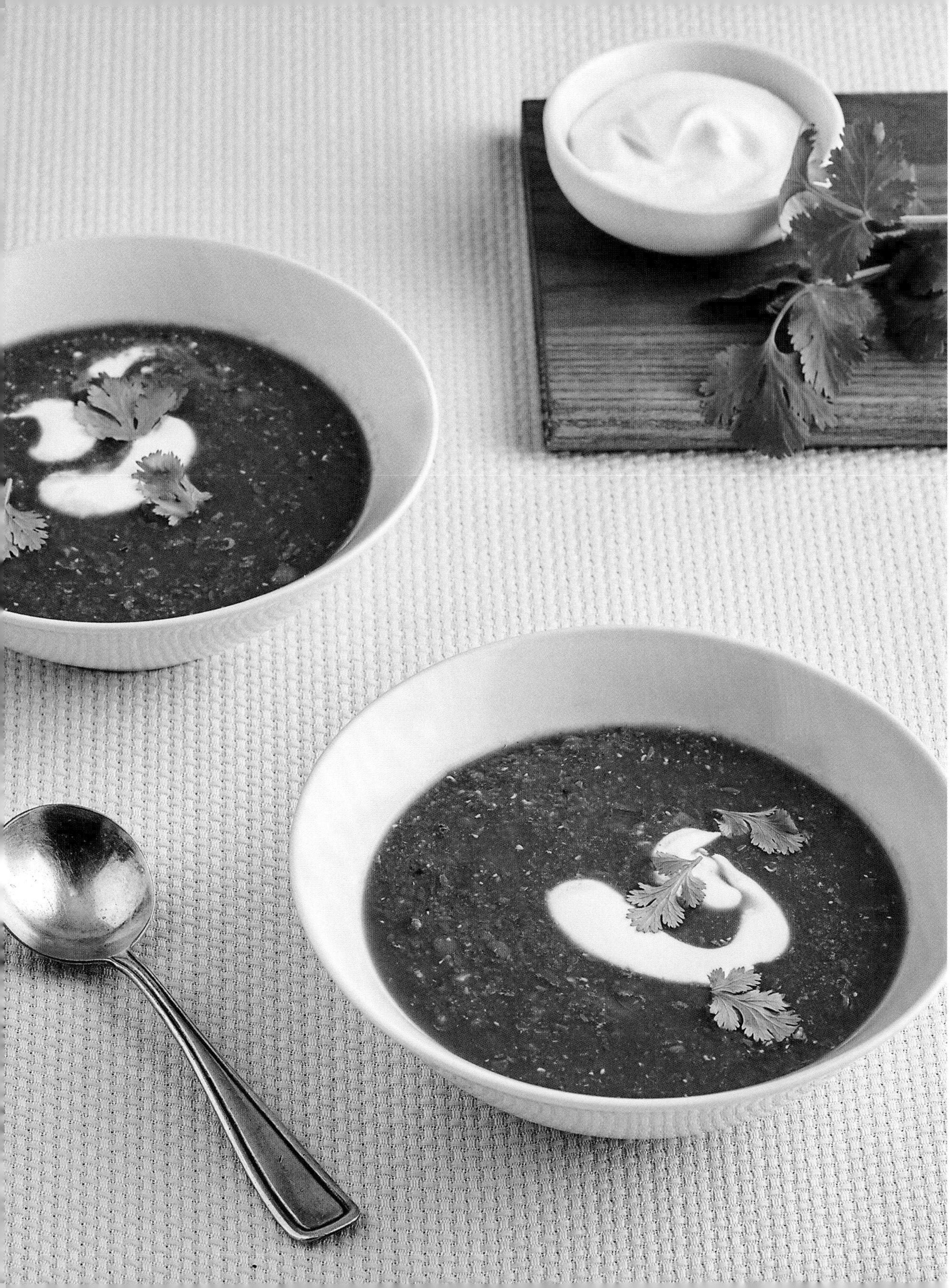

Italian White Bean Soup

If you can find escarole, give it a try. Popular in Italian cooking, it can be enjoyed raw as a salad green and cooked as a vegetable.

PREP TIME	FUNCTION	CLOSED POT TIME	TOTAL TIME	RELEASE
10 minutes	Sauté (Normal); Soup/Broth	1 hour 10 minutes	1 hour 20 minutes	Natural

SERVES: 4 to 6

- 1½ tablespoons olive oil
- 2 tablespoons sliced garlic
- ¼ teaspoon crushed red pepper
- 1 cup dried unsoaked Great Northern or cannellini beans, rinsed and drained
- 1 bay leaf
- 6 cups reduced-sodium chicken broth
- 6 cups coarsely chopped kale or escarole
- ⅓ cup grated Parmigiano-Reggiano or Grana Padano cheese

  Toasted Italian bread (optional)

PREP
Select **SAUTÉ** on the Instant Pot® and adjust to **NORMAL**. When hot, add olive oil, garlic, and crushed red pepper. Sauté for 1 minute. Press **CANCEL**. Add beans, bay leaf, and broth. Secure the lid on the pot. Close the pressure-release valve.

COOK
Select **SOUP/BROTH**. When cooking is complete, use a natural release to depressurize.

SERVE
If desired, use a potato masher to mash some of the beans for a thicker consistency. Stir in kale and cheese. Divide soup among bowls. If desired, serve with toasted Italian bread.

Kathy Hester is the creator of HealthySlowCooking.com and author of *The Ultimate Vegan Cookbook for Your Instant Pot®*.

Vegan Cranberry Bean, Millet & Bulgur Chili

Millet is the crunchy round yellow grain with a cornlike flavor that is often an element in hearty artisan-style whole grain breads. Here it adds texture and interest to a vegan chili.

PREP TIME	FUNCTION	CLOSED POT TIME	TOTAL TIME	RELEASE
10 minutes	Pressure/Manual (High)	1 hour	1 hour 10 minutes	Natural

SERVES: 6 to 8

- 1 pound dried cranberry beans, pinto beans, or black beans (about 2 cups)
- 5 cups water
- 1 14.5-ounce can diced tomatoes with green chiles
- ½ cup bulgur or quinoa
- ¼ cup millet
- 2 tablespoons tomato paste
- 1½ teaspoons ground cumin
- 1 teaspoon chili powder
- 1 teaspoon minced garlic
- 1 teaspoon dried oregano
- ½ teaspoon liquid smoke (optional)
- ½ teaspoon ancho chile or chipotle powder
- Salt and black pepper
- Optional toppings: Cashew cream, vegan shredded cheese, hot sauce, pickled jalapeño peppers

PREP
Combine the beans and 3 cups of the water in the Instant Pot®. Secure the lid on the pot. Close the pressure-release valve.

COOK
Select **MANUAL** and cook at high pressure for 25 minutes. When cooking is complete, use a natural release to depressurize.

Add the remaining 2 cups water, the tomatoes, bulgur, millet, tomato paste, cumin, chili powder, garlic, oregano, liquid smoke (if using), and the ancho chile powder.

Secure the lid on the pot. Close the pressure-release valve. Select **MANUAL** and cook at high pressure for 10 minutes. When cooking is complete, use a natural release to depressurize.

SERVE
Season with salt and black pepper to taste. If desired, serve with optional toppings.

Jill Nussinow blogs at TheVeggieQueen.com and is the author of *Vegan Under Pressure*.

Spicy Brown Rice & Bean Soup

Adding the vegetables to the hot soup after the beans are cooked in the broth preserves their crisp-tender texture and nutritional content.

PREP TIME	FUNCTION	CLOSED POT TIME	TOTAL TIME	RELEASE
20 minutes	Sauté (Normal); Pressure/Manual (High)	1 hour	1 hour 20 minutes + 5 minutes stand	Natural

SERVES: 4 to 6

- 1 tablespoon olive oil
- 1 cup diced onion
- 4 cloves garlic, minced
- 1 Anaheim or jalapeño pepper, seeded and minced (optional)
- 1 tablespoon ground cumin
- 1 tablespoon paprika
- 1 bay leaf
- ¾ cup brown rice
- ¾ cup unsoaked dried pinto beans, rinsed and drained
- ¾ cup unsoaked dried black beans, rinsed and drained
- 6 cups vegetable stock
- 1 to 2 cups chopped summer squash, broccoli, green beans, corn, or any greens
- 3 tablespoons fresh lime juice (about 2 limes)
- 2 tablespoons snipped fresh cilantro
  Salt and black pepper

PREP
Select **SAUTÉ** on the Instant Pot® and adjust to **NORMAL**. When hot, add the oil. Add the onion and cook, stirring occasionally, for 2 minutes. Add the garlic, chile (if using), cumin, and paprika. Cook for 1 minute. Add the bay leaf, rice, beans, and stock. Press **CANCEL**.

Secure the lid on the pot. Close the pressure-release valve.

COOK
Select **MANUAL** and cook at high pressure for 30 minutes. When cooking is complete, use a natural release to depressurize.

SERVE
Remove and discard the bay leaf. Add the summer squash or other vegetables. Cover the pot with the lid. Let stand for 5 minutes.

Add the lime juice and cilantro. Season to taste with salt and black pepper.

Tofu Ramen Bowls

Slurping a steaming bowl of noodles in a garlicky, gingery broth is sublimely satisfying on a cold winter night. This Japanese favorite is so easy to make, serve it any night of the week.

PREP TIME	FUNCTION	CLOSED POT TIME	TOTAL TIME	RELEASE
30 minutes	Pressure/Manual (High)	40 minutes	1 hour 10 minutes + 4 hours marinate	Natural

SERVES: 2

- 6 tablespoons mirin
- 6 tablespoons low-sodium soy sauce
- 2 tablespoons rice vinegar
- 1 tablespoon toasted sesame oil
- 2 teaspoons Asian chili sauce, such as sriracha
- 3 tablespoons minced fresh ginger
- 2 tablespoons minced garlic
- 1 8-ounce block extra-firm tofu
- 4 cups vegetable broth or stock
- 1 tablespoon minced garlic
- 3 tablespoons red miso

GARNISHES

Shredded cabbage

Hard-cooked eggs

Chopped green onions

Thinly sliced daikon

Peeled and thinly sliced English cucumber

- 1 10-ounce package ready-to-eat Asian ramen noodles

PREP

In a medium bowl combine mirin, 3 tablespoons of the soy sauce, the rice vinegar, sesame oil, chile sauce, 1 tablespoon of the gingerroot, and 1 tablespoon of the garlic. Mix well. Add the tofu, turning to cover with marinade. Cover bowl with plastic wrap; let tofu marinate at room temperature for 4 to 6 hours. Remove tofu from marinade and transfer to a cutting board. Cut tofu into ½×1-inch rectangles. Cover and set aside.

Combine broth, remaining soy sauce, gingerroot, and garlic. Secure the lid on the pot. Close the pressure-release valve.

COOK

Select **MANUAL** and cook at high pressure for 5 minutes. When cooking is complete, use a natural release to depressurize.

SERVE

Whisk miso into the hot broth, stirring until it melts.

Ladle broth into large bowls. Garnish ramen bowls as desired with cabbage, halved hard-cooked eggs, green onions, daikon, cucumber, noodles, and tofu.

Laura Pazzaglia blogs at HipPressureCooking.com.

Creamy Split Pea & Bacon Soup

Simple and satisfying, this old-fashioned, creamy green soup is good—and good for you.

PREP TIME	FUNCTION	CLOSED POT TIME	TOTAL TIME	RELEASE
20 minutes	Sauté (Normal); Pressure/Manual (High)	50 minutes	1 hour 10 minutes	Natural

SERVES: 4 to 6

- 5 slices bacon or 3.5 ounces pancetta, chopped
- 1 medium white or yellow onion, diced
- 1 celery stalk, diced
- 1 carrot, large diced
- 2 cups dried green split peas, rinsed
- 6 cups water
- 1 bay leaf
- 1 teaspoon sea salt

PREP

Select **SAUTÉ** on the Instant Pot® and adjust to **NORMAL**. Add the bacon to the pot. When the fat begins to render and bacon begins to fry in the fat, stir until crispy. Using a slotted spoon, remove the bacon to a paper towel-lined plate, leaving any remaining fat in the pot; set aside.

Add the onion, celery, and carrot to the pot. Sauté in the bacon fat until the onions have softened for about 5 minutes, scraping up any browned bits that have formed on the bottom of the inner pot. Press **CANCEL**.

Add split peas, the water, bay leaf, and salt; stir to combine. Secure the lid on the pot. Close the pressure-release valve.

COOK

Select **MANUAL** and cook at high pressure for 5 minutes. When cooking is complete, use a natural release to depressurize.

SERVE

Remove and discard the bay leaf. Stir half of the bacon into the soup. Serve the soup topped with remaining bacon bits.

Chipotle Corn & Sweet Potato Chili

The balance of sweetness from the corn and sweet potato and the smoky, spicy flavor of chipotle gives this vegetarian chili great appeal.

PREP TIME	FUNCTION	CLOSED POT TIME	TOTAL TIME	RELEASE
35 minutes	Sauté (Normal); Pressure/Manual (High)	1 hour 20 minutes	1 hour 55 minutes	Natural

SERVES: 6 to 8

- 2 tablespoons olive oil
- 1 onion, chopped
- 1 red sweet pepper, chopped
- 1 green sweet pepper, chopped
- 1 jalapeño pepper, seeded (if desired) and finely chopped
- 4 cloves garlic, minced
- ½ teaspoon salt
- ⅓ cup tomato paste
- 2 14.5-ounce cans vegetable or chicken broth
- 3 cups diced sweet potatoes
- 2 cups cooked black beans, pinto beans, or kidney beans or two 15-ounce cans black beans, pinto beans, or kidney beans, drained and rinsed
- 1 14.5-ounce can diced tomatoes
- 1 cup frozen corn
- 1 canned chipotle chile, minced
- 2 tablespoons chili powder
- 1½ teaspoons ground cumin
- 1 teaspoon dried oregano

  Shredded cheddar cheese, chopped scallions, and/or chopped fresh cilantro

PREP
Select **SAUTÉ** on the Instant Pot® and add olive oil to pot. When oil is hot, add onion, sweet peppers, jalapeño, and garlic. Season with salt. Cook and stir until softened for about 5 minutes. Add tomato paste. Cook and stir for 1 minute. Press **CANCEL**. Add the broth, sweet potatoes, beans, tomatoes, corn, chipotle pepper, chili powder, cumin, and oregano.

Secure the lid on the pot. Close the pressure-release valve.

COOK
Select **MANUAL** and cook on high pressure for 30 minutes. When cooking is complete, use a natural release to depressurize.

SERVE
Serve chili with cheese, scallions, and/or cilantro.

Creamy Tomato Soup with Lemon & Basil

Lemon and fresh basil give this favorite soup a completely new flavor dimension. Serve it with toasty grilled cheese (of course!) and a glass of wine.

PREP TIME	FUNCTION	CLOSED POT TIME	TOTAL TIME	RELEASE
25 minutes	Sauté (Normal); Pressure/Manual (High)	50 minutes	1 hour 15 minutes	Natural

SERVES: 4 to 6

- ¼ cup butter
- 2 large leeks or 4 small leeks, halved lengthwise, rinsed, and sliced (white and light green parts only)
- 2 cloves garlic, minced
- 1 6-ounce can tomato paste
- 4 cups chicken broth
- 1 28-ounce can whole tomatoes, undrained and cut up
- 1 tablespoon honey or sugar
- 1 cup heavy cream
- ½ cup chopped fresh basil
- 2 tablespoons lemon juice
- 1 teaspoon lemon zest

PREP
Select **SAUTÉ** on the Instant Pot® and adjust to **NORMAL**. Add butter to pot. When the butter is melted, add the leeks. Cook, stirring occasionally, until leeks are softened for about 3 minutes. Stir in garlic. Cook for 2 minutes more. Stir in the tomato paste. Cook and stir for 1 minute. Press **CANCEL**. Stir in the chicken broth, tomatoes, and honey. Secure the lid on the pot. Close the pressure-release valve.

COOK
Select **MANUAL** and cook at high pressure for 5 minutes. When cooking is complete, use a natural release to depressurize.

SERVE
Use an immersion blender to blend soup until smooth (or blend in a blender). Stir in cream, basil, lemon juice, and lemon zest.

Chef AJ blogs at EatUnprocessed.com.

Smoky Butternut Bisque

Choose any nondairy milk you like to add creaminess to this vegan soup. Almond, soy, coconut, and cashew are all good choices.

PREP TIME	FUNCTION	CLOSED POT TIME	TOTAL TIME	RELEASE
10 minutes	Sauté (Normal); Pressure/Manual (High)	20 minutes	30 minutes	Quick

SERVES: 4

- 3 cups chopped onions (about 10 ounces)
- 2 pounds butternut squash, peeled, halved, and seeds removed, cut into chunks
- 6 cloves garlic
- 2 pears, stemmed, halved, and cored
- 1 tablespoon smoked paprika
- 1½ teaspoons salt-free seasoning
- ⅛ teaspoon chipotle powder
- 1 cup plain unsweetened nondairy milk

PREP

Select **SAUTÉ** on the Instant Pot® and adjust to **NORMAL**. When hot, add the onions to the pot. Sauté the onions until browned, adding water if necessary. Add the squash, garlic, pears, paprika, seasoning, and chipotle powder. Press **CANCEL**. Secure the lid on the pot. Close the pressure-release valve.

COOK

Select **MANUAL** and cook at high pressure for 6 minutes. When cooking is complete, use a quick release to depressurize.

SERVE

Add the milk and puree soup in a blender or in the pot using an immersion blender.

Curried Cauliflower Soup

Mild-mannered cauliflower takes beautifully to the intensity of the Thai red curry that flavors this soup. A tablespoon of honey tempers the heat just a bit.

PREP TIME	FUNCTION	CLOSED POT TIME	TOTAL TIME	RELEASE
25 minutes	Sauté (Normal); Pressure/Manual (High)	45 minutes	1 hour 10 minutes	Natural

SERVES: 6

- 2 tablespoons vegetable oil
- 1 medium yellow onion, chopped
- 2 cloves garlic, minced
- 1 tablespoon minced fresh ginger
- 1 teaspoon ground cumin
- ½ teaspoon ground turmeric
- 2 tablespoons red curry paste
- 1 teaspoon finely shredded lemon zest
- 1 large head cauliflower, broken into small florets (about 10 cups)
- 2 cups vegetable broth or chicken broth
- 1½ cups refrigerated coconut milk at room temperature
- 1 tablespoon honey
- ½ teaspoon salt
- ¼ teaspoon black pepper
- ½ cup chopped cilantro

PREP

Select **SAUTÉ** on the Instant Pot® and adjust to **NORMAL**. Add oil to pot. When hot, add the onion. Cook and stir for 3 minutes or until tender. Stir in garlic and ginger. Cook and stir for 1 minute more. Add cumin, turmeric, curry paste, and lemon zest. Cook and stir for 30 seconds. Press **CANCEL**. Add cauliflower florets and broth. Secure the lid on the pot. Close the pressure-release valve.

COOK

Select **MANUAL** and cook at high pressure for 5 minutes. When cooking is complete, use a natural release to depressurize.

SERVE

While cauliflower cooks, in a small bowl combine coconut milk, honey, salt, and pepper. Blend thoroughly. Set aside.

In a food processor or blender puree cauliflower-broth mixture, about 1 cup at a time (or use an immersion blender in the pot). Transfer pureed mixture to a bowl and keep warm. Whisk in coconut milk mixture.

Ladle hot soup into warmed bowls. Sprinkle each serving with cilantro.

Corn Chowder

The consummate soup of summer, this is best made when sweet corn is in season—but if you're craving it in the dead of winter, it's very tasty made with frozen corn as well.

PREP TIME	FUNCTION	CLOSED POT TIME	TOTAL TIME	RELEASE
40 minutes	Sauté (Normal); Soup/Broth	1 hour	1 hour 40 minutes	Natural

SERVES: 6

- 4 slices bacon, chopped
- ¾ cup chopped onion
- ½ cup chopped red sweet pepper
- ¼ cup chopped celery
- 2 cloves garlic, minced
- 1 teaspoon salt
- ¼ teaspoon black pepper
- 1 pound Yukon gold potatoes, peeled and diced (3 cups)
- 4 cups chicken broth
- 3 cups fresh corn kernels or frozen corn, thawed
- 1 cup heavy cream
- 1 teaspoon chopped fresh thyme

PREP

Select **SAUTÉ** on the Instant Pot® and adjust to **NORMAL**. Add bacon to pot. Cook bacon until crisp; remove with a slotted spoon to a paper towel-lined plate; set aside. Add onion, sweet pepper, celery, garlic, salt, and black pepper to bacon drippings in pot. Cook for 3 to 5 minutes until vegetables are softened, stirring frequently. Press **CANCEL**.

Add potatoes and chicken broth. Secure the lid on the pot. Close the pressure-release valve.

COOK

Select **SOUP/BROTH**. When cooking is complete, use a natural release to depressurize. Press **CANCEL**.

Select **SAUTÉ** and adjust to **NORMAL**. Bring soup to a simmer; add corn and cook for 3 to 5 minutes until tender. Press **CANCEL**.

SERVE

Stir in cream and thyme. Season to taste with salt and black pepper. Serve topped with bacon.

Carrot-Ginger Soup

This light and refreshing soup can be served warm or cold. It's lovely in both fall and spring—when gardens and farmers markets are bursting with the sweet orange roots.

PREP TIME	FUNCTION	CLOSED POT TIME	TOTAL TIME	RELEASE
30 minutes	Soup/Broth	50 minutes	1 hour 20 minutes	Natural

SERVES: 6

- 3 cups chicken broth or vegetable broth
- 1 large yellow onion, peeled and cut into 8 wedges
- 3 cloves garlic, peeled and smashed
- 2 tablespoons finely grated fresh ginger
- 1 pound fresh carrots, peeled and cut into thirds
- 1 large Yellow Finn or other gold potato, peeled and quartered
- 1 cup refrigerated coconut milk
- 3 tablespoons freshly squeezed lime juice
- 2 teaspoons finely shredded lime zest

  Plain yogurt (optional)

  Snipped fresh chives (optional)

PREP

Combine broth, onion, garlic, ginger, carrots, and potato in Instant Pot®.

Secure the lid on the pot. Close the pressure-release valve.

COOK

Select **SOUP/BROTH** and adjust cook time to 8 minutes. When cooking is complete, use a natural release to depressurize.

SERVE

Use an immersion blender to blend soup until smooth. (If using a blender or food processor, return all soup to pot.) Stir in coconut milk, lime juice, and lime zest. Serve immediately garnished, if desired, with a dollop of yogurt and chives.

French Onion Soup

The key to perfect onion soup is allowing the natural sugars in the onions to infuse the beef broth with sweetness. The Instant Pot® does that in a fraction of the time of the traditional cooking method for this French favorite.

PREP TIME	FUNCTION	CLOSED POT TIME	TOTAL TIME	RELEASE
25 minutes	Sauté (Normal); Soup/Broth	50 minutes	1 hour 15 minutes + 5 minutes bake	Quick

SERVES: 4 to 6

CHEESE CROUTONS

4 cups 1½-inch bread cubes (cut from Italian country loaf)

1 tablespoon olive oil

½ teaspoon garlic powder

½ cup shredded Gruyère cheese

¼ cup grated Parmesan cheese

SOUP

2 tablespoons olive oil

2 pounds Vidalia onions, sliced ¼ inch thick (8 cups)

1 teaspoon salt

¾ cup cream sherry

6 cups reduced-sodium beef broth

3 sprigs fresh thyme

1 bay leaf

Salt and black pepper

PREP

For the croutons, preheat oven to 375°F. Place bread cubes in a large mixing bowl; drizzle with olive oil and toss to evenly distribute. Place on a foil-lined baking sheet that has been sprayed with nonstick cooking spray. Sprinkle with garlic powder. Set aside.

For the soup, select **SAUTÉ** on the Instant Pot® and adjust to **NORMAL**. Add 2 tablespoons olive oil to the pot. When hot, add onions and salt. Sauté for 3 minutes, stirring frequently. Add sherry and cook for an additional 4 minutes. Press **CANCEL**. Add beef broth, thyme, and bay leaf. Secure the lid on the pot. Close the pressure-release valve.

COOK

Select **SOUP/BROTH**. When cooking is complete, use a quick release to depressurize.

SERVE

Combine both types of cheese and sprinkle over bread cubes. Bake for 5 to 7 minutes until cheese is melted and bubbly. Season soup with salt and pepper to taste. Divide soup among bowls. Top with warm cheese croutons.

Potato-Leek Soup

Velvety and delicately flavored, this creamy soup makes a lovely first course for a nice dinner party—or a yummy lunch accompanied by a roast beef sandwich.

PREP TIME	FUNCTION	CLOSED POT TIME	TOTAL TIME	RELEASE
20 minutes	Sauté (Normal/Less); Soup/Broth	1 hour 5 minutes	1 hour 25 minutes + 5 minutes simmer	Natural

SERVES: 6

- 2 tablespoons butter
- 2 large leeks, halved lengthwise, rinsed, and thinly sliced (white and light green parts only)
- 1 teaspoon salt
- ¼ teaspoon black pepper
- 1 pound russet potatoes, peeled and diced (2¾ cups)
- 4 cups chicken broth
- 1 cup heavy cream
- 2 tablespoons chopped fresh chives

PREP

Select **SAUTÉ** on the Instant Pot® and adjust to **NORMAL**. Melt butter in pot; add leeks, salt, and pepper to pot. Cook for about 5 minutes or until leeks are softened, stirring frequently. Press **CANCEL**. Add potatoes and chicken broth. Secure the lid on the pot. Close the pressure-release valve.

COOK

Select **SOUP/BROTH**. When cooking is complete, use a natural release to depressurize. Press **CANCEL**.

SERVE

Blend soup in pot with an immersion blender or blend in a blender in small batches until smooth; return to pot. Stir in cream.

Select **SAUTÉ** and adjust to **LESS**. Bring soup just to a simmer (do not boil) for about 5 minutes. Stir in chives and season to taste with additional salt and pepper. Press **CANCEL**.

Simple Seafood Bouillabaisse

The ingredient list may look a little daunting, but the recipe is structured in such a way that you're prepping ingredients while the pot is cooking, making this elegant French stew infinitely doable.

PREP TIME	FUNCTION	CLOSED POT TIME	TOTAL TIME	RELEASE
10 minutes	Pressure/Manual (High); Sauté (Normal)	30 minutes	40 minutes	Quick

SERVES: 6

- 1 medium fresh or frozen lobster tail (8 to 10 ounces)
- 12 ounces fresh or frozen jumbo shrimp
- 12 ounces fresh or frozen skinless halibut or sea bass, cut 1 to 1½ inches thick
- 1 medium fennel bulb
- 1 medium red sweet pepper, coarsely chopped
- 1 medium red onion, chopped (about ¾ cup)
- 1 14.5-ounce can diced tomatoes
- 3 cloves garlic, halved
- 3 wide, long strips orange zest (orange-color outer part of the peel only)
- 3 cups seafood stock
- 8 ounces fresh mussels (see Tip, page 147)
- ½ cup dry white wine
- ½ teaspoon dried saffron threads, crushed
- ¼ teaspoon crushed red pepper
- ¼ cup chopped fresh flat-leaf parsley
- 2 tablespoons chopped fresh chives
  Lemon wedges

PREP

Thaw lobster, shrimp, and halibut if frozen. Set aside. Trim tops off fennel bulb; reserve the tops for garnish if desired. Trim a thin slice off the bottom of the bulb; cut bulb in half. Cut out the core and discard. Chop the bulb; add to the Instant Pot®. Add sweet pepper, onion, undrained tomatoes, garlic, and orange zest. Rinse lobster tail with cold water; place lobster tail on top vegetables in the pot. Pour 1 cup of the seafood stock over all in pot.

COOK

Secure the lid on the pot. Close the pressure-release valve. Select **MANUAL** and cook at high pressure for 3 minutes. Once cooking is complete, use a quick release to depressurize. Transfer lobster tail to a cutting board. Transfer vegetables and cooking juices from the pot to a blender or food processor. If necessary, allow mixture to cool for about 10 minutes.* Cover and blend or process vegetable mixture until smooth. Set aside.

While lobster is cooking, clean mussels (see Tip, page 147). Peel and devein shrimp. Rinse shrimp and halibut with cold water; pat dry with paper towels. Cut halibut into 1½-inch cubes. Add mussels, shrimp, and halibut to the pot. Pour remaining 2 cups seafood stock over all. Secure the lid on the pot. Close the pressure-release valve. Select **MANUAL** and cook at high pressure for 2 minutes. Once cooking is complete, use a quick release to depressurize. Press **CANCEL**.

Using kitchen scissors, cut the lobster tail down the center, along the soft side of the shell. Open the shell and remove the lobster meat. Chop lobster meat.

Add pureed vegetable mixture, lobster, wine, saffron, and crushed red pepper to the seafood mixture in the pot. Select **SAUTÉ** and adjust to **NORMAL**. Cook for 1 to 2 minutes or until heated through, stirring gently. Press **CANCEL**.

SERVE

Ladle into shallow bowls. If desired, snip some of the feathery tops of the reserved fennel. Sprinkle over each serving; sprinkle parsley and chives over each serving. Serve with lemon wedges.

*TIP: Some blenders do not require liquid to be cool before blending. Check your blender manufacturer directions.

Desserts

Zinfandel-Poached Pears
with Cinnamon Whipped Cream

This is an ideal dessert for entertaining because it has to be made far ahead of serving time. The overnight soak in the spiced wine syrup allows the flavor to deeply penetrate the pears.

PREP TIME	FUNCTION	CLOSED POT TIME	TOTAL TIME	RELEASE
15 minutes	Sauté (Normal); Pressure/Manual (High)	15 minutes	30 minutes + overnight chill	Quick

SERVES: 4

- 1 750-ml bottle medium-quality Zinfandel wine
- ½ cup sugar
-    Juice from 1 large navel orange (about ⅓ cup)
- 1 strip orange zest, about 1 inch wide by 3 inches long
- 1 cinnamon stick
- 3 whole cloves
- 3 whole allspice berries
- 4 firm, ripe pears

CINNAMON WHIPPED CREAM

- ½ pint heavy whipping cream
- ¼ cup sugar
- ½ teaspoon ground cinnamon

PREP
Combine wine, sugar, orange juice, orange peel, cinnamon stick, cloves, and berries in the Instant Pot®. Select **SAUTÉ** and adjust to **NORMAL**. Allow wine mixture to come to boiling, stirring to dissolve sugar.

While wine mixture cooks, peel pears, taking care that fruit is smooth and retains its shape. Do not remove stems. Cut a ½-inch slice from the bottom of each pear to make it stand upright. When sugar has dissolved, press **CANCEL**. Gently turn pears in wine mixture to coat, then arrange upright in mixture. Secure the lid on the pot. Close the pressure-release valve.

COOK
Select **MANUAL** and cook at high pressure for 5 minutes. When cooking is complete, use a quick release to depressurize. Press **CANCEL**. Open lid; carefully remove the pears to a bowl. Pour wine mixture over the pears. Cover and transfer to refrigerator. Let wine-immersed pears chill for at least 12 hours, turning pears in mixture a few times during chilling time.

Using a slotted spoon, gently remove pears from wine mixture and transfer them to serving plates.

Transfer wine mixture to pot, select **SAUTÉ**, and adjust to **NORMAL**. Cook and stir wine syrup over medium heat for 12 to 15 minutes or until mixture is syrupy. Press **CANCEL**.

SERVE
While syrup is simmering, prepare Cinnamon Whipped Cream: In the chilled bowl of an electric mixer beat cream on high speed until soft peaks form. With mixer running, slowly sprinkle cream with sugar and cinnamon. Continue beating until stiff peaks form.

Spoon syrup over pears. Serve generous dollops of Cinnamon Whipped Cream alongside poached pears.

Mixed Berry Crisp with Ginger & Lemon

No need to heat up the kitchen making this summer fruit crisp—it's slow-cooked until bubbly and delicious in the Instant Pot®. The granola topping is sprinkled on just 30 minutes before serving, so it doesn't get soggy.

PREP TIME	FUNCTION	CLOSED POT TIME	TOTAL TIME
10 minutes	Slow Cook (More)	2 hours	2 hours + 30 minutes stand

SERVES: 8

- 4 **cups fresh blueberries**
- 1 **cup fresh blackberries**
- 1 **cup fresh raspberries**
- ¾ **cup sugar**
- 2 **tablespoons cornstarch**
- ½ **teaspoon ground ginger**
- ½ **teaspoon lemon zest**
- 2 **tablespoons lemon juice**
- 1 **teaspoon vanilla**
- 2 **cups oats and honey granola**
  Vanilla ice cream (optional)

PREP

Combine blueberries, blackberries and raspberries in the Instant Pot®. In a small bowl combine sugar, cornstarch, ginger, and lemon zest; mix well. Add sugar mixture to berries; stir to mix. Add lemon juice. Stir gently to combine.

Secure the lid on the pot. Open the pressure-release valve.

COOK

Select **SLOW COOK** and adjust to **MORE**. Cook for 1 hour. Stir and cook for an additional 1 to 2 hours or until mixture is thickened and bubbly. Stir in vanilla. Sprinkle with granola. Press **CANCEL**. Let stand for at least 30 minutes before serving.

SERVE

Serve warm or at room temperature. Serve with vanilla ice cream if desired.

Apple Brown Betty

Whole wheat bread adds a delicious twist to this old-school dessert.

PREP TIME	FUNCTION	CLOSED POT TIME	TOTAL TIME	RELEASE
25 minutes	Manual/Pressure (High)	25 minutes	50 minutes	Quick

SERVES: 4

- ½ cup + 2 tablespoons brown sugar
- ¼ teaspoon ground cinnamon
- ¼ teaspoon ground nutmeg
- 3 tablespoons butter
- 2 Granny Smith apples, peeled and thinly sliced (about 2 cups)
- 4 cups quality whole wheat bread, cut into ½-inch cubes
- 1 cup water

CARAMEL SAUCE

- ⅓ cup butter
- ⅓ cup granulated sugar
- ⅓ cup packed brown sugar
- ⅓ cup heavy cream
- ½ teaspoon vanilla

Coarse sea salt

Vanilla ice cream (optional)

PREP

Stir ½ cup brown sugar, cinnamon, and nutmeg together in a small bowl; set aside.

Dot the bottom of a 1½-quart casserole dish with 1 tablespoon of the butter. Layer half of the apple slices, ¼ cup of the spiced sugar, and 2 cups bread cubes in the pan. Repeat, pressing down on apple slices and bread cubes if overflowing. (Bread and apples will cook down.) Sprinkle top bread layer with the remaining 2 tablespoons brown sugar. Dot with remaining 2 tablespoons butter.

Place trivet in the Instant Pot®. Add the water to pot. Place casserole dish on trivet. Secure the lid on the pot. Close the pressure-release valve.

COOK

Select **MANUAL** and cook at high pressure for 12 minutes. When cooking is complete, use a quick release to depressurize.

SERVE

While dessert is cooking, prepare Caramel Sauce: In a small saucepan melt butter over medium heat. Stir in sugars and cream. Bring to boiling, stirring constantly. Remove from heat; stir in vanilla.

Spoon Apple Brown Betty into serving bowls. Drizzle with warm Caramel Sauce and sprinkle lightly with coarse sea salt. Serve with vanilla ice cream if desired.

Raspberry-Vanilla Bean Rice Pudding

It's slightly more time-consuming to split and scrape the vanilla bean than to simply measure out vanilla extract, but the more intense flavor is worth a little bit of fuss—and you get the beautiful speckles from the vanilla bean seeds in the pudding.

PREP TIME	FUNCTION	CLOSED POT TIME	TOTAL TIME	RELEASE
10 minutes	Sauté (Normal); Porridge	45 minutes	55 minutes	Natural

SERVES: 6

- 1 cup water
- 2 cups milk
- ¼ cup sugar
- 3 tablespoons seedless raspberry jam
- 1 cup Arborio rice or other desired white rice
- 1 cinnamon stick
- 1 vanilla bean, halved lengthwise, or 1 teaspoon vanilla
- 2 cups fresh raspberries
- ½ cup heavy cream

PREP

Select **SAUTÉ** on the Instant Pot® and adjust to **NORMAL**. Add the water, milk, sugar, and jam to the pot. Cook and stir until sugar and jam dissolve. Press **CANCEL**. Stir in the rice and cinnamon stick. Split the vanilla bean with the tip of a small sharp knife and scrape the seeds into the pot. Add the bean to the pot. Secure the lid on the pot. Close the pressure-release valve.

COOK

Select **PORRIDGE**. When cooking is complete, use a natural release to depressurize.

SERVE

Remove and discard vanilla bean and cinnamon stick. Stir in fresh raspberries and cream.

Chocolate-Cherry Croissant Bread Pudding

Chocolate and cherries complement each other very well. Although dried tart cherries are more common, look for dried sweet cherries to make this decadent bread pudding. They are often available in bulk at health-food stores or in the bulk section of your supermarket.

PREP TIME	FUNCTION	CLOSED POT TIME	TOTAL TIME	RELEASE
15 minutes	Manual/Pressure (High)	35 minutes	1 hour 10 minutes + 20 minutes cool	Natural

SERVES: 6

- 2 cups water
- 1 tablespoon butter, softened
- 2 eggs, beaten
- ½ cup sugar
- 2 cups half-and-half
- 1 teaspoon vanilla
- 4 cups 1-inch day-old croissant pieces
- ⅓ cup dried sweet cherries
- ⅓ cup chopped bittersweet chocolate

PREP

Place trivet in the Instant Pot®. Add the water to the pot. Butter a 1½-quart soufflé dish or casserole that fits in pot.

Whisk together eggs, sugar, half-and-half, and vanilla in a medium bowl. Add croissant pieces and cherries; let stand for 10 minutes. Stir in chocolate and transfer mixture to prepared dish. Cover dish with foil and place on trivet. Secure the lid on the pot. Close the pressure-release valve.

COOK

Select **MANUAL** and cook at high pressure 15 minutes. When cooking is complete, use a natural release to depressurize.

SERVE

Carefully remove dish from pot. Remove foil and let cool for 20 minutes before serving.

Chamomile-Cherry-Poached Peaches

The window for making this dessert is fleeting—peach season doesn't last more than a couple of months in late summer and early fall, so seize the opportunity while you can. The chamomile infuses the wine syrup with a subtle floral flavor.

PREP TIME	FUNCTION	CLOSED POT TIME	TOTAL TIME	RELEASE
5 minutes	Sauté (Normal); Pressure/Manual (High)	10 minutes	50 minutes + 6 hours chill	Quick

SERVES: 4

- 2 cups pink Moscato wine
- ½ cup sugar
- 1 cup dried tart cherries, chopped
- 2 100%-chamomile tea bags, tags removed
- 2 tablespoons freshly squeezed lemon juice
- 4 small firm, ripe peaches, washed, halved, and pitted
- ½ cup plain Greek yogurt
- ¾ cup shelled, salted pistachio nuts, coarsely chopped

PREP
Combine wine, sugar, cherries, tea bags, and lemon juice in the Instant Pot®. Select **SAUTÉ** and adjust to **NORMAL**. Bring mixture to boiling. Press **CANCEL**. Add peach halves, skin sides up, to the pot.

Secure the lid on the pot. Close the pressure-release valve.

COOK
Select **MANUAL** and cook at high pressure for 2 minutes. When cooking is complete, use a quick release to depressurize. Press **CANCEL**.

Using a slotted spoon, gently transfer peaches to a shallow dish and let cool. When cool, cover lightly and chill for at least 6 hours. (Remove skin from peaches before chilling if desired.)

While peaches are cooling, select **SAUTÉ** and adjust to **NORMAL**. Bring liquid in pot to boiling and let mixture simmer, stirring often, for about 12 to 15 minutes or until liquid has a syrupy consistency. Remove and discard tea bags. Press **CANCEL**.

Transfer inner pot to a cooling rack and let syrup cool for 15 minutes. Transfer to a covered container and chill in the refrigerator alongside peaches.

SERVE
To serve, place two peach halves on each plate. Drizzle syrup over peaches. Garnish each peach half with a small dollop of Greek yogurt; sprinkle with pistachios.

Chocolate, Orange & Olive Oil Mini Lava Cake

This warm chocolate dessert is made almost entirely with ingredients you have in your pantry, so it's perfect for satisfying those spur-of-the-moment chocolate cravings. If you don't have an orange, substitute ¼ teaspoon vanilla extract for the ½ teaspoon zest.

PREP TIME	FUNCTION	CLOSED POT TIME	TOTAL TIME	RELEASE
10 minutes	Pressure/Manual (High)	20 minutes	30 minutes + 5 minutes stand	Quick

SERVES: 2 (1 mug)

- 1 **cup water**
- ¼ **cup flour**
- ½ **teaspoon orange zest**
- ¼ **cup sugar**
- **Pinch of salt**
- 1 **tablespoon unsweetened cocoa powder**
- ½ **teaspoon baking powder**
- 1 **egg**
- ¼ **cup milk**
- 2 **tablespoons extra virgin olive oil, plus additional for greasing mug**

PREP

Place the trivet in the Instant Pot®. Add the water to the Instant Pot. Coat a 12-ounce coffee mug, tea cup, or ramekin with olive oil.

Combine flour, orange zest, sugar, salt, cocoa, and baking powder in a 2-cup measuring cup. Mix with a fork. Add the egg, milk, and the 2 tablespoons olive oil. Mix until a batter forms. Pour the batter into the prepared cup. Place the cup in the pot. If you are making more than one cup, arrange them so they are straight and not touching the inside of the pot. Secure the lid on the pot. Close the pressure-release valve.

COOK

Select **MANUAL** and cook at high pressure for 15 minutes. When cooking is complete, use a quick release to depressurize.

SERVE

Let stand for 5 minutes before serving. (Or, for a gooey center, serve immediately. The cake will continue cooking as you let it rest, so the interior will solidify.)

Kathy Hester is the creator of HealthySlowCooking.com and author of *The Ultimate Vegan Cookbook for Your Instant Pot®*.

Vegan Pear & Cranberry Cake

Rustic and not overly sweet, this whole grain fall fruit cake is actually good for you! Not a bad deal for dessert.

PREP TIME	FUNCTION	CLOSED POT TIME	TOTAL TIME	RELEASE
20 minutes	Pressure/Manual (High)	1 hour 15 minutes	1 hour 35 minutes	Natural

SERVES: 6 to 8

Vegetable oil

1¼ **cups whole wheat pastry flour (or use gluten-free baking mix)**

½ **teaspoon ground cardamom**

½ **teaspoon baking soda**

½ **teaspoon baking powder**

2 **tablespoons ground flaxseeds**

⅛ **teaspoon salt**

½ **cup plain unsweetened nondairy milk**

¼ **cup Whole Earth Sweetener Agave 50***

2 **tablespoons vegetable oil (or applesauce to make oil-free)**

1 **cup chopped pear**

½ **cup chopped fresh cranberries**

1½ **cups water**

PREP
Oil a 6- or 7-inch bundt pan and set aside. Stir together the flour, cardamom, baking soda, baking powder, flax, and salt in a bowl. In a large measuring cup mix together the milk, sweetener, and oil. Add the wet ingredients to the dry ingredients and mix well. Fold in the pear and cranberries.

Spread the batter into the prepared pan and cover with foil. Place the trivet in the pot. Pour the water into the Instant Pot®. Place the pan on the trivet. Secure the lid on the pot. Close the pressure-release valve.

COOK
Select **MANUAL** and cook at high pressure for 35 minutes. When cooking is complete, use a natural release to depressurize.

SERVE
Carefully lift the pan out of the pot and remove the foil. Let cool on a cake rack completely before removing the cake from the pan and/or cutting.

***TIP:** If you can't find this product, substitute 2 tablespoons agave nectar and ½ teaspoon liquid stevia.

Peanut Butter-Chocolate Bundt Cake

A much-loved flavor combination shines in this super-moist and rich cake. Choose your glaze—either chocolate or peanut butter—or, if you can't decide, make both.

PREP TIME	FUNCTION	CLOSED POT TIME	TOTAL TIME	RELEASE
25 minutes	Manual/Pressure (High)	35 minutes	1 hour + 2 hours cool	Quick

SERVES: 8

Nonstick baking spray

2 ounces bittersweet chocolate, chopped

½ cup all-purpose flour

½ teaspoon baking powder

¼ teaspoon salt

½ cup butter, softened

½ cup sugar

2 eggs

1 teaspoon vanilla

¼ cup creamy peanut butter

1 cup water

Ganache or Peanut Butter Glaze

Chopped honey-roasted peanuts (optional)

GANACHE

¼ cup whipping cream

3 ounces milk, semisweet, or bittersweet chocolate, chopped

PEANUT BUTTER GLAZE

½ cup powdered sugar

3 tablespoons creamy peanut butter

2 to 3 tablespoons milk

PREP
Generously coat a 3-cup fluted tube pan with baking spray. In a small saucepan melt the chocolate over low heat. Set aside to cool.

In a small bowl stir together the flour, baking powder, and salt; set aside. In a medium bowl beat the butter on medium speed for 30 seconds. Add the sugar and beat on medium for 1 to 2 minutes or until well combined. Add the eggs, one at a time, beating well after each addition. Beat in the vanilla. Add flour mixture and beat just until combined. Transfer half of the batter (about 1 cup) to a small bowl; stir in the melted chocolate. Stir peanut butter into the remaining batter.

Alternately drop spoonfuls of chocolate and peanut butter batters into the prepared pan. Using a table knife, gently cut through batters to swirl them together (do not overmix).

Place the trivet in the Instant Pot®. Add the water to pot. Place the cake pan on the trivet. Secure the lid on the pot. Close the pressure-release valve.

COOK
Select **MANUAL** and cook at high pressure for 25 minutes. When cooking is complete, use a quick release to depressurize.

SERVE
Carefully remove the cake from the pot. Let the cake cool on a wire rack for 10 minutes, then remove cake from pan and let cool completely on a wire rack. Drizzle with Ganache or Peanut Butter Glaze. If using Peanut Butter Glaze, sprinkle with peanuts if desired.

GANACHE: In a small saucepan bring whipping cream just to boiling over medium heat. Remove from heat and add the chocolate. Do not stir. Let stand for 5 minutes. Stir until smooth. Cool for 15 minutes before using.

PEANUT BUTTER GLAZE: In a small bowl stir together the powdered sugar, peanut butter, and enough milk to make a thick drizzling consistency.

Mocha Pots de Crème

Coffee and cocoa come together in this silky custard. Pronounced POH-duh-KREM (think fancy French dessert), it can be made in the morning and chilled all day before serving.

PREP TIME	FUNCTION	CLOSED POT	TOTAL TIME	RELEASE
15 minutes	Sauté (Normal); Pressure/Manual (High)	15 minutes	30 minutes + 20 minutes cool + 3 hours chill	Quick

SERVES: 4

½ teaspoon espresso powder

½ teaspoon vanilla extract

1¼ cups half-and-half

3 ounces bittersweet chocolate, grated

¼ cup sugar

3 egg yolks

1½ cups water

Whipped cream (optional)

Cinnamon (optional)

PREP
Combine espresso powder, vanilla, and half-and-half in the Instant Pot®. Whisk to dissolve espresso powder. Select **SAUTÉ** and adjust to **NORMAL**. Bring half-and-half mixture just to boiling. Press **CANCEL** and stir in chocolate.

In a medium bowl combine sugar and egg yolks. Whisk until thick and well combined.

Ladle approximately ⅓ cup hot chocolate mixture into the egg mixture. Whisk well. Pour all of egg mixture into the chocolate mixture; mix until smooth.

Ladle custard into four 6-ounce ramekins; set aside. Remove inner pot and wash. Carefully cover pots de crème with foil.

Return clean inner pot to the cooker. Place trivet in the pot, tucking handles underneath. Add water to pot. Arrange three of the ramekins evenly on the trivet. Set remaining ramekin on top of the other three. Secure the lid on the pot. Close the pressure-release valve.

COOK
Select **MANUAL** and cook at high pressure for 6 minutes. When cooking is complete, use a quick release to depressurize.

SERVE
Carefully remove pots de crème from pot. Transfer to a wire rack. Cool for 20 minutes, then transfer to the refrigerator. Let chill for at least 3 hours.

To serve, remove foil from ramekins. If desired, top each dessert with a dollop of whipped cream and a sprinkle of cinnamon. Serve cold.

Crème Brûlée

If you have a kitchen torch, caramelize the sugar on top of the custards. If not, it can be done in a pan on the stove.

PREP TIME	FUNCTION	CLOSED POT TIME	TOTAL TIME	RELEASE
15 minutes	Pressure/Manual (High)	25 minutes	40 minutes + 30 minutes cool + 2 hours chill	Natural

SERVES: 3

1⅓ cups whipping cream

3 tablespoons sugar

4 egg yolks

1 teaspoon pure vanilla extract

Dash salt

1 cup water

2 tablespoons sugar

PREP

In a medium bowl combine ⅓ cup of the whipping cream, the sugar, egg yolks, vanilla, and salt. Whisk until well combined. Slowly whisk in the remaining 1 cup whipping cream until smooth. Evenly pour cream mixture into three 6-ounce custard cups or ramekins. Cover cups or ramekins with foil.

Place trivet in the bottom of the Instant Pot®; add the water to the pot. Arrange filled custard cups on the trivet. Secure the lid on the pot. Close the pressure-release valve.

COOK

Select **MANUAL** and cook at high pressure for 10 minutes. When cooking is complete, use a natural release to depressurize.

SERVE

Use pot holders to transfer custard cups to a wire rack; uncover cups. Let stand for 30 to 60 minutes or until completely cool. Cover; chill for at least 2 hours or for up to 3 days.

To serve, sprinkle 2 tablespoons sugar evenly over surface of the custards (use about 2 teaspoons sugar per custard). Using a small handheld kitchen torch,* slowly and evenly melt the sugar, allowing it to turn a deep golden brown.

***TIP:** If you don't have a kitchen torch, pour 2 tablespoons sugar into a heavy small skillet. Heat sugar over medium-high heat until sugar begins to melt, shaking the skillet occasionally for even melting. Do not stir. When sugar starts to melt, reduce heat to low; continue to cook until all sugar is melted and golden brown, stirring with a wooden spoon so all sugar melts evenly. Immediately pour the melted sugar over custards. If the sugar starts to harden in the skillet, return to heat and stir until melted.

MAPLE-GINGER CRÈME BRÛLÉE: Prepare as directed except substitute 3 tablespoons pure maple syrup for the 3 tablespoons sugar and add ¼ teaspoon ground ginger with the salt. If desired, sprinkle tops of custards with 2 teaspoons finely chopped crystallized ginger just before serving.

Barbara Schieving is the creator of the blog PressureCookingToday.com.

Raspberry Cheesecake

Just a little bit of raspberry extract boosts the flavor of the filling of this cheesecake, but it's not crucial.

PREP TIME	FUNCTION	CLOSED POT TIME	TOTAL TIME	RELEASE
30 minutes	Pressure/Manual (High)	1 hour	1 hour 30 minutes + 1 hour cool + 4 hours chill	Natural

SERVES: 8

Nonstick cooking spray

1 cup Oreo cookie crumbs (about 12 Oreos, filling removed)

2 tablespoons butter, melted

16 ounces cream cheese, softened

¼ cup sugar

1 tablespoon all-purpose flour

¼ teaspoon raspberry extract (optional)

½ cup seedless raspberry jam

¼ cup sour cream

2 eggs, room temperature

Red food coloring (optional)

2 cups water

6 ounces milk chocolate, finely chopped

⅓ cup heavy cream

Fresh raspberries

PREP

Spray a 6- or 7-inch springform pan with nonstick spray. Cut a piece of parchment paper to fit the bottom of the pan. Place in pan and spray again; set aside. Combine cookie crumbs and butter in a bowl. Press into the bottom and 1 inch up the side of the pan. Place in the freezer for 10 minutes.

In a large bowl beat the cream cheese, sugar, flour, and extract (if using) until smooth and creamy. Mix in the jam and sour cream. Add eggs, beating just until combined. Add a drop or two of red food coloring to tint to desired hue if desired. Stir gently until combined. Pour into prepared crust.

Pour the water into the Instant Pot®. Place the trivet in the bottom of the pot. Cut a piece of foil the same size as a paper towel. Place the foil under the paper towel and place the pan on top of the paper towel. Wrap the bottom of the pan in the foil with the paper towel as a barrier.

Fold an 18-inch-long piece of foil into thirds lengthwise. Place under the pan and use the two sides as a sling to place cheesecake in the pot. Secure the lid on the pot. Close the pressure-release valve.

COOK

Select **MANUAL** and cook at high pressure for 35 minutes. When cooking is complete, use a natural pressure release to depressurize.

SERVE

Remove the cheesecake from the pot using the sling. Cool on a wire rack for 1 hour and then refrigerate for at least 4 hours. Carefully remove pan sides.

When cheesecake is chilled, prepare the topping: Place half the chocolate in a bowl. Heat heavy cream in a small saucepan over medium-high heat until it comes to a boil. Remove from heat and immediately pour cream over chocolate, stirring until chocolate is completely melted. Add remaining chocolate and stir until completely melted. Cool until ganache is thickened but still thin enough to drip down the sides of the cheesecake.

Spoon ganache on top of cake, spreading to edges and letting it drip down sides. Decorate top of cake with raspberries. Refrigerate until ready to serve.

Triple Citrus Cheesecake

This is the lightest, fluffiest cheesecake you'll taste anywhere. The moist cooking environment in the Instant Pot® makes it super creamy and greatly reduces the chances it will crack or dry out. Be sure to beat the eggs just until combined to ensure the cake won't sink in the middle as it cools.

PREP TIME	FUNCTION	CLOSED POT TIME	TOTAL TIME	RELEASE
30 minutes	Manual/Pressure (High)	1 hour	1 hour 30 minutes + 1 hour cool + 4 hours chill	Natural

SERVES: 8

Nonstick cooking spray

1½ cups graham cracker or vanilla wafer crumbs

2 tablespoons sugar

4 tablespoons melted butter

16 ounces cream cheese, softened

½ cup sugar

1 tablespoon flour

¼ teaspoon salt

2 teaspoons vanilla

2 tablespoons orange juice

2 eggs

½ teaspoon freshly grated orange zest

½ teaspoon freshly grated lemon zest

½ teaspoon freshly grated lime zest

2 cups water

Fresh orange segments (optional)

PREP

Lightly spray a 6- or 7-inch springform pan with cooking spray. Cut a piece of parchment paper to fit the bottom of the pan. Place in the pan and spray again; set aside.

Combine crackers, the 2 tablespoons sugar, and butter in a bowl; mix well. Press into bottom and about 2 inches up the sides of the pan.

In a large bowl beat cream cheese, the ½ cup sugar, flour, salt, vanilla, and orange juice until smooth and creamy. Add eggs, beating just until combined. Stir in citrus zests. Pour into prepared crust.

Pour the water into the Instant Pot®. Place the trivet in the bottom of the pot. Cut a piece of foil the same size as a paper towel. Place the foil under the paper towel and place the pan on top of the paper towel. Wrap the bottom of the pan in the foil, with the paper towel as a barrier.

Fold an 18-inch-long piece of foil into thirds lengthwise. Place under the pan and use the two sides as a sling to place cheesecake in the pot. Secure the lid on the pot. Close the pressure-release valve.

COOK

Select **MANUAL** and cook at high pressure for 35 minutes. When cooking is complete, use a natural pressure release to depressurize.

SERVE

Remove the cheesecake from the pot using the sling. Cool on a wire rack for 1 hour and then refrigerate for at least 4 hours. Carefully remove pan sides. Top cheesecake with fresh orange segments if desired.

Sauces, Spreads & Jams

Quick & Easy Marinara Sauce

You can buy jarred sauce, but it doesn't taste as fresh as sauce you make yourself. By cooking it in the Instant Pot®, you not only you get rich flavor in the fraction of the time it takes to cook it on the stovetop, but there's no spattering, either!

PREP TIME	FUNCTION	CLOSED POT TIME	TOTAL TIME	RELEASE
20 minutes	Sauté (Normal); Pressure/Manual (High)	55 minutes	1 hour 15 minutes	Natural

MAKES: 10 cups

- 3 tablespoons extra virgin olive oil
- 6 cloves garlic, minced
- 2 28-ounce cans whole tomatoes
- 2 15-ounce cans no-salt-added tomato sauce
- ¼ cup water
- 2 teaspoons dried Italian seasoning
- ½ teaspoon salt
- ¼ teaspoon black pepper
- ⅛ to ¼ teaspoon crushed red pepper
- ¼ cup chopped fresh basil
- ¼ cup chopped fresh flat-leaf parsley

PREP

Select **SAUTÉ** on the Instant Pot® and adjust to **NORMAL**. When hot, add 1 tablespoon of the oil and the garlic. Cook and stir for 10 to 20 seconds or until garlic is fragrant but not brown. Press **CANCEL**. Add undrained tomatoes, tomato sauce, the water, Italian seasoning, salt, black pepper, and crushed red pepper to the pot. Secure the lid on the pot. Close the pressure-release valve.

COOK

Select **MANUAL** and cook at high pressure for 10 minutes. When cooking is complete, use a natural release to depressurize.

SERVE

Using a potato masher, mash sauce to desired consistency (or for a smooth sauce, use an immersion blender or regular blender to blend sauce until smooth). Stir in remaining olive oil, the basil, and parsley. Serve as desired.

Chipotle Barbecue Sauce

If you don't want the touch of smoke and heat the chipotle brings to this sauce, simply leave it out.

PREP TIME	FUNCTION	CLOSED POT TIME	TOTAL TIME	RELEASE
20 minutes	Sauté (Normal); Pressure/Manual (High)	20 minutes	40 minutes + 5 minutes simmer	Quick

MAKES: 2½ cups

- 1 tablespoon cooking oil
- ½ cup finely chopped onion
- 2 cloves garlic, minced
- 1½ cups ketchup
- 1 cup water
- ⅓ cup packed brown sugar
- ⅓ cup apple cider vinegar
- 2 tablespoons honey
- 1 canned chipotle chile in adobo, finely chopped
- 2 teaspoons chili powder
- 2 teaspoons Dijon mustard
- ¼ teaspoon black pepper

PREP
Select **SAUTÉ** on the Instant Pot® and adjust to **NORMAL**. Heat oil in pot; add onion and cook for 2 minutes or until softened, stirring frequently. Add garlic; cook and stir for 1 minute more. Press **CANCEL**.

Add ketchup, water, brown sugar, vinegar, honey, chipotle, chili powder, mustard, and black pepper; stir well. Secure the lid on the pot. Close the pressure-release valve.

COOK
Select **MANUAL** and cook at high pressure for 10 minutes. When cooking is complete, use a quick release to depressurize. Press **CANCEL**.

SERVE
For a thicker sauce, select **SAUTÉ** and adjust to **LESS**. Bring sauce to a simmer. Cook for 5 to 10 minutes or until mixture reaches desired consistency, stirring frequently. Press **CANCEL**.

Honey-Cinnamon Applesauce

This silky applesauce is so delicious, you'll forget that it's actually good for you. Use a mix of apples for a more complex flavor.

PREP TIME	FUNCTION	CLOSED POT TIME	TOTAL TIME	RELEASE
10 minutes	Pressure/Manual (High)	45 minutes	55 minutes	Natural

MAKES: 4½ cups

- 4 pounds apples, such as Jonathan, McIntosh, Golden Delicious, Cortland, and/or Fuji
- ½ cup apple cider
- ½ cup water
- ¼ cup honey
- 2 tablespoons lemon juice
- 3 cinnamon sticks
- ¼ teaspoon salt

PREP

Core, peel, and chop the apples. Combine the apples, cider, the water, honey, lemon juice, cinnamon sticks, and salt in the Instant Pot®. Secure the lid on the pot. Close the pressure-release valve.

COOK

Select **MANUAL** and cook at high pressure for 8 minutes. When cooking is complete, use a natural release to depressurize. Press **CANCEL**.

SERVE

Remove cinnamon sticks. Use a potato masher to mash the applesauce or, working in batches, transfer to a food processor and process until smooth (or use an immersion blender in the pot).

If applesauce is thin, select **SAUTÉ** and adjust to **LESS**. Cook and stir for 10 to 15 minutes or until desired consistency. Press **CANCEL**.

Bacon-Onion Jam

Sweet, smoky, salty, and tangy, this mélange of caramelized onions and bacon is the perfect way to top a wheel of baked Brie or a burger. This recipe makes a fairly chunky jam. If you want it a little smoother, transfer the finished jam to a food processor and pulse a few times.

PREP TIME	FUNCTION	CLOSED POT TIME	TOTAL TIME
40 minutes	Sauté (Normal/Less); Slow Cook (Less)	6 hours	6 hours 40 minutes

MAKES: 4 cups

- 1 **pound thick-cut bacon, diced into ½-inch pieces**
- 3 **large onions, halved and thinly sliced (about 4 cups)**
- 3 **garlic cloves, minced**
- ½ **cup packed brown sugar**
- ¼ **cup apple cider or apple juice**
- ¼ **cup apple cider vinegar**
- 1 **teaspoon fresh thyme leaves**
- ¼ **teaspoon ground cinnamon**
  Dash cayenne pepper

PREP
Add bacon to Instant Pot®. Select **SAUTÉ** and adjust to **NORMAL**. Cook and stir until bacon is cooked through but not crisp for about 8 minutes. Remove bacon to a paper towel-lined plate; refrigerate. Remove all but 1 tablespoon of the bacon grease from the pot.

Add onions and garlic to drippings in the pot. Cook and stir for 5 minutes until just tender. Press **CANCEL**.

Add brown sugar, apple cider, vinegar, thyme, cinnamon, and cayenne. Stir to combine. Secure the lid on the pot. Open the pressure-release valve.

COOK
Select **SLOW COOK** and adjust to **LESS**. Cook for 6 to 7 hours. Press **CANCEL**.

Add cooked bacon to pot. Select **SAUTÉ** and adjust to **LESS**. Cook jam until most of the liquid has been evaporated for 5 to 10 minutes. Press **CANCEL**.

STORE
Cool and refrigerate for up to 1 week. (Jam can also be frozen.)

Orange Marmalade

Using a mandoline to slice the oranges will give you the thinnest, most even slices.

PREP TIME	FUNCTION	CLOSED POT TIME	TOTAL TIME	RELEASE
15 minutes	Pressure/Manual (High); Sauté (Normal)	40 minutes	55 minutes	Natural

MAKES: about 4 cups

- 3 **medium oranges (about 1½ pounds)**
- 1½ **cups water**
- 3 **cups sugar**

PREP
Thinly slice the oranges, removing and discarding any seeds. Cut the orange slices into quarters. Add oranges and the water to the Instant Pot®. Secure the lid on the pot. Close the pressure-release valve.

COOK
Select **MANUAL** and cook at high pressure for 10 minutes. When cooking is complete, use a natural release to depressurize. Press **CANCEL**.

Remove the lid and stir in sugar. Select **SAUTÉ** and adjust to **NORMAL**. Bring mixture to a full boil. Boil for 5 to 10 minutes or until mixture reaches gel stage (220°F), stirring frequently. Press **CANCEL**.

STORE
Ladle into half-pint glass jars. Seal jars. Store for up to 3 weeks in the refrigerator.

Apple Butter

Rich and fragrant with cinnamon and nutmeg, this old-school spread is delicious on a slice of warm buttered toast—especially if it's made with raisin-walnut bread.

PREP TIME	FUNCTION	CLOSED POT TIME	TOTAL TIME	RELEASE
25 minutes	Pressure/Manual (High); Sauté (Less)	45 minutes	1 hour 10 minutes + 10 minutes simmer	Natural

MAKES: 6 or 7 half-pints

- 4 pounds apples, such as Jonathan, McIntosh, Golden Delicious, Granny Smith, Gala, and/or Braeburn, cored and chopped (peel on if desired)
- ¼ cup apple cider
- ½ cup packed brown sugar
- ½ cup granulated sugar
- 2 teaspoons ground cinnamon
- ½ teaspoon ground nutmeg
- 1 teaspoon vanilla

PREP
Add apples, cider, brown sugar, granulated sugar, cinnamon, and nutmeg to the Instant Pot®. Secure the lid on the pot. Close the pressure-release valve.

COOK
Select **MANUAL** and cook at high pressure for 8 minutes. When cooking is complete, use a natural release to depressurize. Press **CANCEL**.

Use a potato masher or immersion blender to blend the apples until fairly smooth. Select **SAUTÉ** and adjust to **LESS**. Simmer apple butter for 10 to 15 minutes or until thickened to desired consistency. Stir in the vanilla. Press **CANCEL**. Cool completely.

STORE
Transfer to half-pint glass jars. Seal jars. Store for up to 3 weeks in the refrigerator or freeze for up to 3 months. (If frozen, it will have a thinner consistency upon thawing.)

Strawberry Jam

Fully ripe strawberries—sweet, juicy, and red all of the way through—make the best jam. Visit a pick-your-own farm in late spring and early summer and give jam making a whirl.

PREP TIME	FUNCTION	CLOSED POT TIME	TOTAL TIME	RELEASE
20 minutes	Sauté (Normal); Pressure/Manual (High)	40 minutes	1 hour	Natural

MAKES: about 3 cups

4 **cups quartered fresh strawberries**

2½ **cups sugar**

¼ **cup lemon juice**

PREP
Combine strawberries, sugar, and lemon juice in the Instant Pot®.

Select **SAUTÉ** and adjust to **NORMAL**. Bring mixture to a full boil for about 8 minutes, stirring frequently. Press **CANCEL**. Secure the lid on the pot. Close the pressure-release valve.

COOK
Select **MANUAL** and cook at high pressure for 8 minutes. When cooking is complete, use a natural release to depressurize. Press **CANCEL**.

Remove the lid. Mash berries with a potato masher. Select **SAUTÉ** and adjust to **NORMAL**. Bring mixture to a full boil. Boil for 5 minutes or until mixture reaches gel stage (220°F), stirring frequently. Press **CANCEL**.

STORE
Ladle into half-pint glass jars. Seal jars. Store for up to 3 weeks in the refrigerator.

Strawberry-Rhubarb Sauce

Spoon this sweet-tart sauce over angel food cake, ice cream, and waffles.

PREP TIME	FUNCTION		CLOSED POT TIME	TOTAL TIME
1 hour 10 minutes	Slow Cook (More)		1 hour 30 minutes	1 hour 40 minutes

MAKES: 2¾ cups

8   ounces (2 cups) ½- to ¾-inch diced frozen or fresh rhubarb

1   pound whole strawberries, stems removed, halved

¼   cup sugar

¼   teaspoon almond extract

1   teaspoon fresh lemon juice

PREP
Place rhubarb, strawberries, and sugar in the Instant Pot®. Secure the lid on the pot. Open the pressure-release valve.

COOK
Select **SLOW COOK** and adjust to **MORE.** Cook for 1½ hours.

SERVE
When cooking is complete, mash berries and rhubarb with a fork or potato masher. Stir in almond extract and lemon juice; cool. Cover and chill before serving.

Kathy Hester is the creator of HealthySlowCooking.com and the author of *The Ultimate Vegan Cookbook for Your Instant Pot®*.

Cranberry Sauce with Apple Brandy

Don't settle for boring cranberry sauce. This version—spiced with orange, cardamom, cinnamon, and maple syrup—is super simple to make and so much better than canned.

PREP TIME	FUNCTION	CLOSED POT TIME	TOTAL TIME	RELEASE
20 minutes	Pressure/Manual (High); Sauté (Less)	30 minutes	50 minutes	Natural

MAKES: 2½ cups

- 3 **cups fresh cranberries**
- 2 **cups peeled, minced apple**
- ½ **cup orange juice (about 2 medium oranges)**
- 1 **tablespoon orange zest**
- 10 **cardamom pods**
- 2 **cinnamon sticks**
- ¼ **teaspoon salt**
- ½ **cup water**
- 2 **tablespoons apple brandy or spiced rum**
- 2 **to 4 tablespoons maple syrup or other sweetener**
- ¼ **teaspoon ground cardamom**

PREP
Combine cranberries, apple, orange juice and zest, cardamom pods, cinnamon sticks, salt, and the water in the Instant Pot®. Secure the lid on the pot. Close the pressure-release valve.

COOK
Select **MANUAL** and cook at high pressure for 6 minutes. When cooking is complete, use a natural release to depressurize. Press **CANCEL**.

Select **SAUTÉ** and adjust to **LESS**. Stir in the brandy, maple syrup, and ground cardamom. Cook and mash the fruit pieces. Cook until sauce reaches desired consistency. Press **CANCEL**.

SERVE
Remove the cardamom pods and cinnamon sticks. Store in a tightly sealed container in the refrigerator for up to 1 week.

Mango-Ginger Chutney

The combination of heat and sweet is classic in mango chutney. How much heat it has is up to you—just vary the amount of crushed red pepper according to your taste. To seed a mango, stand it on its end and slice down either side of the large seed, discarding the center that contains the seed.

PREP TIME	FUNCTION	CLOSED POT TIME	TOTAL TIME	RELEASE
25 minutes	Pressure/High; Sauté (Less)	30 minutes	55 minutes	Natural

MAKES: 3½ cups

- 4 ripe mangoes, seeded, peeled, and chopped (4 cups)
- 1 cup chopped red onion
- ½ cup diced red sweet pepper
- ½ cup golden raisins
- ¼ cup minced fresh ginger
- ½ teaspoon ground cinnamon
- ¼ teaspoon ground cardamom
- ½ to 1 teaspoon crushed red pepper
- ½ cup apple cider vinegar
- ½ cup pineapple juice or apple juice
- ½ cup sugar
- ½ teaspoon kosher salt

PREP
Place all of the ingredients in the Instant Pot® and stir to combine. Secure the lid on the pot. Close the pressure-release valve.

COOK
Select **MANUAL** and cook at high pressure for 5 minutes. When cooking is complete, use a natural release to depressurize. Press **CANCEL**.

Select **SAUTÉ** and adjust to **LESS**. Cook chutney for 10 minutes or until desired consistency. Press **CANCEL**.

SERVE
Serve with turkey, chicken, pork, and ham. Store in a tightly sealed container in the refrigerator for up to 1 week.

Basics

Pressure-Cooked Chicken Broth

The amount of flavor this broth takes on being cooked under pressure is amazing—without hours of simmering on the stovetop.

PREP TIME	FUNCTION	CLOSED POT TIME	TOTAL TIME	RELEASE
10 minutes	Soup/Broth	1 hour 40 minutes	1 hour 50 minutes	Natural

MAKES: about 9 cups

- 2½ pounds bony chicken pieces (wings, backs, and/or necks)
- 3 stalks celery with leaves, cut up
- 2 medium carrots, scrubbed, trimmed, and cut in half (leave peel on)
- 1 large onion, unpeeled and cut into large chunks
- 1 medium tomato, halved
- 4 sprigs fresh flat-leaf parsley
- 2 bay leaves
- 4 cloves garlic, unpeeled and lightly crushed
- 1 teaspoon salt
- 1 teaspoon dried sage, thyme, or basil, crushed
- ½ teaspoon whole black peppercorns
- 7½ cups cold water

PREP
If using wings, cut each wing at joints into three pieces. Place chicken pieces in the Instant Pot®. Add celery, carrots, onion, tomato, parsley, bay leaves, garlic, salt, dried herb, peppercorns, and the water. Secure the lid on the pot. Close the pressure-release valve.

COOK
Select **SOUP/BROTH**. When cooking is complete, use a natural release to depressurize.

Remove chicken pieces from pot.* Using a slotted spoon, remove as many vegetables as you can. Line a colander with four layers of cheesecloth. Set colander over a large bowl or stockpot and strain broth through cheesecloth; discard vegetables and seasonings.

SERVE
If using the broth immediately, skim the fat from the top. Or chill broth for at least 6 hours. Remove fat with a spoon and discard. Store broth in airtight containers in the refrigerator for up to 3 days or freeze for 6 months.

*TIP: If desired, remove meat from bones when they are cool enough to handle. Chop the meat and discard the bones. Store meat in an airtight container in the refrigerator for up to 3 days or freeze for up to 3 months.

Slow-Cooked Chicken Broth

Toss all of the ingredients in the pot in the morning and then walk away. At the end of the day you'll be rewarded with a rich, delicious stock that can be used in soups, stews, risotto, and all kinds of other recipes.

PREP TIME	FUNCTION	CLOSED POT TIME	TOTAL TIME
10 minutes	Slow Cook (More)	6 hours	6 hours 10 minutes

MAKES: about 9 cups

2½ **pounds bony chicken pieces (wings, backs, and/or necks)**

3 **stalks celery with leaves, cut up**

2 **medium carrots, scrubbed, trimmed, and cut in half (leave peel on)**

1 **large onion, unpeeled and cut into large chunks**

1 **medium tomato, halved**

4 **sprigs fresh flat-leaf parsley**

2 **bay leaves**

4 **cloves garlic, unpeeled and lightly crushed**

1 **teaspoon salt**

1 **teaspoon dried sage, thyme, or basil, crushed**

½ **teaspoon whole black peppercorns**

7½ **cups cold water**

PREP

If using wings, cut each wing at joints into three pieces. Place chicken pieces in the Instant Pot®. Add celery, carrots, onion, tomato, parsley, bay leaves, garlic, salt, dried herb, peppercorns, and the water. Secure the lid on the pot. Open the pressure-release valve.

COOK

Select **SLOW COOK** and adjust to **MORE**. Cook for 6 hours.

Remove chicken pieces from pot.* Using a slotted spoon, remove as many vegetables as you can. Line a colander with four layers of cheesecloth (or use a fine-mesh strainer). Set colander over a large bowl or stockpot and strain broth through cheesecloth; discard vegetables and seasonings.

SERVE

If using the broth immediately, skim the fat from the top. Or chill broth for at least 6 hours. Remove fat with a spoon and discard. Store broth in airtight containers in the refrigerator for up to 3 days or freeze for 6 months.

*TIP: If desired, remove meat from bones when they are cool enough to handle. Chop the meat and discard the bones. Store meat in an airtight container in the refrigerator for up to 3 days or freeze for up to 3 months.

Pressure-Cooked Beef Broth

Beef broth can be difficult to make at home and get a good, rich taste. Some recipes call for roasting the bones before making broth to intensify the beefy flavor, but with this recipe, there's no need for that additional step.

PREP TIME	FUNCTION	CLOSED POT TIME	TOTAL TIME	RELEASE
10 minutes	Soup/Broth	3 hours 20 minutes	3 hours 30 minutes	Natural

MAKES: about 9 cups

1½ **pounds beef soup bones (knuckle, neck, and marrow bones)**

2 **medium carrots, scrubbed, trimmed, and cut in half (leave peel on)**

1 **large onion, unpeeled and cut into large chunks**

1 **medium leek, white part only, cut into 2-inch chunks**

3 **stalks celery with leaves, cut up**

1 **tablespoon dried thyme, crushed**

1½ **teaspoons salt**

1 **teaspoon whole black peppercorns**

8 **sprigs fresh flat-leaf parsley**

2 **bay leaves**

4 **cloves garlic, unpeeled and lightly crushed**

8 **cups cold water**

1 **tablespoon cider vinegar**

PREP
Combine bones, carrots, onion, leek, celery, thyme, salt, peppercorns, parsley, bay leaves, garlic, the water, and the vinegar in the Instant Pot®.

COOK
Secure the lid on the pot. Close the pressure-release valve. Select **SOUP/BROTH** and adjust cook time to 120 minutes. When cooking is complete, use a natural release to depressurize.

Remove bones from broth.* Using a slotted spoon, remove as many vegetables as you can. Line a colander with four layers of cheesecloth. Set colander over a large bowl or stockpot and strain broth through cheesecloth; discard vegetables and seasonings.

SERVE
If using the broth immediately, skim the fat from the top. Or chill broth for at least 6 hours. Remove fat with a spoon and discard. Store broth in an airtight container in the refrigerator for up to 3 days or freeze for 6 months.

*TIP: If desired, remove meat from bones when they are cool enough to handle. Chop the meat and discard the bones. Store meat in airtight containers in the refrigerator for up to 3 days or freeze for up to 3 months.

Slow-Cooked Beef Broth

A little bit of vinegar helps draw minerals out of the bones as they simmer in the liquid, making the finished broth more flavorful and nutrient-rich.

PREP TIME	FUNCTION	CLOSED POT TIME	TOTAL TIME
10 minutes	Slow Cook (More)	8 hours	8 hours 10 minutes

MAKES: about 6 cups

- 1½ pounds beef soup bones (knuckle, neck, and marrow bones)
- 2 medium carrots, scrubbed and trimmed (leave peel on)
- 1 large onion, unpeeled and cut into large chunks
- 1 medium leek, white part only, cut into 2-inch chunks
- 3 stalks celery with leaves, cut up
- 1 tablespoon dried thyme, crushed
- 1½ teaspoons salt
- 1 teaspoon whole black peppercorns
- 8 sprigs fresh flat-leaf parsley
- 2 bay leaves
- 4 cloves garlic, unpeeled and lightly crushed
- 8 cups cold water
- 1 tablespoon cider vinegar

PREP
Combine bones, carrots, onion, leek, celery, thyme, salt, peppercorns, parsley, bay leaves, garlic, the water, and the vinegar in the Instant Pot®.

COOK
Secure the lid on the pot. Open the pressure-release valve. Select **SLOW COOK** and adjust to **MORE**. Cook for 8 hours.

Remove bones from broth.* Using a slotted spoon, remove as many vegetables as you can. Line a colander with four layers of cheesecloth. Set colander over a large bowl or stockpot and strain broth through cheesecloth; discard vegetables and seasonings.

SERVE
If using the broth immediately, skim the fat from the top. Or chill broth for at least 6 hours. Remove fat with a spoon and discard. Store broth in airtight containers in the refrigerator for up to 3 days or freeze for 6 months.

*TIP: If desired, remove meat from bones when they are cool enough to handle. Chop the meat and discard the bones. Store meat in airtight containers in the refrigerator for up to 3 days or freeze for up to 3 months.

Jill Nussinow blogs at TheVeggieQueen.com and is the author of *Vegan Under Pressure*.

Dark Vegetable Stock

This richly flavored vegan stock is infused with the earthy essence of mushrooms. Use it in soups or stews—or sip on a cup of it alone as an energizing hot beverage.

PREP TIME	FUNCTION	CLOSED POT TIME	TOTAL TIME	RELEASE
20 minutes	Sauté (Normal); Pressure/Manual (High)	60 minutes	1 hour 20 minutes	Natural

MAKES: about 8 cups

- 1 **tablespoon olive oil**
- 2 **red onions, peeled and quartered**
- 3 **cloves garlic, smashed**
- 2 **carrots, peeled and coarsely chopped**
- ½ **cup shiitake mushroom stems (from about 16 mushrooms) or 4 whole dried shiitake mushrooms**
- 6 **ounces cremini or shiitake mushrooms, sliced**
- 2 **celery stalks with leaves, chopped**
- 1 **sprig rosemary**
- 3 **sprigs thyme**
- 2 **bay leaves**
- ¼ **teaspoon whole black peppercorns**
- 8 **cups water**
- ½ **teaspoon salt**

PREP
Select **SAUTÉ** on the Instant Pot® and adjust to **NORMAL**. When hot, add the oil. Add the onions and cook for 4 minutes.* Add the garlic and cook 6 minutes longer or until the onions start turning brown. Press **CANCEL**. Add carrots, shiitake mushrooms, cremini mushrooms, celery, rosemary, thyme, bay leaves, peppercorns, and the water. Secure the lid on the pot. Close the pressure-release valve.

COOK
Select **MANUAL** and cook at high pressure for 10 minutes. When cooking is complete, use a natural release to depressurize.

SERVE
Pour stock through a strainer, pressing on the solids with a spoon to extract all the liquid and flavor. Stir salt into the stock.

Use immediately or store in a tightly covered container in the refrigerator for up to 1 week or for up to 3 months in the freezer.

*NOTE: The onion and hot oil will spatter a bit while it's being sautéed.

Perfectly Cooked Eggs

Steaming eggs in the shell gives you the very best results, whether you want soft-, medium-, or hard-cooked eggs. An extra benefit of steaming: Your hard-cooked eggs will never acquire a green ring around the yolk—a sign of overcooking.

PREP TIME	FUNCTION	CLOSED POT TIME	TOTAL TIME	RELEASE
5 minutes	Manual/Pressure (Low)	Varies	Varies	Natural

SERVES: Varies

1 **cup water**

1 **to 6 large or jumbo eggs**

PREP
Pour the water into the Instant Pot®. Place a steamer basket or the trivet in the pot. Carefully arrange eggs in the steamer basket. Secure the lid on the pot. Close the pressure-release valve.

COOK
For soft-cooked eggs, select **MANUAL** and cook at low pressure for 3 minutes. When cooking time is complete, use a natural release to depressurize. (For medium-cooked eggs, cook for 4 minutes; for hard-cooked eggs, cook for 5 minutes.)

SERVE
Remove the lid from the pot and gently place eggs in a bowl of cool water for 1 minute to serve warm.

Classic Oatmeal

Get this oatmeal cooking before you jump in the shower. By the time you're ready for the day, your oatmeal will be ready for you.

PREP TIME	FUNCTION	CLOSED POT TIME	TOTAL TIME	RELEASE
5 minutes	Manual/Pressure (High	10 minutes	15 minutes	Natural

SERVES: 2 or 3

Nonstick cooking spray

2 **cups water**

2 **cups unsweetened plain or vanilla almond, soy, or cashew milk (or 1 cup nondairy milk and 1 cup water)**

⅛ **teaspoon salt**

1 **cup rolled oats**

1 **tablespoon butter (optional)**

½ **teaspoon vanilla extract (optional)**

¼ **teaspoon ground cinnamon (optional)**

1 **tablespoon honey, pure maple syrup, or agave nectar (optional)**

¼ **cup raisins, dried cranberries, dried cherries, or chopped dried apricots (optional)**

3 **tablespoons chopped toasted almonds, walnuts, or pecans (optional)**

PREP
Spray the inner pot of the Instant Pot® with cooking spray (this helps reduce foaming and aids in cleanup). Pour the 2 cups water into the Instant Pot®. Place the trivet in the pot. Place an 8-cup heatproof bowl on top of the trivet. Combine the water, milk, salt, and oats in the bowl. Secure the lid on the pot. Close the pressure-release valve.

COOK
Select **MANUAL** and cook at high pressure for 5 minutes. When cooking is complete, use a natural release to depressurize.

SERVE
If desired, stir in the butter, vanilla, cinnamon, sweetener, dried fruit, and nuts. Top with additional milk (dairy or nondairy) if desired.

Steel-Cut Oatmeal

It's important to use a nondairy milk in this oatmeal because the natural sugars in cow's milk will cause it to scorch. Top the cooked oatmeal with dairy milk if you like.

PREP TIME	FUNCTION	CLOSED POT TIME	TOTAL TIME	RELEASE
5 minutes	Manual/Pressure (High)	20 minutes	25 minutes	Natural

SERVES: 4 to 6

Nonstick cooking spray

2 cups water

1 cup unsweetened plain or vanilla almond, soy, or cashew milk

⅛ teaspoon salt

1 cup steel-cut oats

2 tablespoons butter (optional)

1 teaspoon vanilla extract (optional)

1 teaspoon ground cinnamon (optional)

1 to 2 tablespoons honey, brown sugar, pure maple syrup, or agave nectar (optional)

⅓ cup raisins, dried cranberries, dried cherries, or chopped dried apricots (optional)

¼ cup chopped toasted almonds, walnuts, or pecans (optional)

Milk (optional)

PREP
Spray the inner pot of the Instant Pot® with cooking spray (this helps reduce foaming and aids in cleanup). Combine the water, milk, salt, and oats in the pot. Secure the lid on the pot. Close the pressure-release valve.

COOK
Select **MANUAL** and cook at high pressure for 10 minutes. When cooking is complete, use a natural release to depressurize. (If oats are not tender, place the lid on the pot and let stand for 5 to 10 minutes.)

SERVE
If desired, stir in the butter, vanilla, cinnamon, sweetener, dried fruit, and nuts. Top with additional milk if desired.

Homemade Yogurt

When you open the pot after 8 hours of incubation, the yogurt will appear very firm and the whey—a pale yellow liquid—will be separate from the milk solids. Just give the mixture a stir before you pour into the strainer.

PREP TIME	FUNCTION	CLOSED POT TIME	TOTAL TIME	RELEASE
5 minutes	Steam; Yogurt	9 hours	9 hours 5 minutes + 6 hours chill	Quick

MAKES: about 9 cups

3 **cups water**

1 **gallon milk (whole, 2%, 1%, or skim)***

3 **tablespoons powdered milk (optional)**

¼ **cup plain, unsweetened yogurt with active cultures**

Vanilla (1 or 2 tablespoons extract or 1 vanilla bean, split and scraped) (optional)

½ **cup granulated sugar or honey (optional)**

Cheesecloth

PREP
To sterilize the Instant Pot®, pour the water into the pot. Secure the lid on the pot. Close the pressure-release valve. Select **STEAM** and adjust cooking time to 5 minutes. When cooking time is complete, use a quick-release to depressurize. Press **CANCEL**. Remove the lid and pour water out of the pot. Dry and cool pot.

COOK
Pour the milk into the completely cooled pot. Stir in powdered milk if using. Secure the lid on the pot. Open the pressure-release valve. Select **YOGURT** and adjust until display reads "Boil."

When boil and cool-down cycles are complete (about 1 hour), check the temperature with an instant-read thermometer. If it is not 185°F, select **SAUTÉ** and adjust to **NORMAL** to warm it to 185°F. Press **CANCEL**. Remove inner pot and place on a cooling rack to cool. (Or speed the cooling process by setting the inner pot into a sink full of cool water.) Cool milk to 110°F, whisking occasionally. Return inner pot to Instant Pot®.

Whisk in yogurt and, if desired, vanilla and sugar. Secure the lid on the pot. Open the pressure-release valve. Select **YOGURT** and adjust incubation time to 8 hours, making sure display says **NORMAL**. (If a more tart flavor is desired, you can adjust the time up to 10 hours.)

When incubation time is complete, cool yogurt in the pot in the refrigerator, covered and undisturbed, for at least 6 hours or overnight.

In a large bowl place a colander lined with a double layer of cheesecloth. Transfer yogurt to the cheesecloth-lined strainer and strain in the refrigerator for about 1 to 2 hours for regular yogurt or at least 8 hours or overnight for Greek-style yogurt. Store in tightly sealed containers in the refrigerator.

SERVE
Enjoy yogurt plain or with fruit, preserves, nuts, or granola.

*NOTE: Milk that is higher in fat will produce thicker, creamier yogurt than 1% or skim milk—but you can also thicken yogurt by straining it for a longer period of time. The powdered milk is optional, but it, too, helps thicken the yogurt—as well as adding protein.

Pressure Cooking Charts

Because people have preferences in the taste and texture of their foods, these timings offer a range so you can experiment and find the timings you like. All are based on the high-pressure setting.

Fish & Shellfish

Cook times are generally short to preserve the delicate flavors and textures. Steaming is the ideal method, though it does depend somewhat on the recipe. You will needs at least 1 cup of water in the bottom of the pot and the trivet and/or a vegetable steamer basket. Use a quick release.

Fish & Shellfish	Fresh Cooking Time (minutes)	Frozen Cooking Time (minutes)
Crab	3–4	5–6
Fish, whole	5–6	7–10
Fish, fillet	2–3	3–4
Fish, steak	3–4	4–6
Lobster	3–4	4–6
Mussels	2–3	4–5
Seafood soup or stock	6–7	7–9
Shrimp or prawns	1–2	2–3

Poultry

In general, removing the skin from poultry before pressure cooking yields the best results. Raw poultry is highly perishable. Never set the delay cook time for more than 1 hour. We recommend instead cooking the poultry immediately and using the **KEEP WARM** function to main food at serving temperature. Use a natural release for larger, bone-in pieces and a quick release for smaller, boneless pieces.

Poultry	Cooking Time (minutes)
Chicken, breasts	8–10
Chicken, whole	20–25
Chicken, dark meat	10–15
Cornish hen, whole	10–15
Duck, cut up with bones	10–12
Duck, whole	25–30
Pheasant	20–25

Poultry	Cooking Time (minutes)
Turkey, boneless breast	15–20
Turkey breast, whole with bones	25–30
Turkey, drumsticks	15–20
Quail, whole	8–10

Rice & Grains

The pre-set **RICE** and **MULTIGRAIN** functions generally provide the optimum timing for cooking rice and other grains, but the **MANUAL** setting may also be used. Use the following grain:water ratios. Use a natural release.

Rice & Grains	Grain to Water Ratio (cups)	Cooking Time (minutes)
Type		
Barley, pearl	1:4	25–30
Barley, pot	1:3-1:4	25–30
Couscous	1:2	5–8
Kamut, whole	1:3	10–12
Millet	1: 1⅔	10–12
Oats, quick-cooking	1: 1⅔	6
Oats, steel-cut	1: 1⅔	10
Quinoa	1:2	8
Rice, basmati	1: 1½	4–8
Rice, brown	1: 1¼	22–28
Rice, jasmine	1:1	4–10
Rice, white	1: 1½	8
Rice, wild	1:3	25–30
Sorghum	1:3	20–25
Spelt berries	1:3	15–20
Wheat berries	1:3	25–30

Vegetables

Steaming vegetables—whether fresh or frozen—helps preserve vitamin and minerals, as well as maintain their bright colors and crisp-tender textures. When steaming vegetables, you need at least 1 cup of water in the bottom of the pot and the trivet and/or a vegetable steamer basket. Use a quick release.

Vegetables	Fresh Cooking Time (minutes)	Frozen Cooking Time (minutes)
Artichoke, whole, trimmed	9–11	11–13
Artichoke, hearts	4–5	5–6
Asparagus, whole or cut	1–2	2–3
Beans, green/yellow or wax, whole, ends trimmed	1–2	2–3
Beets, small, whole	11–13	13–15
Beets, large, whole	20–25	25–30
Broccoli, florets	2–3	3–4
Broccoli, stalks	3–4	4–5
Brussels sprouts, whole	3–4	4–5
Cabbage, red or green, shredded	2–3	3–4
Cabbage, red or green, wedges	3–4	4–5
Carrots, sliced or shredded	1–2	2–3
Carrots, whole or chunks	2–3	3–4
Cauliflower florets	2–3	3–4
Celery, chunks	2–3	3–4
Collards	4–5	5–6
Corn, kernels	1–2	2–3
Corn, on the cob	3–4	4–5
Eggplant, slices or chunks	2–3	4–5
Endive	1–2	2–3
Escarole, chopped	1–2	2–3
Greens (beet, collards, kale, spinach, Swiss chard, turnip greens), chopped	3–6	4–7

Vegetables	Fresh Cooking Time (minutes)	Frozen Cooking Time (minutes)
Leeks	2–4	3–5
Mixed vegetables	2–3	3–4
Okra	2–3	3–4
Onions, sliced	2–3	3–4
Parsnips, sliced	2–3	2–3
Parsnips, chunks	2–4	4–6
Peas, snow pea or sugar snap	1–2	2–3
Peas, green	1–2	2–3
Potatoes, cubed	7–9	9–11
Potatoes, whole, baby	10–12	12–14
Potatoes, whole, large	12–15	15–19
Pumpkin, small slices or chunks	4–5	6–7
Pumpkin, large slices or chunks	8–10	10–14
Rutabaga, slices	3–5	4–6
Rutabaga, chunks	4–6	6–8
Spinach	1–2	3–4
Squash, acorn, slices or chunks	6–7	8–9
Squash, butternut, slices or chunks	8–10	10–12
Sweet potato, cubed	7–9	9–11
Sweet potato, whole, small	10–12	12–14
Sweet potato, whole, large	12–15	15–19
Sweet pepper, slices or chunks	1–3	2–4
Tomatoes, quartered	2–3	4–5

Meat

Browning meats on the **SAUTÉ** setting before pressure cooking helps to seal in the juices. Raw meat is highly perishable. Never set the delay cook time for more than 1 to 2 hours. We recommend instead cooking the meat immediately and using the **KEEP WARM** function to main food at serving temperature. Use a natural release for larger cuts and a quick release for smaller cuts.

Meat	Cooking Time (minutes)
Type	
Beef, stew meat	15–20
Beef, meatballs	10–15
Beef, whole: pot roast, steak, rump, round, chuck, blade, or brisket	35–40
Beef, small chunks: pot roast, steak, rump, round, chuck, blade, or brisket	25–30
Beef, ribs	25–30
Beef, shanks	25–30
Beef, oxtail	40–50
Ham, slice	9–12
Ham, picnic shoulder	25–30
Pork, loin roast	45–50
Pork, butt/shoulder roast	55–60
Pork, ribs	20–25
Lamb, stew meat	10–15
Lamb, leg	35–45
Veal, chop	5–8
Veal, roast	35–45

Fruit

Steaming fresh or dried fruits best preserves their taste, texture, and nutrients. When steaming fruits, you need at least 1 cup of water in the bottom of the pot and the trivet and/or a vegetable steamer basket. Use a quick release.

Fruits	Fresh Cooking Time (minutes)	Dried Cooking Time (minutes)
Apples, slices or pieces	2–3	3–4
Apples, whole	3–4	4–6
Apricots, whole or halves	2–3	3–4
Peaches	2–3	4–6
Pears, whole	3–4	4–6
Pears, slices or halves	2–3	4–5
Plums	2–3	4–5 (prunes)
Raisins	NA	4–5

Dried Beans, Legumes & Lentils

Dried beans double in volume and weight after soaking or cooking. Do not fill the inner pot more than half full to allow for expansion. Use enough liquid to cover the beans. Use a natural release.

Dried Beans & Legumes	Dry Cooking Time (minutes)	Soaked Cooking Times (minutes)
Type		
Adzuki beans	20–25	10–15
Anasazi beans	20–25	10–15
Black beans	20–25	10–15
Black-eyed peas	20–25	10–15
Chickpeas/ garbanzo beans	35–40	20–25
Cannellini beans	35–40	20–25
Pigeon peas	20–25	15–20
Great Northern beans	25–30	20–25
Lentils, French green	15–20	NA
Lentils, green/brown	15–20	NA
Lentils, yellow, split (moong dal)	15–18	NA
Lima beans	20–25	10–15
Kidney beans, red	25–30	20–25
Kidney beans, white	35–40	20–25
Navy beans	25–30	20–25
Pinto beans	25–30	20–25
Scarlet runner beans	20–25	10–15
Soybeans	25–30	20–25

Index